Think Ahead
to First Certificate

Teacher's Book

Donald Adamson
and Jon Naunton

LONGMAN

Addison Wesley Longman Limited
Edinburgh Gate
Harlow
Essex CM20 2JE
England

and Associated Companies throughout the World.

ISBN 0 582 30608 6

Printed in Spain by Gráficas Estella

Illustrated by Susannah English and James Fewell

Contents

Think Ahead to First Certificate is designed for students who have successfully followed general English courses to intermediate level and now require the special training necessary to help them progress to a full First Certificate course with confidence. Recognising the specific needs of such students, it provides them with a solid foundation in essential language and skills and trains them to focus on the accuracy so crucial to exam success.

The comprehensive and challenging syllabus of *Think Ahead to First Certificate* combines the vital skills of reading, writing, listening and speaking with a clear emphasis throughout on grammar and vocabulary (including phrasal verbs).

Think Ahead to First Certificate consists of a Coursebook, two accompanying Cassettes, Teacher's Book and Workbook offering together a full programme of essential language training and practice at pre First Certificate level. It can be used independently of, or as a lead-in to, its sequel, *Think First Certificate*.

(Note: In the following, the Cambridge First Certificate in English is referred to as 'FCE'.)

Components and organisation

Coursebook

The Coursebook provides approximately 100 – 120 hours of classroom material. It contains fifteen topic-based units divided into double-page teaching sets. Each set focuses on a particular aspect of the unit topic and provides a logical and integrated sequence of language and skills, making it suitable as the basis for a lesson.

A 'Pairwork Section' offers information-gap activities to develop transactional language skills while reinforcing the importance of accuracy.

A special 'Reference Section' covering irregular verbs, prepositions, phrasal verbs, functions and grammar enables students to engage actively in building their own record of these key language areas.

Tapescripts of the listening materials are included to allow students to refer to and revise particular items of language and vocabulary embedded in them. (See also the note on tapescripts under 'Listening' below.)

Coursebook Cassettes

The two Cassettes contain all the listening material included in the course: the listening texts themselves and the items focusing on stress, intonation and pronunciation.

Teacher's Book

The Teacher's Book provides detailed teaching notes as well as answers and tapescripts for the Coursebook material. The material is arranged in units and sets, following the Coursebook, and an overview of contents is provided at the beginning of each unit. The teaching notes for each set are completed by a 'Homework Suggestion' relating specifically to the set. A 'Homework Suggestion' will generally be a fresh writing task following on from the classroom activity/activities. Occasionally, it will suggest that students complete a writing task which they have begun in class but are unlikely to have finished in the lesson time available. The Teacher's Book also contains the answer key for the Workbook (pages 92 – 104).

Workbook

The Workbook is arranged into units and sets relating directly to the topics and language of the Coursebook. Each Workbook set further practises and consolidates the language introduced in the Coursebook through a variety of tasks designed for individual study in the classroom or at home. It also introduces students to the exercise types found in the FCE exam. Additionally, the Workbook contains three quick-check tests, each focusing on the key FCE-related language and skills of the preceding five units and allowing students to monitor their progress.

A 'Study Guide' at the end of the Workbook shows students ways of developing their own study skills in vocabulary, grammar and reading. References at various points throughout the Workbook direct students to the Study Guide and encourage them to work further on a particular area of language, as appropriate.

Approach and methodology

Think Ahead to First Certificate's challenging syllabus revises and teaches key language and skills while gradually familiarising students with the approach, techniques and task formats they will meet when they follow an FCE-preparation course.

Think Ahead to First Certificate combines the essential elements of a communicative methodology with language presentation and task types which train students in accuracy and the more formal approach to language used in FCE preparation.

Recognising the fact that a class of intermediate students using *Think Ahead to First Certificate* may previously have followed different courses, a number of sets begin with diagnostic activities which allow the teacher to assess the need for any remedial and revision work in key areas (e.g. Unit 1, Set C).

Think Ahead to First Certificate is committed to the concept of encouraging students to use their own resources and resourcefulness to help them towards confidence with the language and language-learning. Where appropriate, therefore, students are guided towards working out the rules of the language for themselves, to lead to a keener awareness of the way the language works and deeper and longer-lasting learning.

Coursebook headings and contents

The headings 'Reading', 'Writing', 'Listening', 'Speaking', 'Language Study' and 'Vocabulary' occur throughout the Coursebook. These indicate the focus of the activities and their relation to key areas of preparation for the FCE Examination.

Reading

Reading texts include a variety of narratives, stories, newspaper/magazine-type articles, informational texts (e.g. brochures, programmes, menus), and instructions. They are pitched at a level and length designed to challenge intermediate students and lead them towards FCE-level texts. Many of these texts are 'modified-authentic' and so stretch students without presenting them with the impossible. The nature of the texts means that they frequently contain incidental vocabulary, whose meaning students should generally be able to deduce from context. Reading tasks include traditional comprehension questions, true/false statements, multiple-choice, gap-fill, and the new task types introduced in the FCE Exam in 1996 – multiple matching and gapped text. They are designed to increase students' mastery of extensive and intensive reading comprehension skills and to prepare them for the formats they are likely to meet at FCE level.

Writing

Writing is at the heart of *Think Ahead to First Certificate*. It looks ahead to the importance of writing in the First Certificate Examination and recognises the considerable preparation which students at this level often need in order to cope confidently and competently with composition writing and other types of writing tasks.
'Writing Preparation' tasks require students to analyse written texts and become aware of points of style, appropriacy, format, coherence, etc. Controlled and guided writing tasks establish, practise and consolidate good writing habits before students go on to freer writing practice. They are also taught the importance of writing sub-skills such as expressing cause and effect, linking and sequencing.
To provide maximum opportunity for writing practice and reinforcing good writing habits, the course contains a variety of writing pay-offs – writing tasks which round off other activities (e.g. role plays, discussions).
This Teacher's Book contains other suggestions to guide and assist the process of writing: ideas on planning, collecting thoughts, organising ideas, etc.

Listening

Listening passages range from everyday conversations (including functional language) to interviews, commentaries and narratives. Two main listening skills are developed: extensive and intensive.
For extensive listening, students listen to passages for overall understanding. The tasks are similar to those used in the FCE Examination but are designed to train rather than test students in the understanding of the essential message of the text.
Intensive listening skills are developed by tasks designed to concentrate students' attention on specific language points. As well as items of grammar, vocabulary and pronunciation, these tasks focus on functional language, particularly in the everyday conversations. In earlier units especially, intensive listening activities often require the students to complete gapped passages, thus highlighting the salient points.
Listening activities are identified by the heading 'Listening' and the appropriate symbol or, when they form part of an activity with another main focus (e.g. 'Reading' or 'Writing'), by a cassette symbol.
Tapescripts for the listening activities are found on pages 153 – 167 of the Coursebook. Tapescripts are also included in the Teacher's Book at the appropriate points in the teaching notes.

Speaking

Most sets include speaking activities which allow students to practise the skill of speaking for both fluency and accuracy. Speaking activities range from discussions and debates to role plays and story-telling.
Certain activities require students to work in pairs and refer to the 'Pairwork Section' on pages 138 – 145. Here, they do information-gap activities. These activities are designed to encourage real communication and transactional language, but also to make students aware that the accuracy of what they say is crucial to the success of these activities.

Language Study

The challenge students face when confronted with grammar varies according to its familiarity, conceptual difficulty and complexity of form. For this reason, the course takes a pragmatic attitude towards the treatment of grammar and draws on the following approaches:
– presenting and explaining new language overtly (e.g. Unit 1, Set E)
– leading students to formulate their own rules through guided discovery activities (e.g. Unit 3, Set A)
– using a diagnostic approach to identify areas of residual difficulty and providing a back-up revision (e.g. Unit 4, Set A).
In the majority of cases, items of grammar focused on are introduced in a strong context within reading or listening passages.

Vocabulary

The course builds students' topic vocabulary and deals with a range of common phrasal verbs in the thematic contexts of the units.
Students' understanding of the vocabulary is helped by strong contextualisation in texts and by illustrations. The part of the 'Reference Section' which concentrates on phrasal verbs encourages students to review the relevant course material and collate the items they have encountered.

Pairwork section

See 'Speaking' above.

Tapescripts

See 'Listening' above.

Reference section

See 'Coursebook' and 'Vocabulary' above.
Students are directly referred in Unit 2, Set C, to the Irregular Verbs section and in Unit 3, Set A, to the Prepositions section. It is recommended that the students deal with the remaining sections – Phrasal Verbs, Functions, 'Language Study' (grammar) Index – when they have completed the course, since these sections encourage an overall review and research of the material they have covered.

Practical classroom advice

The teacher's notes for Unit 1 of this Teacher's Book spell out the recommended approaches and procedures for the tasks in the Coursebook by giving detailed descriptions of the ways in which they should be handled. These approaches and procedures will then generally apply for similar tasks throughout the course.
The following notes provide further advice and suggestions on how to deal with particular areas in the classroom and on making classroom learning with the course both varied and enjoyable.

Reading and listening

Context and purpose

Recognising that in real life we rarely read or listen without context or purpose, *Think Ahead to First Certificate* encourages pre-reading and pre-listening activities to stimulate and prepare students and to lend the context and purpose which will aid understanding.
• Always begin a reading or listening task by creating some sort of context. For example, you can use the illustrations which accompany most of the tasks to set the scene and stimulate the class. Ask students what they think has happened/is going to happen, etc.
• At this point, pre-teach any vocabulary which you feel will be crucial to the students' understanding and accomplishment of the task.
Frequently, suggestions for pre-reading activities and vocabulary are included in this Teacher's Book.

Extensive reading/listening

Students are usually asked to read or listen to a passage at least twice, and initial tasks are designed to encourage reading or listening for general understanding.
How to help students develop extensive reading/listening skills:
• Avoid trying to explain the meaning of every unknown word within passages.
• Encourage students to use the context to help them understand the gist.
• Encourage them to focus on the task and what it requires of them.
• Discourage them from getting stuck on unimportant

language or language not relevant to the task. (One way of doing this in reading tasks is by giving them a time limit – enough time to read the text and do the task but not so much time that they begin to get caught up in unknown vocabulary or irrelevant detail. You can vary such time limits according to the level or ability of the class or group.)
• As a general rule, encourage students to read silently, as they would in real life.

Intensive reading/listening

Following the tasks designed to develop general comprehension are more detailed comprehension tasks. These help the students understand the texts in more depth and/or focus on particular points of language and vocabulary. These tasks vary accordingly, but it is always important to check general comprehension through the initial tasks beforehand.

Gapped listening passages

Shorter listening passages representing more everyday situations often form a basis for work on functional language (e.g. apologising, making suggestions) and opportunities for work on e.g. stress and intonation. A number of these passages are dialogues for completion, particularly in the earlier units.
How to approach gapped dialogues:
• Ensure that work on general comprehension is done before students fill in the gaps. (It is recommended that students keep their books closed for the general tasks so that they are not tempted to focus on the gaps immediately.)
• You will generally need to pause the tape to allow students enough time to fill in each gap.
• You will probably find that you have to play the recording three or four times.
• You may want to suggest that your students write on a separate piece of paper rather than in the book itself.

Feedback and follow-up

• It is usually a good idea to get students to discuss their answers for most tasks in groups or pairs before you ask for general class feedback. In this way you can listen in and assess how many individuals have been able to complete a task successfully. This allows you to monitor individual progress and the different levels of ability within a class or group, and assess where perhaps more work or revision is required.
• Use follow-up discussion activities after the comprehension and language tasks to encourage students to relate the text to their own experience and opinions.
• With a listening text, it is often useful to encourage the students to read the tapescript after completing the listening tasks as a way of rounding off, perhaps highlighting the use of certain structures and items of vocabulary embedded within it.

Writing

Writing is a *skill*, which, in common with most others, improves with practice. Some students have a poor self-image as writers, even in their own language, and easily become disheartened. They read successful finished texts and wonder how they will ever be able to achieve a comparable level themselves. It is therefore important that we as teachers show them that successful writing is the culmination of a *process* which includes thinking, planning, 'false starts', and re-writing.

How to achieve this:

• We should not expect them to produce perfect written work at the first attempt.

• We should therefore try to be far less critical of error in the early stages, and concentrate instead on helping them to develop their ideas with confidence.

• In laying the necessary foundations for successful writing, it is important to budget enough time to help students with the less tangible process of planning, drafting and editing.

In *Think Ahead to First Certificate*, the skill of writing is generally taught through a problem-solving approach. Students prepare for writing by correcting or re-arranging texts to arrive at finished texts. These, in turn, can be used as a basis for analysis of discourse features and ultimately as a model for their own writing.

Speaking

The course contains different types of speaking activities which can broadly be identified as follows:

– the incidental speaking which occurs when students are replying to questions.

– discussion activities.

– communication and information-gap activities which are usually done in pairs.

– role-play activities.

To cope with this variety, different abilities and levels of confidence, good classroom management is essential.

Discussion activities

It is sometimes a problem to get students to talk enough. The following suggestions are to help you achieve more volume of speaking practice and maximise students' speaking time:

• As a rule, avoid leading class discussions yourself as this will mean that you will do most of the speaking and ask most of the questions.

• Do all you can to encourage students to work in groups and/or pairs. Perhaps it will prove useful to explain to them that by doing so, they are maximising their personal talking time.

• Try, if possible, to arrange chairs and desks so that students are physically working in pairs or groups.

• Avoid very large groups, as one or two students are likely to dominate. (Groups of three or four are usually best.)

The following suggestions are designed to help you to manage freer speaking practice:

1 Preparing for group discussion

Imagine a class of twelve students, A – L.

• First put the students into four groups of three each:

ABC DEF GHI JKL

They talk about the discussion points and reach some kind of agreement.

• Then rearrange the groups into three groups of four by taking one student from the original groups for each of the new groups, e.g.:

ADGJ BEHK CFIL

They can then compare what they decided in their original groups.

2 Pyramid discussion

These work best when students have the opportunity to select and rank their choices.

• First, students agree choices in pairs:

AB CD EF GH IJ KL

• Then they agree their choices in groups of four:

ABCD EFGH IJKL

• Then in groups of six:

ABCDEF GHIJKL

• Then they agree their choices as a whole class.

Information-gap activities

Most units contain a speaking activity which depends upon some kind of information gap. For such activities, students are generally divided into pairs and referred to the Pairwork Section on pages 138 – 145.

• It is generally far simpler to demonstrate rather than explain how these activities should be carried out.

• For activities which involve describing, drawing and 'telephoning', try to arrange the pairs so that Students A and B are sitting or standing back-to-back.

• It is often a good idea to encourage all the As and all the Bs to confer and help each other with ideas, question-formation and possible replies to anticipated questions before you arrange them into pairs.

Role-play activities

Imagine that there are twelve students and four roles:

A B C D

• First put students into four groups, according to their role:

AAA BBB CCC DDD

Get them to pool their ideas, work out what they are going to say and how they are going to act.

• Go round the groups and help them, where necessary, with ideas and vocabulary.

• Then put students into their role-play groups, e.g.:

ABCD ABCD ABCD

• Start the role play off but then sit in the background and let the students get on with the task. (It is often a good idea, particularly in small classrooms, to play some fairly loud music so that students concentrate on what is going on in their own groups rather than being distracted by other groups.)

• Only interrupt and correct if a serious error appears to have caused a breakdown in communication and if the students are unable to correct it themselves.

• Introduce a short correction spot at the end of the interaction, when all students have finished.

• At the end of the role play, you may choose to ask one of the groups to act it out again in front of the class.

The Art of Deception

Aims and content

The overall aim is to see how familiar students are with intermediate level structures, and how capable they are of performing a challenging writing task based around picture prompts. Throughout the unit there is considerable emphasis on accuracy work for FCE Paper 2 (Composition).

Set A
Aims: To provide speaking practice and launch the topic of fashion through a class questionnaire; to teach a lexical set around the topic of fashion; to practise the listening skill; parallel writing.
Speaking: Fashion survey
Vocabulary: Clothes and fashion [P]
Listening: Women's fashions since the 1950s
Writing: Describing how someone is dressed

Set B
Aims: To practise the reading skill (scanning, then reading for inference, related to FCE Paper 1); to introduce phrasal verbs.
Speaking: Discussion around a cartoon
Reading: The fashion fraud
Vocabulary: Introduction to phrasal verbs

Set C
Aims: To practise the listening skill (first gist, then intensive listening); to revise/introduce language for making complaints; to teach vocabulary related to 'damage' (FCE Paper 3); to practise the speaking skill based on a structured communication activity.
Listening: Making complaints – dialogue completion
Vocabulary: Damage
Speaking: Making complaints

Set D
Aims: To provide a diagnostic activity to assess students' manipulation of intermediate-level structures and forms; to teach ways of opening and closing letters (FCE Paper 2, Part 1 + 2); to provide freer writing practice through a picture composition (FCE Paper 2, Part 2) – again, a challenging diagnostic activity.
Language study: Tense review
Writing: Opening and closing letters – composition around picture prompts.

Set E
Aims: To show how events can be sequenced (important for FCE Paper 2, Writing); to teach students how to write a sequence of instructions (FCE Paper 2, Writing); to practise listening and note-taking (FCE Paper 4, Part 2).
Listening: A 'Mentalist Act'
Language study: After and afterwards
Writing: How to perform a trick – giving instructions

Set A

SPEAKING: Fashion survey

• The first activity in the book is a speaking activity. Point out the importance of speaking for FCE, and explain how important it is for students to practise the speaking skill by working in pairs and groups with each other during the course.
• Introduce the topic of fashion. Are students interested in or knowledgeable about fashion?
• Read out the questions. You can take some opinions from students as examples to demonstrate the kind of points which might be raised.
• You can get the class to work first in pairs, then in larger groups, and finally in whole class discussion (see Introduction, 'Pyramid discussions'). But as this is the first task, do not let the discussion drag on too long.

VOCABULARY: Clothes and fashion [P]

1 Read out the instructions and briefly discuss the example. Then set students to find the other odd-ones-out. They can work individually or in pairs.
• Take answers from the class as a whole. Discuss reasons for the answers and possibilities of more than one answer.

KEY

Example: **C** (*gloves*) The other two are worn around the neck and shoulders.
1 **C** (*tie*) The other two are worn on the head.
2 Two possibilities: **C** (*shirt* – other two worn by women) or **A** (*skirt* – covers lower part of the body).
3 **A** (*vest*) In British English a vest is an item of underwear which covers the upper part of the body. The other items cover the legs and feet.
4 **C** (*belt*) All the others are footwear.
5 Two possibilities: **A** (*jacket* – usually a larger, heavier item worn over the other choices) or **B** (*pullover* – both a jacket and cardigan have buttons).
6 Two possibilities: **B** (*suit* – the others are items of sportswear) or **C** (*trainers* – worn on the feet).
7 **B** (*purple*) This is the only word referring to a definite colour. All the other words refer to patterns.

2 Make sure that students have a partner to work in pairs, that they find the page that relates to their part, and that they know what to do. Help with any difficult words in the instructions for A and B (e.g. dummy, 'dress' a dummy). As this is the first activity of this kind, you could choose a student as your 'partner' to demonstrate at least part of the task. (Other students look and listen as you demonstrate.)

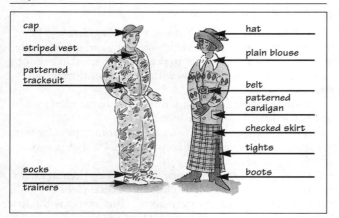

cap	hat
striped vest	plain blouse
patterned tracksuit	belt
	patterned cardigan
	checked skirt
	tights
socks	boots
trainers	

3   This is a quick exercise to test vocabulary. Students can work individually or in larger groups. When you go through the answers, get students to give examples of sentences or items to illustrate the words filled in.

KEY

1 make-up; **2** smart; **3** tight; **4** high-heeled; **5** old-fashioned

LISTENING: Women's fashions since the 1950s

1   Give students a few moments to look at the photographs. Then obtain opinions about the fashions shown. Count the number of students who like each fashion most or least – the results can go on the board. A is from the 1950s, B the 1960s, C the 1980s and D the 1990s.

2   Introduce the Listening task. If necessary, play part of the tape so that students get the idea of the matching task.
• Play the tape through. Observe students and see if they are finding the task difficult. You will probably need to play the tape two or three times and if the class is weak you may have to stop the tape between descriptions.

TAPESCRIPT

1 In this photograph she's wearing a pinkish patterned shirt and trousers. They're quite short and stop above her ankle. She's also wearing a pair of sandals. Her hair is up and she seems to be wearing a lot of make-up and, um, false eyelashes. Looks quite nice, I suppose.
2 Um, I think this is really fashionable. Really simple but very smart and practical too. She has just got on a black one piece suit and a pair of white trainers. She has got long straight hair and is wearing some bright red lipstick. Apart from that no other make-up.
3 She looks really weird in this one. I mean, lots of black lipstick and her hair is in a mess. She is wearing trousers and a loose yellow top with a scarf tied around her waist. She looks a bit like a pirate. Awful.
4 Wow! This one is really too much. She is wearing a really short skirt and high-heeled shoes. She has also got on a

leopard skin top. Hope it wasn't from a real leopard. You could have worn this to a party but not for anything else surely.
5 This must be the oldest one. She is formally dressed and looks terribly old fashioned. She is wearing a matching skirt and jacket with high-heeled shoes and she is carrying a tiny bag and has got a funny little hat on her head. Her clothes look really tight and uncomfortable.

• Discuss answers. See if students can quote the relevant part of the tape to support the answers. Play relevant parts of the tape after students have given their ideas.

KEY

1 – B; **2 – D**; **3 – C**; **4** – the missing photo; **5 – A**
The missing photo shows fashions from the 1960s. See tapescript for description.

3   Read out the instructions and get students to turn to the tapescript on page 153 of their books. Play part of the tape again and elicit ideas, so that students know what they are supposed to underline. Then play the whole tape, with pauses if students are having difficulties. Go through answers in the normal way.

KEY

Introducing what the women are wearing:
1 She's wearing/She's also wearing/She seems to be wearing
2 She has just got on/She has got long
3 She is wearing
4 She is wearing/She has also got on
5 She is formally dressed/She is wearing/She is carrying/has got

Giving opinions:
1 Looks quite nice, I suppose.
2 I think this is really fashionable. Really simple but very smart and practical too.
3 (a) She looks really weird in this one. (b) Awful.
4 (a) This one is really too much. (b) You could have worn this to a party but not for anything else, surely.
5 (a) This must be the oldest one. (b) ... looks terribly old fashioned. (c) Her clothes look really tight and uncomfortable.

WRITING: Describing how someone is dressed

Make sure that students undertake this activity in a friendly spirit and that no-one gets hurt or embarrassed. If there is any teasing it should be directed at students with plenty of self-confidence.
• Read the model description aloud, slowly. Students follow as you read.
• Elicit the main structures from the description and write them on the board, as follows:
She is _____ dressed and looks very _____ .
She is _____ .
She is carrying _____ .
Her clothes look _____ .
• Elicit different ways of expanding the structures, with different words and expressions to match the blanks (e.g.

informally dressed; looks very fashionable; etc.) There is no need to relate the expressions to any particular person in the class at this point.

• If necessary, take a person in the class as an example (with the person's agreement) and elicit ways of describing the person.

• Students write the descriptions as indicated. They can do this individually or in pairs. Then the descriptions are read out and other students guess who is being described.

HOMEWORK SUGGESTION

Imagine it is the year 2020. You are at a fashion show. Write two fifty-word paragraphs describing what men and women are wearing.

Set B

SPEAKING

Check that students understand what they have to do. Then give students a few moments to work out the correct order for the speech bubbles (working in pairs or individually). Obtain answers.

KEY

The order is: top right; bottom right; top left; bottom left

• Students can then read the three questions for themselves. It will be good if students can take time to frame their answers in sentences, and find words to express their ideas from dictionaries. They can work in pairs or groups for this.

KEY (suggested answers)

Penny probably feels embarrassed at the way Alex is dressed. Alex is proud because it shows he can afford a holiday in an exotic and faraway place like Thailand.
An open-ended question. Answers will lead students into the reading passage which comes next.

READING: The fashion fraud

1 Comment as necessary on the vocabulary items *fake* and *counterfeit*. Pre-teach the word *label*.

• Write on the board the 'gist' question: 'Who are Vincent, Gerry and Miguel?'

• Give students time to read the passage and answer the question (but not too much time, since students do not need to understand the passage in depth). Students answer in their own words. Ask questions if students need further prompting to supply the information asked for (e.g. 'What does the detective agency do?').

KEY

Vincent is Vincent Carratu, the head of a detective agency specialising in uncovering counterfeiting fraud. Gerry is one of his agents, an experienced and crafty ex-policeman. Miguel is a

Mafia-style gang member involved in the manufacture of fake whisky.

2 Read out the questions which require a closer reading of the passage, and give students time to find the answers. If time allows, you could get students to answer in writing.

KEY

1 The writer doesn't really seem to care much about fashion fraud. S/he feels that big-name manufacturers exploit the snobbery of their customers.

2 Gerry's assignment was to uncover a gang of fake whisky manufacturers. It was dangerous because the informer who gave Carratu's agency the initial information was certainly murdered by the gang.

3 Miguel's trap was to ask Gerry about how whisky was made. If Gerry had appeared knowledgeable then Miguel could have guessed he was some kind of spy. After all, Gerry was supposed to be a rough gang member who would have known nothing about these things. When Gerry said he just drank the stuff, Miguel was no longer suspicious.

3 This task tests students' general understanding of the text and their ability to distinguish the main point of each paragraph. Students need to learn to interpret the heading and look for evidence in the paragraph.

KEY

1 B (Evidence: Don't we pay far too much for fashion goods anyway?)

2 D (Evidence: ... they ... employ investigator Vincent Carratu to find out who is making ...)

3 A (Evidence: It is a dangerous game, ...)

4 C (Evidence: Naturally, Gerry knew all about the process but realised that the kind of criminal he was playing wouldn't.)

4 Word search
Students work out how many words there are in the text which express the idea of 'authentic' and 'not authentic'.

KEY

authentic: real, genuine (the genuine article = the real thing)
not authentic: fake, counterfeit, imitation

VOCABULARY: Phrasal verbs

1 Write the example sentences on the board. Read through the explanations and examples, using the examples on the board to point out particular items (verbs, prepositions and particles). Check that students understand the idea of phrasal verbs by eliciting a few further examples, writing them on the board and getting students to explain their meanings.

2 Students match phrasal verbs and definitions. While checking answers, you could get students quickly to provide a sentence to bring out the meaning of the phrasal verb.

KEY

1 – E; 2 – F; 3 – C; 4 – B; 5 – A; 6 – D

3 Students can do this exercise individually or in pairs. They should correct the sentences in which the phrasal verb is used incorrectly, and be able to say how the 'incorrect' phrasal verb should be used, with examples.

KEY

1 Wrong. He *found* some money ... (You find out information, or a secret.)
2 Correct.
3 Correct.
4 Wrong. Where did you *find* it? (If you look for something, you search for it.)
5 Correct.
6 Wrong. Why don't you *give* it *up*? (If you give something away, you let someone else have it, without asking for money.)
7 Correct.
8 Correct.
9 Correct.

4 Students choose four phrasal verbs (e.g. any of the phrasal verbs already mentioned in the lesson) and make sentences of their own. This can be done as a quick writing task.
• Go round the class monitoring students individually. Concentrate on appropriate contexts for the phrasal verbs. Do not try to correct everything.

HOMEWORK SUGGESTION

Write ten sentences using the phrasal verbs you have already come across.

Set C

LISTENING: Making complaints

1 Read out the questions. Give students a few moments to think about them. Students can exchange ideas briefly among themselves (pairs or small groups). Then elicit some experiences from members of the class as a whole. But do not spend too much time on this lead-in activity.

2 Ask students to describe the picture and elicit from them what is going on. Get students to cover the dialogue or close their books. Introduce the situation and read out the questions which students must answer from the listening. (You could write these on the board.) It will be useful to get students to guess what problems Colin might have had with the shirt, and what he might want the store to do. Pre-teach the word *receipt*.

• As usual, adapt the playing of the tape (and any pauses while playing) to the level of the class. A good class may be able to answer the questions after a single play-through. Students could answer initially by writing notes; this will make it easier for you to do a quick check on the understanding of individual students. Then you can take answers from the class as a whole.

TAPESCRIPT

ASSISTANT:	Can I help you?
COLIN:	Yes, it's (1) *about* this sports shirt. I washed it the other day. The colour ran and it shrank.
ASSISTANT:	Oh dear, I see. Do you have the (2) *receipt* ?
COLIN:	I'm (3) *afraid not* , but it was in one of your bags.
ASSISTANT:	I'm sorry, (4) *but I'm not allowed to change anything* without a receipt.
COLIN:	(5) *Do you think I could speak* to the Manageress?
ASSISTANT:	Yes of course. I'll fetch her for you.
MANAGERESS:	Are you the gentleman who brought this shirt in?
COLIN:	Yes, could you change it? It is a (6) *well-known brand*.
MANAGERESS:	Where did you get it? Did you buy it here?
COLIN:	Actually, it was a present from my girlfriend. Is (7) *something the matter* ?
MANAGERESS:	I'm afraid there is. You see, (8) *it's an imitation* .
COLIN:	An imitation? Are you sure?
MANAGERESS:	I'm absolutely positive. The crocodile is even the wrong way round.
COLIN:	I don't know (9) *what to say* .
MANAGERESS:	Forget it. But if I (10) *were you, I'd have a word* with my girlfriend!

KEY

1 The colour ran and it shrank.
2 No, his complaint is unsuccessful.
3 Embarrassed, and probably rather angry with his girlfriend.

3 Students look at the blank-filling dialogue, listen again, and try to fill in the missing words.

KEY

See tapescript above. The missing words are in italics.
Introducing the complaint: It's about this sports shirt ...
Supporting the complaint: It is a well-known brand.

4 Intonation in questions
• Play the questions from the tape. Students follow in their books and listen to the intonation patterns. Check if students can imitate the patterns. Ask students what they notice about the patterns.

KEY

What the students should notice is that the *wh*-question finishes with a falling intonation, whereas the *yes/no* question starts high, drops, then rises again at the end.

• Drill the questions as necessary, adding some further examples of simple wh- and yes/no questions.

VOCABULARY: Damage

Read out the 'damage' words in the box. Quickly check if students can give examples of goods which might be scratched, broken, etc. Then students do the exercise.

KEY

1 stained; 2 broken; 3 torn; 4 scratched; 5 cracked

SPEAKING: Making complaints

1 Take situation 1 as an example. Read through the roles for Student A and Student B. Elicit suggestions from students for things that might be said, suitable for each role.
• With a weak class you can get a good pair of students to give a complete demonstration of the role play as an example, while other students listen.
• Divide the class into pairs. Students do the role-play task. Go round the class and listen as students speak. When they have had enough time to do the task you can comment briefly on any general problems that have arisen.
• Introduce Situation 2. This time students should be able to do the role play with less preparation. Try to organise different pairs than for Situation 1.

2 Take the first situation as an example. Students from the class give their ideas about whether they would complain or not, and what they might say.
• Students discuss the remaining situations in pairs. Go round quickly and discuss briefly with each pair if possible.
• Round off with a brief discussion with the class as a whole.
• As a follow-up, you could perhaps (a) get students to role play one of the situations, or (b) set students to write a 'playlet' on one of the situations for homework.

KEY (POSSIBLE ANSWERS)

1 Excuse me, but I think there is a hair in my food.
2 Do you think we could have the window open just a little bit? It's terribly hot in here.
3 I'm terribly sorry, but you're not allowed to smoke in here.
4 Hey, come on. I was first. I'm in a hurry too!
5 Excuse me. Are you sure this is mineral water? It tastes like tap water to me.

HOMEWORK SUGGESTION

Choose one of the two situations from the speaking exercise and write a conversation similar to the one Colin had in the shop.

Set D

LANGUAGE STUDY: Tense review

1 Give students a moment to look at the task and find the letter. Tell them they have to think of a title for the letter. Give them a limited time to read through the letter. (They should not try to understand the letter in detail.) Briefly discuss possible titles and write them on the board. (Adjectives such as crooked, fraudulent, dishonest could appear in the title, and nouns such as boyfriend, crook, confidence-trickster.)

2 Students read the letter and write the correct form of the verbs given. Go round and check as students work. Quickly go through the answers when students have had time to do the exercise.

KEY

1 are getting on; 2 sounds; 3 were; 4 would leave; 5 ask; 6 will/'ll find; 7 needs; 8 have had/have been having; 9 do you remember; 10 was sent; 11 stealing; 12 knew; 13 wanted to be; 14 said; 15 had; 16 had given; 17 to buy; 18 thought; 19 would never see; 20 was walking; 21 saw; 22 told; 23 thought; 24 was lying; 25 managed to; 26 told; 27 lived/was living; 28 found; 29 had taken in; 30 had known; 31 was; 32 would never have given; 33 will not trust; 34 am picking up/am going to pick up; 35 finish; 36 'll/will write

3 If necessary, check that students understand the grammar terms by getting them to give examples (preferably not from the letter). Then get them to pick out examples of the different forms from the letter.

KEY

1 Present simple 35; also verbs that don't take the continuous 2, 7, 9
2 Present continuous 1, 34 (for future)
3 Present perfect 8. Past perfect 16, 29
4 Past simple 12, 14, 15, 18, 21, 22, 23, 26, 28
5 Past continuous 20, 24, 27 (reported speech)
6 Simple (will) future 33, 36
7 Conditional sentences:
   1st conditional 5 and 6
   2nd conditional 3 and 4
   3rd conditional 30 – 32
8 The passive 10
9 Reported speech 14 and 15. 18 uses the reporting verb 'thought'.
10 Infinitive construction 13, 17 (infinitive of purpose), 25. Gerund construction 11

• Now discuss with students the areas they find most difficult. You may be able to plan remedial work on problem areas.

WRITING: Opening and closing letters

1 Introduce the subject of letters. With books closed you could elicit opening and closing expressions known to students.

- Students look at the opening and closing expressions and match them. Discuss briefly, checking that students know that 'Yours faithfully' is used with 'Dear Sir', 'Dear Madam', or 'Dear Sir or Madam'.

KEY

1 – D; 2 – C; 3 – B; 4 – A

2 Students can read through this short exercise and do it for themselves. But point out that they may not be able to use the items in (1) above word for word.

KEY

1 Dear Ann, Dear Bill (students can invent a name); Lots of love, With best wishes
2 Dear Mr Brown, Dear Mrs Black; Yours sincerely
3 Dear Sir, Dear Madam, Dear Sir/Madam, Dear Sir or Madam; Yours faithfully
4 Dear Mr and Mrs White; Yours sincerely

3 Students look at the letter and answer the questions. Comment briefly, using the board if you wish.

KEY

1 Kirsten puts her address in the top right hand corner.
2 Her signature goes at the end of the letter.

4 Students work in pairs or groups, find useful expressions and write them down for their own later use. Write items on the board when you discuss answers.

KEY (examples)

It was so nice to hear from you ...
I hope you are getting on better.
Anyway, I must go now.
I'll write again soon.

5 Practice
- Explain the task. Point out that the paragraph below is only the *first* paragraph of Monika's reply – students will have to write the rest of the reply from the pictures.
- Read through the opening paragraph. Then take the first picture as an example. Elicit ideas about what Monika might write in the letter. Students can then continue, telling the story shown in the pictures (working individually or in pairs). Go round, check and help. You may want to take the writing in for correction.

KEY (examples)

I met a really nice guy at a discothèque on Saturday. We danced and talked a lot. He was very fit and athletic, and so I asked him what he did. He told me that he was a professional cyclist and that he rode for England! I didn't want to tell him that I was just a sales assistant in a fashion shop, so I told him that I was a top model! Then on Monday, something really embarrassing

happened. I was taking a dress from the window when I saw him outside. He was cleaning the shop window! (He did have a bicycle, though.) When he saw me he was surprised too! Afterwards we went to a café and had a cup of coffee and laughed about it all. We have arranged to see each other again next weekend.

HOMEWORK SUGGESTION

Write the story from exercise 5; base your composition around the pictures and any work you have done in class.

Set E

LISTENING: A 'Mentalist Act'

- Write *telepathy* on the board. Elicit what it means. Students use their own words or give examples.
- Students discuss briefly in pairs or groups whether or not they believe in telepathy. Have some brief whole-class discussion and find out how many students believe in it. Give students a few moments to read the situation for themselves. Go through it briefly. Check that they understand *magician* and *blindfold*.
- Play the tape through for general understanding.
- Play again, several times if necessary. Students complete the notes. They may check their answers in pairs if you wish.
- Go through answers, playing the tape and pausing as necessary.

TAPESCRIPT

INT: How did you start in show business, Arthur?
AC: As a magician's assistant for 'The Great Marvella'. I helped out mostly with the mentalist act.
INT: What was that?
AC: Oh, a kind of telepathic act where she guessed the names of objects while wearing a blindfold. Um... I put the blindfold on her. Afterwards I went into the audience. People handed me objects like watches or rings and things and then 'The Great Marvella' guessed what they were.
INT: And how did this trick work then? She didn't have any special powers, did she?
AC: No, not at all. Actually she could see through the cloth.
INT: So it was as simple as that!
AC: Not really. After I had blindfolded her she couldn't actually see the objects. They were too small, and don't forget the theatres were dark.
INT: So how was it done?
AC: I spelled out the name of the object by the way that I was standing. For example, if I had my head on the left, that told her that it began with 'r', or if both of my arms where bent that there was a 'ing' sound in the word ...
INT: So she could guess that you'd been given a ring. And did anybody ever realise what you were doing?
AC: No. Never. I also misled the audience. I said things in a funny way – you know – changed my intonation so that people would think I was signalling with my voice.
INT: Clever. And did it work? I mean did the boss always manage to guess the objects which were handed to you?

AC: Oh yes. Ninety-five per cent of the time.
INT: And for the other five?
AC: She just said that the vibrations weren't right. The audience loved it.

KEY

1 telepathic act; **2** guess the names of; **3a** watches; **3b** rings; **4** see through the cloth; **5** the way that he was standing; **6** began with 'r'; **7** an 'ing' sound; **8** saying things in a funny way; **9** ninety-five; **10** that the vibrations weren't right

LANGUAGE STUDY: *After* and *Afterwards*

1 Write the example on the board, pointing out the sequence of actions.

2 Again, go through the example sentences, writing them on the board, and pointing out the uses of *afterwards, after* and *after that;* also the tenses and the use of the *-ing* form. Note the use of the past perfect to make the sequence of actions clear: *After I **had** put ... .* It is worth pointing out that most problems occur when students put *after* between the two actions. Then it is often extremely unclear which actions happened first and second, e.g. She went to the bank *after* she went to the shops.

3 Practice
Read out the actions. Elicit some ways of showing the sequence of actions in sentences. You can write these on the board. Then get students to continue with further sentences showing the sequences (working individually or in pairs).

KEY

1 She ate fire. Afterwards she cut Arthur in half.
After eating/After she had eaten fire, she cut Arthur in half.
She ate fire; after that she cut Arthur in half.
2 She threw knives. Afterwards she caught a bullet between her teeth.
After throwing/After she had thrown knives, she caught a bullet between her teeth.
She threw knives; after that she caught a bullet between her teeth.

WRITING: How to perform a trick

1 Introduce the task. Read out the expressions in the box. You can elicit the answer for the first blank as an example. Students continue with the rest of the exercise themselves. Go round and check, then conduct feedback in the usual way.

KEY

1 the following
2 First of all
3 After that
4 What you do is this
5 and then

6 Now this is the tricky bit
7 Obviously
8 Now all you have to do

2 Giving instructions
• Ask students to say what they can tell about the card trick from the pictures.
• Take the first note or two as an example. You can write the expanded note on the board. Then students write instructions for the whole trick, expanding the notes. Go round and help in the usual way. You might want to take the work in for correction.

KEY *(example)*

You'll need an assistant to help you with this trick. First of all arrange nine cards face down in a square. And now for the trick. What you do is this. You invite a member of the audience to come up and you leave the room. The person chooses a card, turns it over and looks at it. Afterwards you come back and ask the person if they have chosen a card. Now this is the tricky bit! As you are asking the question your assistant casually places his/her finger on any card to show its position in the square. Obviously, your assistant must do this without too much fuss. For example, if your 'guest' has chosen the top right hand card then your assistant will put his/her finger on the top right hand corner of one of the cards. Then all you have to do is turn over the card and wait for the reaction of your 'guest'.

HOMEWORK SUGGESTION

Write a 'speech' telling someone how to perform a trick you know.

Aims and content

The overall aim is to develop writing skills. Relative pronouns which give texts cohesion are revised. Ways of sequencing, expressing reason and purpose, and planning compositions are also dealt with.

Set A

Aims: To teach film vocabulary; to practise pronunciation (word stress); to revise functional areas; suggestions, preferences, agreeing with what has been said; to practise listening and deciding who said what (FCE Paper 4, Part 4).
Vocabulary: Types of films
Speaking: Discussing films
Listening: Organising an evening out – making and responding to suggestions
Speaking: A telephone conversation

Set B

Aims: To test, revise and teach the simple past and past participle forms of the most common irregular verbs; to practise the listening skill (FCE Paper 4, Part 4); to contrast the two most common uses of *used to*.
Language study: Revision of past forms
Listening: Cartoon Characters
Language study: Uses of *used to*
Speaking: An interview with Chris Caine [P]
Writing: A magazine article

Set C

Aims: To practise intensive reading (FCE Paper 1, Part 3); to practise question making; to revise/teach basic sequencing, and expressing reason and purpose.
Speaking: Maxine Guest
Reading: Aardman animations
Writing: Completing an open dialogue
Language study: Sequencing/Reason and purpose; sentence patterns using *so* and *such*

Set D

Aims: To show how relative pronouns such as *which, who, when* can be used to achieve cohesion in a written text; to present a model for a written description of a film or play; to provide additional topic vocabulary which would help students to write a description for themselves; to practise some basic elements of punctuation.
Reading: Describing a film (including relative pronouns)
Writing: Describing a film
Listening: People in films

Set A

VOCABULARY

This activity is part of the overall vocabulary build-up required for First Certificate. It presents a lexical set of items related to films.

1 As a lead-in (books closed), ask students the name of the last film they saw and the names of favourite film stars, directors, etc. See if students can also give some words for different types of film.
• Students open books at page 18. They work individually or in pairs and match the photographs from the films with the different types of film. Some films have more than one word to describe them, i.e. D is a horror story and a comedy.
• Quickly obtain answers to the exercise. Do not bother too much about pronunciation at this stage.

KEY

A – cartoon; B – western; C – musical; D – horror story and comedy; E – science fiction; F – documentary

2 Main stress in words
• Word and sentence stress are important factors in the evaluation of candidates in FCE Paper 5 (Interview).
• Elicit students' ideas about how to pronounce the 'film' words, and especially where the stress occurs. Start by asking how many syllables the word has. Then go on to show the stress on the board. A useful technique is to mark the stress using 'bubbles': a big bubble shows the stressed syllable, a little bubble the unstressed syllable, as follows:

western	Oo
thriller	Oo
cartoon	oO
comedy	Ooo
musical	Ooo
adventure	oOo
documentary	ooOo
horror film	OoO
love story	OOo
science fiction film	OoOo O

NOTE: We CANNOT say 'I went to see a horror at the cinema'.
• Play the tape (tapescript as in list of film types above). Students listen to the stress. Play again as necessary and get students to repeat the stress on the words.

SPEAKING

Divide students into groups of three or four. Read the questions out and obtain a few example answers. Students can then discuss the questions in their groups as you go round and listen. Allow some time at the end for brief whole-class discussion.

LISTENING: Organising an evening out

1 Read out the instructions and briefly get students to comment on the people in the picture, who they are and where they are. Then play the tape and conduct feedback as suggested in the Introduction.

TAPESCRIPT

ANNABEL: What (1) *shall we do* this evening?

MARTIN: (2) *Why don't we* go out for a meal? Or maybe we (3) *could* go and see a film.

RICK: I think (4) *I'd rather* go to the cinema.

ANNABEL: So would I.

MARTIN: OK. That's fine by me. (5) *What's on?*

ANNABEL: Well, there's (6) *Robocop*. It's a (7) *kind of* science fiction thriller.

RICK: Mm, I know. It's great but I've already seen it.

MARTIN: Well, (8) *let's* go and see (9) *Back to the Future III* then.

ANNABEL: That (10) *sounds like* a good idea. I haven't seen it yet.

RICK: (11) *Neither have* I. I really enjoyed the first two.

ANNABEL: Look. It's 6 o'clock now and the film doesn't start until 8.30. I'm going home to change.

MARTIN: ... and I'd like to get something to eat!

RICK: Me too. Why (12) *don't you come back to my place* for a snack?

MARTIN: Thanks. That (13) *would be really nice.*

RICK: What about you, Annabel?

ANNABEL: Thanks for the offer, but (14) *I'd like to go home* and change first. But I can pick you up at Rick's place in my parents' car if I can borrow it. (15) *Would 7.45 be OK?*

RICK: Great. We'll see you then. (16) *Could you give us a ring* if there's a problem?

ANNABEL: I promise ... See you later then. 'Bye.

KEY

1 Rick
2 Rick
3 Annabel
4 Rick
5 Annabel

2 Give students a few moments to look at the dialogue for completion. Play the tape once through. Then play the tape a little at a time (see Introduction). Students write down the words that go in the blanks.

KEY

See tapescript above – the missing words are in italics.

3 **Making suggestions and agreeing**
Elicit the expressions from the students and write them on the board, as follows:
Asking for suggestions: What shall we do this evening?
Making suggestions: Why don't we ...?
                We could ...
                Let's go and ...
                Why don't you ...?
                Would 7.45 be OK?

Agreeing: OK.
         That's fine by me.
         That sounds like a good idea.
         Thanks. That would be really nice.
         Great.
         (with positive sentence) Me too. So would I.
         (with negative sentence) Neither would I.

4 **Pronunciation:** *don't you/could you*
Drill these sentences for pronunciation:
Why don't⁀you come back to my place? (/tʃ/: 'ch' sound as in *church*)
Could⁀you give us a ring if there's a problem? (/dʒ/: 'j' sound as in *judge*)

SPEAKING

Demonstrate the activity using a bright student, then put the class into pairs to role play. Afterwards, let them swap parts. As the aim of this activity is to promote fluency, keep any correction to a minimum.

HOMEWORK SUGGESTION

Using the conversation between Annabel, Rick and Martin as a model, write one between Pat and Jo based on the prompts.

Set B

LANGUAGE STUDY: Revision of past forms

This section also relates to FCE Paper 2 (Composition). To do most of the composition questions students must know the past simple and past participle forms of the most frequently used irregular verbs; weaknesses in this area can lead to failure in this part of the examination.

1 Ask students to turn to the table on page 146. Allow them five or six minutes to complete the list on a separate piece of paper. Students can work alone or in pairs.
• Go through answers, drilling pronunciation and checking spelling. The full version of the table can be found on Teacher's Book page 88.

2 Introduce the passage on Walt Disney, briefly eliciting some information about Disney's films. Which of Disney's films and cartoon characters are most famous? Ask if anyone has been to Disneyland or Eurodisney.
• Students change the forms in italics into the past tense. Go round and check as students work to note any common mistakes.

KEY

1 was; **2** began; **3** broke; **4** drove; **5** got; **6** met; **7** went; **8** made; **9** lost; **10** gave; **11** came; **12** saw; **13** held; **14** built; **15** felt; **16** took; **17** spent; **18** brought; **19** paid; **20** were

NOTE: As well as rounding off work on irregular verbs, this exercise sets the scene for the listening which follows.

LISTENING: Cartoon characters

1 Students read the paragraph for themselves. You can allow brief discussion in pairs about what *Tom and Jerry* and *The Flintstones* are called in their country (or countries).
• Have some brief whole-class discussion. Get students to write on the board the names given to *Tom and Jerry* and *The Flintstones* in their country. Students talk about these or other cartoons which they especially like.

2 Students read through the task. If necessary, play part of the tape to make the task clear, and help students to work out who the speakers are.
• Play the tape, two or three times if necessary. Students fill in the answers.

TAPESCRIPT

RACHEL:	Oh great. *The Flintstones* are on telly. I used to watch *The Flintstones* when I was a kid.
BARRY:	Me too. My favourite's *Tom and Jerry* though.
RACHEL:	That's because of all the violence!
BARRY:	Don't be silly. It's just a cartoon!
JOHN:	But they are really cruel. I agree with Rachel.
BARRY:	It's just harmless fun!
RACHEL:	But kids still copy them. I mean, these things have, um, more of an effect than we like to think. *Tom and Jerry* seems to get more and more violent too.
BARRY:	Oh come off it! They're exactly the same.
JOHN:	That's not true, you know. Characters do change. Take Mickey Mouse.
BARRY:	Mickey Mouse?
RACHEL:	Yeah, I read an article. It – the article – said in the old days, in the early cartoons he was really horrible. You know, he was always doing cruel things.
RACHEL:	Yeah. Like, in one, erm, cartoon he makes the animals play a tune by pinching and squeezing them, to, erm make them squeal.
JOHN:	That's right. We're not used to seeing that kind of Mickey these days. He is too busy being nice to everybody.
BARRY:	Goody goody.
JOHN:	Right. He never does anything naughty.
BARRY:	Even so. This article, did it say anything else?
RACHEL:	I'm trying to think. Oh yeah – it said that his face gets rounder and softer as time goes on. How can I explain? Have you seen any of the early cartoons?
JOHN AND BARRY:	Yes.
RACHEL:	Well, in the early ones he looks quite rat-like, doesn't he? He has got this long pointed nose and little eyes.
BARRY:	And?
RACHEL:	Well, later on his face changes. His head gets as big as his body. Or almost. His eyes get bigger, too.
BARRY:	Strange, isn't it?
RACHEL:	Yeah, he grows backwards! He gets younger instead of older. I wonder if they did it on purpose?
JOHN:	Mm, it makes him much cuter I suppose.
BARRY:	An acceptable symbol for the US of A.

• The questions about character and appearance cover the 'gist' of the listening. After the first play-through obtain students' ideas.

2 Play the tape again. Students complete the notes, working on their own. They can check their answers in pairs.

3 Go through answers. Have the table on the board. Get students to fill in answers on the board.

LANGUAGE STUDY: Uses of *used to*

1 Go through the explanations and examples as suggested in the Introduction. Elicit answers to the questions. (The first sentence, *I used to watch The Flintstones*, describes a past habit. The second sentence, *We're not used to seeing that kind of Mickey these days*, describes a present habit.)

2 Pronunciation of *used to*
Point out that we do not say 'useD to' with a 'd' sound, but rather 'use To' /juːstə/. In other words, the 'd' sound in 'used' is assimilated to the 't' of 'to'. Students practise the pronunciation.

3 Obtain answers to the questions. Write questions and answers on the board. Show the relationship between the auxiliary verb in the question and the answer.

| Did you | use to watch *The Flintstones*? No, | I didn't |.

| Are you | used to watching a lot of TV? Yes, | I am |.

4 Make sure the task is understood. Take sentence 1 orally if necessary.
• Students do the exercise. They can check their answers in pairs. Go round and check as they work.
• Go through answers. Try to elicit reasons why the forms are used in each case.

SPEAKING: An interview with Chris Caine

This is an information gap task, related to FCE Paper 5 (Speaking). Candidates may well be asked to role play a situation with the other candidate. Present the task and get students to work in pairs in the normal way, see Introduction. Student A may need some help to absorb his/her part, as there is quite a lot of information to take in.

KEY (Notes on Chris Caine's career)

Background: born in poor part of London; life was hard; poor but happy child
Early career: singer in London club; drama school (many plays); small parts in Hollywood films
Number of films made: 30
Reputation as a bad driver: 6 accidents through driving on the left
Reputation for being nervous before acting: always used to be sick before going on stage

WRITING: A magazine article

• Read through the instructions. You can start by getting students to make a list of things they might want to say about Chris Caine in their article, including the information obtained by Student B above (see Key), but adding any other points that would interest readers.
• Elicit some examples of sentences continuing the article. Then students continue writing the article for themselves. Go round, check and help as students work. Pay particular attention to *used to* forms for HABITUAL behaviour in the past (not specific events or actions).
• If time allows, conduct feedback, obtaining sentences that students have written, writing them on the board and discussing points as they arise.

HOMEWORK SUGGESTION

Rewrite and improve the magazine article about Chris Caine.

Set C

SPEAKING

• Give students a few moments to look at the photograph. Elicit some suggestions about her job.
• Students work in pairs and describe the picture to each other. Go round quickly and listen to the kinds of sentences they are producing. Keep this activity brief.

READING

1 Students skim the article. Quickly check a few ways in which students were right in their assumptions and, more interestingly, examples of ways they were wrong.

2 Give students a few moments to read through the task for themselves. Check that they understand the idea of fitting in the missing sentences. Take A as an example if necessary.
• Students read and decide where the sentences go. They may check their answers in pairs if you wish.
• Discuss answers.

KEY

1 C (Evidence: *The same principle guides both techniques ...* refers to animators and Aardman)
2 A (Evidence: *in order to keep them rigid* refers back to *difficult to control*)
3 B (Evidence: *They are also given a sound track.* The heading refers to sound.)
4 D (Evidence: *afterwards it has to be carefully cut and edited* is evidence that *the job is far from over.*)

WRITING

1 Present the task, taking the first question as an oral example if necessary.
• Students work out the questions, then compare their ideas, working in pairs.
• Go through answers with the whole class.

KEY

1 successful are they/successful have they been
2 are the models made of
3 frames is a forty second advertisement made up of
4 long has Maxine been making models
5 responsibility does Maxine have

2 Students reread the last paragraph of the text and make similar questions and answers.

LANGUAGE STUDY: Sequencing/Reason and purpose

1 Get students to recall ways of showing the sequence of actions from Unit 1. Then students work in pairs or individually and pick out the sequencing words and expressions from paragraph 2 of the text.

KEY

First of all; After that

2 Students find expressions in paragraph 2 which introduce reason or purpose.

KEY

in order to; so that; That's why; (takes over) to produce (= in order to produce)

3 Go over the example with the class as a whole. Students then transform the remaining sentences working individually or in pairs.

KEY

1 Chris wanted to develop her career; that's why she went to Hollywood.
2 She had so many accidents because she wasn't used to driving on the right.

3 She slept in car parks in order to save money.
4 She's studying hard so that she can pass the exam.

4 Go through the examples and elicit students' ideas about the use of *such* (before a noun phrase) and *so* (before an adjective). Use the board to show the form:
It was such a challenge …
such + noun
It was so challenging …
so + adjective

5 Students do the exercise, working individually or in pairs.

KEY

1 It was such a sad film that it made us miserable.
2 He screamed so loudly that everyone jumped.
3 She laughed until she cried because the film was so funny.
4 It was banned because it was such a violent film.
5 He used to be a famous actor.
6 She still is not used to signing her autograph.
7 They went to Hollywood in order to become film stars.

HOMEWORK SUGGESTION

Write eight true/false statements for the text about Maxine Guest.

Set D

READING: Describing a film

1 Explain that the text is a description of a film with words missed out. Briefly introduce the actual film described – check if students have seen it and if they can remember any of the main characters, but do not get them to describe the story in detail. Then give students time to look at the text and the picture.

2 Explain that the words missed out are words like *which*, *who*, etc. Briefly check if students can give any information about these words (e.g. that they are called 'relative pronouns', that *who* relates to people, *which* to things). If necessary, take one or two examples of blanks to launch the students into the exercise. Then get students to work at filling in the blanks, in pairs or individually.
Conduct feedback by asking students to 'vote' for which relative pronoun belongs in each blank. Then get students to match relative pronouns with 'people', 'things', etc.

KEY

1 which; **2** which; **3** where; **4** who; **5** whose; **6** who; **7** who; **8** which; **9** which/that; **10** when; **11** who; **12** who; **13** why; **14** where
people: who, whose
things and animals : which, that
times: when
places: where
reasons: why

3 Word search
Read out the meaning and give students time to find the matching words in the text. Obtain answers and write them on the board.

KEY

plot; character; is set in; the script; the hero; the villain

WRITING

• Go through the task, and the sequence of points to be covered. Encourage students to make notes and prepare a plan. Monitor closely and supply any vocabulary they may need. Elicit some examples of sentences that might be used at each point. Get students to think of which tense will mainly be used (the simple present tense).
• After this, students can write out the complete description of their favourite film, based on the models they have studied. This could be done as homework, to be corrected by you and handed back in a later lesson.

HOMEWORK SUGGESTION

Write about your favourite film using the notes you have made in class.

LISTENING: People in films

1 Read out the list of people, A – G, slowly. Students try to point to the appropriate pictures as you read.
• Give students time to match any pictures they have not already matched with people. They can discuss this in pairs.
• Go through answers, briefly.
• In pairs or groups, students discuss the duties and responsibilities of the different people, and who they would most/least like to be. The pairs or groups report back to the class, giving answers in their own words. Have some brief whole-class discussion. (NOTE: Further indications of the kinds of things the people do are given in the listening extracts which follow in Task 2.)

2 Make sure the task is clear. Play the tape, several times if necessary. You can allow discussion in pairs between plays.
• Take answers, but do not discuss in detail at this point, as there is a further task to follow.

TAPESCRIPT

1 Cut, cut. We're going to have to do it again. That was just fine but you need to concentrate on the feelings. Now Angela, remember this is the man who you think murdered your brother, but you've got to try hide your suspicions 'cos you're afraid something might happen to you. OK, let's have another go, shall we? When you're ready …. action.

2 Yeah, it was a really difficult shot. It was continuous, from the moment Angela leaves the place where she has hidden the money to when she gets to work, about four minutes in all. We did it all with one camera as a single take. It took two days to get it right.

3 One of the, erm, biggest problems we had was how to explain the motivation of the main character, Angela. In the original book, the writer describes her inner emotions, so it is quite clear why she does such crazy things later on. After all, on the surface she is a really ordinary housewife, the kind of person who you meet every day. But ordinary housewives don't steal drug money from the Mafia. So for the film we had to create an extra character, someone she worked with who was involved, so that Angela had someone to talk to.

4 I've got to say Angela was one of the most difficult roles I've ever had. One thing which made it really tough was the leading man. He had such an ego, you know, such a high opinion of himself. Although, to be fair, I found the part challenging too. I'd always been in comedies before and found changing to drama very hard.

5 Of course these days there's a lot that you can do with video and with, er, computers – lots of the special effects are generated by computer. Having said that, I think that there will always be a need for people like me who can jump out of high windows and fast cars because somehow it makes the film look much more realistic. It was me, by the way, in the helicopter scene in *Angela*. It can be dangerous but it is a calculated risk.

6 There's a lot of waiting around but it's fun. It means that I can make a few dollars to help get me through college. You also see some of the stars close up... Anyway, it's a beginning and who knows, some day, a director may notice me in the crowd and give me a bigger part. You know, one day you're a face in the crowd and then you might get a small part with a couple of lines, and then who knows? Lots of the big names in Hollywood started out just the same way so why not me?

7 Well, I suppose I'm the guy everybody loves to hate. The one with the big cigar except that I don't smoke any more. Once we decide to make the film, I have to get the money together to do it, which means convincing a lot of people who are going to expect a good profit too. Then I have to sort out the contracts and locations and make sure that we can get the support of the theatres. Film making is an art, it is creative but it's big business too and you need someone like me who really knows what they're doing ... .

KEY

A – **4** (star); **B** – **5** (stuntman/woman); **C** – **2** (cameraman/woman); **D** – **7** (producer); **E** – **6** (extra); **F** – **1** (director); **G** – **3** (scriptwriter)

3 Give students time to look at the questions. They may be able to work out answers from what they remember. You can take one or two of the questions orally if you wish.
• Play the tape again. Students decide on answers.
• Go through answers with the whole class. If necessary, play the tape and pause at relevant information.

KEY

1 – A; 2 – A; 3 – A; 4 – A; 5 – A; 6 – B; 7 – B

3 Great Escapes

Aims and content

The overall aim is to explore the language and sequencing of narrative.

Set A

Aims: To review, teach and test prepositions of position and direction.
Speaking: Tara the Tarantula (picture story) (FCE Paper 5, Part 3)
Language study: Prepositions of position and direction
Listening: She's leaving home

Set B

Aims: To practise prediction in reading; to compare and contrast the infinitive and gerund; to deduce meanings of words from contexts.
Reading: A bowl of macaroni
Language study: The infinitive and the gerund

Set C

Aims: To examine the grammar of intransitive phrasal verbs; to practise gist and intensive listening (FCE Paper 4, Part 4).
Vocabulary: Phrasal verbs
Language study: Subjects, verbs and objects
Listening: A narrow escape

Set D

Aims: To practise the skill of speaking based on a simulation; to introduce students to the language of telephone conversation.
Speaking: The Wall
Listening: Booking by telephone
Speaking: Booking a hotel [P]

Set E

Aims: To analyse narrative composition and the use of narrative tenses; to give practice in writing narratives.
Writing preparation: Narrative composition – an introduction to which tenses are used and when
Language study: Narrative tenses 1
Speaking: Collective story telling
Writing: Narrative composition (FCE Paper 2, Part 2)

Set A

SPEAKING: Tara the Tarantula

• This activity relates to Part 3 of Paper 5 (Speaking). It is also a diagnostic activity which will allow you to check how much remedial work students need on prepositions.
• Read out the title. Find out if any students are especially afraid of spiders, or at least of large spiders such as tarantulas. Do students know anything about the habits of tarantulas?

NOTE: It is possible that some students may have an extreme fear of spiders. If this is the case, try to handle the matter sensitively; above all, do not make fun of the students concerned.
• Students look at the pictures. If necessary, take some examples of notes orally, and write them on the board. Then students work on the notes by themselves. Go round and check the notes they produce as they work.
• Put students into pairs. They tell the story to each other, helping each other where there are difficulties. Try to listen to some pairs as they do this.
• Get students in turn to tell parts of the story to the class as a whole.

KEY (example)

Deep in the banana plantations of Guacarica, Tara is asleep in a bunch of green bananas. A plantation worker cuts off the bunch where she is sleeping.

The bananas are loaded onto a ship which is sailing to New York.

Some weeks later in New York, Tara wakes up. She is in a fruit bowl. A child sees her and screams.

Tara leaves the skyscraper in New York and climbs down her web, into the street.

Tara hides herself on the coat of a woman who is taking a taxi to the airport.

At the airport, Tara climbs onto a man who is going to Guacarica.

On the plane, she lies curled up like a wig, on the man's bald head.

An air stewardess tries to hit Tara with a tray, but she only hits the head of the bald man. The bald man is astonished. Tara escapes.

At Guacarica, Tara floats down to the ground on her web parachute.

The other tarantulas welcome her. 'Home at last!' says Tara.

LANGUAGE STUDY: Prepositions of position and direction

1 Read out the prepositions. Give students time to look at the pictures.
• Students make sentences about the pictures, using the prepositions.
• You could very briefly elicit some examples of *other* prepositions, with sentences to illustrate their meaning, e.g. selecting from the prepositions in Exercises 2 and 3. However, do not spend too much time on this, as the exercises below are themselves designed for revision.

2 Students complete the text on page 147 as indicated. See Teacher's Book page 89 for the key.

3 This activity relates to FCE Paper 3 Part 1 (choosing from alternatives) and also Paper 1 Part 2. It also provides a lead-in to the Reading and Listening which follows.
• Students read the paragraph and choose the correct preposition from the alternatives given.

1 out of; **2** through; **3** on; **4** out of; **5** into; **6** against; **7** inside; **8** between; **9** into; **10** out of; **11** onto; **12** along; **13** past; **14** down; **15** into; **16** towards; **17** behind; **18** across; **19** over; **20** at

LISTENING: She's leaving home

• Direct students to the text they have completed in ex. 3 and get them to read it through carefully. This could be done by asking the students to read the text aloud as a form of feedback to the exercise. The completed text basically tells the story of the song which follows. Students should now be able to concentrate on listening and interpretation as most of its 'information' is embedded in the preceding exercise.

• Now play the song 'She's leaving home'. Find out if any students have heard it, or know the group that sang it. (*Answer:* The Beatles)

• Present the questions. Check that students understand *guilty* and *react*. Give students a few moments to think about the questions (you can allow students to discuss the questions briefly among themselves). Then see if students can make any kind of prediction about what the song will be about.

• Play the tape, several times if necessary. If the class is weak, on the third or fourth play-through you may want to stop the tape after each verse or chorus. After playing the tape, do not ask questions immediately, and do not put the questions to the class as a whole. Instead, give students time to consider their answers to the questions. They can discuss their answers in pairs or groups.

• Observe the class or listen as students discuss. (You can quietly check comprehension with individual students if you wish.) When it appears that most students have understood the gist of the song and have a reasonable idea of the answers to the questions, briefly conduct general feedback (see Introduction).

TAPESCRIPT

She's leaving home
Wednesday morning at 5 o'clock as the day begins.
Silently closing the bedroom door,
Leaving the note that she hoped would say more,
She goes downstairs to the kitchen clutching her handkerchief.
Quietly turning the back door key,
Stepping outside, she is free.

She is leaving home
We gave her most of our lives.
Sacrificed most of our lives.
We gave her everything money could buy.
She's leaving home after living alone for so many years.

Father snores as his wife gets into her dressing gown.
Picks up the letter that's lying there.
Standing alone at the top of the stairs,
She breaks down and cries to her husband
'Daddy, our baby's gone.

Why would she treat us so thoughtlessly?
How could she do this to me?'

She is leaving home.
We never thought of ourselves.
Never a thought for ourselves.
We struggled hard all our lives to get by.
She's leaving home after living alone for so many years.

Friday morning at 9 o'clock she is far away,
Waiting to keep the appointment she made,
Meeting a man from the motor trade.

She is leaving home.
What did we do that was wrong?
We didn't know it was wrong.
Love is the one thing that money can't buy.
Something inside that was always denied for so many years.
She's leaving home.
Bye, bye.
She's leaving home.
Bye, bye.
She's leaving home.
Bye, bye.

KEY

1 She is going to meet her lover (a man in the motor trade).

2 She probably doesn't feel guilty because she wants the fun she has been denied for so many years. (However, do allow the students to say what they think here.)

3 She may not be very young, since we are told that she has been 'living alone for so many years', and the song mentions 'something inside that was always denied for so many years'. She could even be in her late twenties or thirties. But all we really know is that her parents treated her as younger than she is.

4 Somewhere far away.

5 Her parents are very upset. They wonder how she can be so cruel after everything they have done for their 'baby' over the years.

6 Yes, they do think they have been good parents. They think they have sacrificed all of their lives for her.

HOMEWORK SUGGESTION

Look at the speaking activity about Tara the tarantula again and write one or two sentences for each picture. Be sure to use the prepositions of place and direction we have revised.

Set B

READING: A bowl of macaroni

1 Briefly introduce the reading text 'A bowl of macaroni'. Find out if students have heard of Casanova. Point out that this text isn't connected with Casanova's fame as a great lover. Students read the first paragraph to find out why Casanova is in prison.

KEY

Casanova was in prison because in his youth he had written a book which attacked the church, so his enemies had arrested him and locked him up.

2 Point out the illustrations, and see if students can say what any of the items are in English (a spike, a Bible, a bedsheet, a bowl of macaroni).

• At this point you could get students to work in groups (books closed) and produce theories about how the items helped Casanova to escape. The more amusing or unrealistic the theories the better.

• Students read through the text in the normal way to check their answers.

KEY

The spike was hidden in the Bible. The dish of macaroni was used as a decoy. The jailer was so busy trying not to spill it, he didn't notice how heavy the Bible was. The spike was used to dig a hole in the cell floor. The bedsheet was used as a rope to climb along the roof tops and escape.

3 If you wish, ask students to draw a diagram of the escape route. Help them to isolate the pieces of information in the text they will need to do this. (See 1–7 below)

KEY (example)

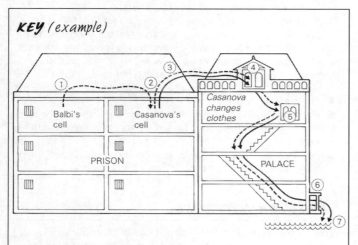

1 Balbi makes a hole in his ceiling.
2 He makes a hole in Casanova's ceiling and pulls him up.
3 They climb along the rooftop.
4 They find an open window into the palace.
5 Casanova looks out of a window.
6 They go through the door.
7 They go to the waterfront.

Key
– – – – –   Casanova
————   Balbi

4 Word search

• Students read the text again to find the words, working quietly (individually or in pairs).

• Go through answers. To reinforce the meanings you could get students to use the words to write further sentences of their own.

KEY

Para. 1: famous in a bad way = notorious
Para. 2: very angry = furious
Para. 3: clever like a fox – crafty
to move something to another place illegally = smuggle
Para. 4: to move along on your hands and knees = crawl
to walk slowly and silently to avoid detection = creep
(past tense *crept*)
Para. 5: to look very closely = peer
to walk purposefully, with big steps = stride (past tense *strode*)

5 Students read the text and decide on the correct choice. When you go through the answers, get students to quote evidence from the text in support of the correct answer, or against the wrong answer.

• This task will give students some insight into the way multiple choice tests are constructed. Discuss the task briefly to make sure it is understood. Begin by asking for (or giving) one or two examples of further incorrect choices, so that students get the idea.

• Students work in pairs and try to invent further incorrect choices.

• Elicit choices from different pairs. Write good examples on the board.

KEY

1 A
2 A
3 B
4 A
5 B (A is wrong: 'Casanova saw Balbi's hand ...')
6 B (claim of spending the night in the Chief of Police's house)

LANGUAGE STUDY: The infinitive and the gerund

1 Briefly revise the terms 'infinitive' and 'gerund'. Elicit examples. If students seem to require it, go through the verbs listed and elicit some examples of infinitives and gerunds coming after them, within complete sentences (e.g. 'I managed to pass my exams', 'I succeeded in passing my exams').

2 Students complete the sentences.

KEY

1 managed; 2 offered; 3 looking forward to; 4 succeeded in;
5 risked; 6 promise; 7 hope; 8 plans/hopes; 9 consider;
10 denied; 11 avoid; 12 pretended

HOMEWORK SUGGESTION

Write the story of the escape from Balbi's point of view. Try to
use as many of the verbs which take the infinitive and gerund as
you can.

Set C

VOCABULARY: Phrasal verbs

1 If necessary, remind students what phrasal verbs are,
eliciting some examples and writing them on the board.
Then go through the instructions to the task.
• Students read the paragraph individually and match the
highlighted verbs with the meanings given.

KEY

to leave = set off; to recover consciousness = come to; to finish
= run out; to arrive = turn up; to begin suddenly = break out; to
escape = get away

2 Students use the phrasal verbs to complete the
sentences.

KEY

1 comes to; 2 get away; 3 turn up; 4 set off; 5 runs out;
6 broken out

• If time allows, you can get students to use the phrasal
verbs in a 'story' of their own, as an extension activity.

LANGUAGE STUDY: Subjects, verbs and objects

• Find out if students have come across the terms
'transitive' and 'intransitive' and can provide any examples.
• Go through the explanations in the normal way (see
Introduction). Give or elicit examples to explain technical
words (*transitive, intransitive, direct object, passive*).
• If necessary for reinforcement, elicit further examples of
sentences containing transitive, intransitive and transitive-
intransitive verbs.

LISTENING: A narrow escape

1 **Key words**
Students look at the key words and decide on the kind of
context in which they might occur. (*Answer:* You might find
them in a description of a riot or a demonstration.)

2 As a pre-listening activity, generate interest and set the
scene by discussing the three questions.

3 Set the main-point question ('Whose fault ...?') and
play the tape in the normal way (see Introduction). Students
decide on their answers.

TAPESCRIPT

JANICE:	Goodness! That was lucky ... It reminds me of one I had years ago. I was studying Italian in Rome.
CAROLE:	Huh, huh.
JANICE:	One, erm, night I went to a to a pop concert in an indoor stadium. We all set off in a party mood; we'd been looking forward to it for ages. Anyway, around this time people used to invade cinemas and theatres without paying because they said prices were just too high.
CAROLE:	Sounds like a good idea.
JANICE:	Not if you'd paid. Well that evening, about two hundred of them got in. Every seat was taken. It was packed.
CAROLE:	Go on.
JANICE:	So then the riot police turned up and told everybody to leave. Then the troublemakers started throwing things at the police. They'd come prepared for a fight, they had sticks and helmets. Fighting broke out around the stadium.
CAROLE:	Wow!
JANICE:	Then the police started hitting their sticks against their shields. It was a really terrifying noise. Anyway, the troublemakers kept throwing things at them and several got hurt by flying chairs and things. Eventually they just ran out of patience and started firing tear gas and hitting people.
CAROLE:	What, just the troublemakers?
JANICE:	No, anybody ... Discipline just broke down.
CAROLE:	... and did you get hurt?
JANICE:	Almost. A policeman told me to move but I answered back in English. Roberto did though. He got hit on the head so I stayed by him until he came round. Finally we got away – they hadn't blocked off one of the exits. Of course we were coughing and blind from the tear gas but it was great to get outside.

KEY

It was partly some of the demonstrators' fault, as some
troublemakers clearly wanted a fight. However, if we believe
Janice's account, the police got out of control.

4 Present the true/false exercise. Students can look
through the questions individually before you play the tape
again and check if they can answer any of them. Do not let
students shout out answers.
• Play the tape again, give students time to work out their
answers, and conduct feedback. Students should be able to
correct the false sentences.

KEY

1 False. She was studying there.
2 False. It was an indoor stadium.
3 True.
4 True.
5 False. The riot police arrived later.
6 False. They left one exit free.
7 True.
8 False. The troublemakers started throwing things at the police.
9 False. Janice was fine although one of her friends was hurt.
10 False. She just pretended she couldn't understand.

5 Speaking

Put the students into pairs or small groups to discuss the questions; then lead into a group discussion.

HOMEWORK SUGGESTION

Write a short article either defending or attacking the behaviour of the police in the stadium. Use the tapescript for 'A narrow escape' for ideas.

Set D

SPEAKING: The Wall

1 Present the task, get students to look at photographs, and encourage discussion in the normal way (see Introduction).

KEY

In the left-hand picture, a man is helping a woman escape by putting her onto some kind of chair made of ropes. Perhaps she is going along an underground tunnel into West Berlin. In the right-hand picture, there is a big round thing (a drum for a cable) and there is a hole in the middle where people could hide. They would hide in the drum and then would be smuggled into West Berlin.

2 Students look at the map of Berlin and read individually the description of Berlin.
• Students can briefly discuss any particular vocabulary problems in pairs or groups before going on to the main task of planning how they would spend a weekend in Berlin.
• Deal with the discussion in the normal way (see Introduction). Where students decide to go and what they choose to see will depend on their own preferences. But do make sure that students choose logical and manageable itineraries. Listen for accurate use of functional language for making suggestions and stating preferences. (Items to express these functions have been introduced in earlier units.)

LISTENING: Booking by telephone

1 Present the situation so the students are ready to write a note. Then play the tape in the normal way.

TAPESCRIPT

Part A

TELEPHONIST:	Breakaway Travel.
MRS ROBERTS:	Good morning, I'm phoning about your weekend escapes to Berlin.
TELEPHONIST:	I'll put you through to someone who can help you. Hold the line please, madam. I'm afraid all lines are busy. If you'd like to leave me your name and number I'll get someone to return your call as soon as possible.
MRS ROBERTS:	The name is Mrs Roberts, and my number is 675982.
TELEPHONIST:	Right, Mrs Roberts. I'll pass the message on.

Part B

Five minutes later

MRS ROBERTS:	Hello. 675982.
SHARON GREY:	Hello. This is Sharon from Breakaway Travel ...
MRS ROBERTS:	Oh hello, thanks for ringing back. I'd like to know about your weekend escapes to Berlin for the last weekend of next month.
SHARON GREY:	Let me see. Yes, madam, three nights departing the 27th is available. That's £320 per person for scheduled flights, and a double room in a three star hotel with continental breakfast is also included.
MRS ROBERTS:	That sounds fine. I'll come in to book this afternoon.
SHARON GREY:	I look forward to seeing you then, Mrs Roberts.
MRS ROBERTS:	Goodbye.

• Check the messages that students have written.

KEY (the ideal note)

Sharon
Call Mrs Roberts a.s.a.p. Tel: 675982
Re: weekend breaks in Berlin

2 Read out question 1 (How does Mrs Roberts tell the telephonist what she wants to know?). Play the tape again, several times if necessary. Students try to write down the phrases used.
• Obtain answers, writing out the correct phrases on the blackboard.
• Deal with question 2 in the same way.

KEY

1 How does Mrs Roberts tell the telephonist what she wants to know?
Good morning, I'm phoning about your weekend escapes to Berlin.
2 How does the telephonist:
a ask Mrs Roberts to wait? *Hold the line please, madam.*
b ask Mrs Roberts for her name and telephone number? *If you'd like to leave me your name and number ...*

c tell Mrs Robert's someone will call her? *I'll get someone to return your call as soon as possible.*

3 Point out the notes. Explain that Mrs Roberts made the notes after the second conversation, but that the details in the notes are wrong.
• Play the tape of Part B, several times if necessary. Students correct the notes.

KEY

Mrs Roberts' notes	Correct version
£340 per person	£320 per person
charter flight	scheduled flight
full English breakfast	continental breakfast

4 Questions 1 and 2. Proceed as for the previous conversation (Task 2, above).

KEY

1 How does Sharon:
   a introduce herself? *This is Sharon from Breakaway Travel.*
   b show she is trying to find the information? *Let me see.*
2 How does Mrs Roberts:
   a show she is pleased that Sharon has returned her call? *Thanks for ringing back.*
   b ask for information? *I'd like to know about your weekend escapes to Berlin for the last weekend of next month.*
   c show that she is happy with the information Sharon gives her? *That sounds fine.*

SPEAKING: Booking a hotel

This is an information-gap task, related to, but slightly varying from, the 'booking by telephone' conversations students have just heard. Present it and get students to work in pairs. The aim here is fluency and completing the task successfully. Do not worry about minor errors.

HOMEWORK SUGGESTION

Using the tapescript for 'Booking by telephone' as a guide, write a dialogue between the receptionist of the Avonbury Hotel and the caller.

Set E

WRITING PREPARATION: Narrative composition

• Introduce the model narrative composition. Ask the students to read it through quickly to find out what the story is about. (A fire in a hotel.)
• Get students to underline the verb forms used in the composition.
• Briefly get students to identify the tenses used. (Do not discuss why they are used at this point.)
• Students think of ways of ending the story, discussing their ideas with their classmates. If time permits you can get

students to write a complete ending to the story for themselves.

LANGUAGE STUDY: Narrative tenses 1

1 The past simple and past continuous
• Go through the explanations and examples in the normal way (see Introduction). Elicit further examples as necessary.
• Students do the exercise, changing the verbs in bold type to their correct form.

KEY

1 The guard entered the cell as he was digging the tunnel.
2 When they found her she was cutting a hole in the fence.
3 He arrived while I was trying to phone him.
4 I was walking in the woods when I heard a shot.
5 He fell over as he was crossing the road.

• Discuss the uses of *while, when, as.* Generally speaking, *while* comes before the past continuous, *when* comes before the past simple, and *as* comes before either tense.

2 The past simple and past perfect
Go through the explanations and examples. Elicit further examples as necessary. Then students do the exercise, deciding if the past perfect is used correctly or incorrectly.

KEY

1 Correct.
2 Correct.
3 Wrong. He must have climbed down the rope before he disappeared into the trees.
4 Correct.
5 Wrong. The past perfect is not needed here. There is a clear sequence of actions in the past, following each other. The sequence does not finish with an idea which would require a past perfect, e.g. 'We had washed, dressed and eaten breakfast by the time they arrived'.

3 The past perfect continuous
• Check if students are familiar with the term 'past perfect continuous' and can give examples of it.
• Write the examples given at (a) and (b) on the board. Underline the *had* and the *-ing*.
• Go through the explanations. Elicit further examples of past perfect continuous forms if necessary.
• Students do the exercise. Go through answers with the whole class. Get students to say whether the form they give is past simple or past perfect continuous.

KEY

1 had been going out; happened
2 had been waiting; turned up
3 said; had been playing; had been making; behaving; began

• Tell students to turn to page 148 in their books.
• Students can do this individually or in pairs. It could also be done as a homework task.

1 had; **2** had been studying; **3** was; **4** was watching; **5** felt; **6** went; **7** fell; **8** became; **9** woke; **10** made; **11** had been having; **12** saw; **13** looked; **14** tried; **15** could not; **16** took; **17** felt; **18** realised; **19** had been kidnapped; **20** travelled; **21** wondered; **22** would ever; **23** held; **24** explained; **25** were; **26** had exploded; **27** had travelled; **28** was coming; **29** started; **30** knew; **31** was; **32** was shaking

4   The class should be able to look back at the Casanova story (pages 28 – 29) and explain why each narrative tense is used. They can find the narrative tenses in pairs and work out why the tenses are used, before you elicit answers from the whole class.

SPEAKING

• This activity should be enjoyable, and it acts as a lead-in to the written task which follows. Read out the instructions. Get students to suggest some details to make the story interesting. Each suggestion should add to (not contradict) those that were given before. (But aim at a balance between the bare facts and too much information.) Write down the suggestions in note form on the board.

• Divide students into groups. Give groups time to look through points 1–18 and to work out their ideas. (NOTE: Most of the points are 'independent' – they do not depend very closely on earlier points – but some exceptions to this may emerge in the course of the activity.)

• If the class is weak you may have to help students by writing more notes on the board yourself. But try to keep the activity moving along briskly.

WRITING: Narrative composition

Students write compositions based on the notes they have made. They work individually, then compare their efforts with those of other group members (exchanging compositions, or reading out what they have written). Go round, check and help as students work. You may want to take the work in for correction, or discussion in a later lesson.

HOMEWORK SUGGESTION

Imagine that you are one of the people in one of the pictures from Set D Speaking: The Wall. Write the exciting story of your escape from East to West Berlin.

4 Treasure

Aims and content

The overall aims are to revise countables and uncountables; to examine the grammar of phrasal verbs; to teach sentence patterns using *despite* and *although*; to teach/revise the language of describing objects and practise writing descriptions of objects; to practise the reading skill through a variety of texts highlighting the use of discourse markers and linkers.

Set A
Aims: To launch the topic; to test students' use of quantifiers and countable/uncountable expressions.
Speaking: Spot the difference
Language study: Countable and uncountable

Set B
Aims: To practise the reading skill; to practise determiners.
Reading: The history of Captain William Kidd
Vocabulary: Colonel Blood
Speaking: Captain Kidd or Colonel Blood?

Set C
Aims: To practise describing a picture; to practise the reading and listening skills; to teach clauses of concession using *although* and *despite*; to revise narrative tenses; to examine the grammar of separable and inseparable phrasal verbs.
Reading: Shipwreck!
Language study: Despite and *although* – narrative tenses 2
Listening: Sunken treasure
Vocabulary: Phrasal verbs

Set D
Aims: To teach words related to personal objects, with work on their pronunciation; to test/practise adjectives relating to the shape, texture and quality of objects; to practise the listening skill; to introduce and practise 'polite' questions (using indirect forms).
Vocabulary: Personal treasures
Listening: Treasure in our attic
Language study: Indirect questions

Set E
Aims: To practise the reading skill; to write a descriptive text based around a model; to practise the reading skill through separating out and reordering two texts; to raise awareness of informal and formal features within letters.
Reading: Pirates!
Reading: Lost property – re-assembling a jumbled text.
Writing: Lost property

Set A

SPEAKING: Spot the difference

• Introduce the topic of the unit. Do students know any stories about buried treasure? Or the names of any famous sea pirates? What did pirates do? What flag did they use? (*Answer:* The skull and crossbones) Can students draw the flag?
• Find one difference between the two pictures as an example. Then students work in pairs and find the remaining differences. Go round and listen as students work. Listen especially for how they use uncountable, singular and plural forms, as this will help you to decide how to approach the task which follows.

KEY

A (left-hand picture):
The pirate with the parrot has no tattoo on his arm; The eye patch on the pirate in the painting is on his right eye; The woman has some rings on her fingers and one string of pearls; The pirate in the foreground has no scar on his face and two hands; There are six coins on the table in front of the pirate with the striped T-shirt; There is a full bottle on the table; The pirate in the striped T-shirt is hiding the Ace of Diamonds; The woman's glass is empty.

B (right-hand picture):
The pirate with the parrot has a tattoo on his arm; The eye patch on the pirate in the painting is on his left eye; The woman has no rings on her fingers and two strings of pearls; The pirate in the foreground has a scar on his face and a hook instead of his hand; There are four coins on the table in front of the pirate with the striped T-shirt; There is a little drink in the bottle on the table; The pirate in the striped T-shirt is hiding the Ace of Hearts; The woman's glass is full.

LANGUAGE STUDY: Countable and uncountable

• Give students time to look at the diagram and go through the explanations with them as necessary.
• Elicit some sentences about the picture of the girl and boy on the beach – what they are doing and what they are looking for. Obtain the answer to the first multiple-choice item to demonstrate the exercise. Then set students to do the rest of the exercise (individually or in pairs). Tell students to refer to the diagram above to help them. Go round and check for problems occurring with uncountable and countable forms.
• Conduct feedback in the usual way, discussing problem areas. Finally you can get students to act out the complete conversation.

KEY

1 – C; 2 – A; 3 – B; 4 – A/C; 5 – C/D; 6 – B; 7 – C; 8 – B; 9 – A;
10 – A; 11 – A; 12 – A; 13 – B; 14 – C; 15 – C; 16 – C;
17 – A/B; 18 – B; 19 – A/B; 20 – A; 21 – C; 22 – A/C

HOMEWORK SUGGESTION

Write ten sentences fully explaining the differences between the two pictures in the speaking activity. Make sure that you use *some* and *any*!

Set B

READING: The history of Captain William Kidd

1 Find out if any students have heard of Captain Kidd (a famous pirate), or can give any information from their own knowledge. Then set students to read the text and decide if the sentences are true or false. Students should try to write true sentences where a correction has to be made. Conduct feedback, getting students to refer to relevant parts of the text.

KEY

1 False. He was a gentleman with friends in high places.
2 True.
3 True.
4 True.
5 False. It seems it would have made no difference to his fate.
6 False. His friends refused to help him.
7 False. No map shows the exact location of the treasure.
8 True.

2 Get students to look at the words in the box. Obtain an example completion for the first blank. Then students continue with the exercise themselves. Conduct feedback in the usual way.

KEY

1 been; **2** the; **3** with; **4** than; **5** several; **6** employed; **7** little; **8** him; **9** for; **10** by; **11** no; **12** down; **13** since; **14** once; **15** does

VOCABULARY

1 Ask students what kind of man someone called 'Colonel Blood' might be. Elicit some ideas. Then read through the task.
• Students read the text quickly and find answers. Do not give them too long for this.

KEY

1 Because he brutally attacked Edwards and left him for dead.
2 His attempt to steal the crown jewels.
3 Because he was pardoned by the king and his property was returned to him.

2 Students can do this vocabulary task in pairs. You may want to encourage students to use a dictionary. When you go through answers, see if students can explain why a particular choice is correct.

KEY

0 destiny (*Destination* means a real place you are travelling to.)
1 priceless (= very valuable)
2 stolen (You *rob* a person, you *steal* a thing.)
3 amazing
4 trustworthy
5 fact (*In fact* = in reality)
6 hidden (*Hide* is transitive, *disappear* is intransitive.)
7 chance (The expression is *by chance*)
8 killed (transitive)
9 raised (idiom: to *raise* the alarm)
10 reached (transitive)
11 trial
12 certain (adjective)
13 unfairly
14 come up with (= invented, discovered)
15 delightful
16 sympathetically
17 Nowadays
18 opportunity (idiom: *take the opportunity* to do something)

SPEAKING

Students discuss the questions in groups.

Set C

READING: Shipwreck!

1 The picture is part of a large painting showing a stormy coast and a shipwreck. The people in this detail are survivors being attacked by a band of men on the shore. The woman is raising her arm because she is about to be killed. Very possibly, they have made the captain steer his ship onto the rocks by using lights (lanterns). With no witnesses they will be able to steal any cargo which survives the wreck.
You might also see the ship wrecked on the rocks, people pulling things out of the sea, dead bodies on the beach.
NOTE: The picture has no factual connection with the text.

2 Read out the headings. Make sure the task of matching headings with paragraphs is understood.
• Students read the text and try to match headings with paragraphs. They can check their answers in pairs.
• Discuss answers with the whole class.

KEY

A 2 (Evidence: *any survivors were usually murdered*)
B 4 (Evidence: *The admiral ... had believed he was near France.*)
C 5 (Evidence: *he was murdered by local women* is a *kind* of justice as he had unjustly hanged a sailor)
D 1 (Evidence: *local people changed the name*)
E 3 (Evidence: *at least half of any of the silver ... would have to be given to the government.*)

3 Point out the first sentence in the key. Take it as an example to make the task clear. Students will have to form

questions, based on the reading passage, to which sentences 1 – 5 are answers.
• Students read the text and work out questions, working individually or in pairs. Go round the class as students read. Check if students are able to form suitable questions, and help them as appropriate.
• Discuss possible questions with the class as a whole.

KEY (examples of questions)

1 What dangers did sailors face at sea?
2 What did the admiral do?/What mistake did the admiral make?
3 What sort of person was the admiral?/What was the admiral like?
4 Why did local people change the name of the rock?
5 Where is the rest of the treasure?

LANGUAGE STUDY: *Despite* and *although*

1 Go through the examples and explanations in the usual way. Give or elicit further examples, writing them on the board, and pointing out noun phrases, verb phrases and gerunds.

2 If necessary, elicit examples based on sentence 1. Students continue with the exercise themselves. Notice that students should be able to give two – or even three – sentences in each case.

KEY

1a) Although he was a gentleman, he became a pirate.
b) Despite being a gentleman, he became a pirate.
2a) Although he offered to say where his treasure was, he was hanged.
b) Despite his offer to say where the treasure was, he was hanged.
c) Despite offering to say where the treasure was, he was hanged.
3a) Although he had important friends, they refused to help him.
b) We cannot make a sentence with 'Despite' *in this case.*
4a) Although there are maps of Kidd's 'Treasure Island', nobody has found it.
NOTE: The following sentences are also possible:
b) Despite the existence of maps of Kidd's 'Treasure Island', nobody has found it. (using noun phrase)
c) Despite there being maps of Kidd's 'Treasure Island', nobody has found it. (using gerund)

LISTENING: Sunken treasure

1 Introduce the listening. Tell students to have a look at the notes for completion, and the table with notes for completion.
• Play the tape through once for general understanding.
• Play the first part of the tape through (as far as 'get covered in sand') several times if necessary. Students complete the notes.
• Go through answers, writing them on the board.

TAPESCRIPT

PJ: So, Francis, is there very much pirate treasure left?
FG: I'm not sure. You see, they mostly spent what they stole or else it was taken back. Kidd's famous treasure might not even exist. But there are lots of sunken wrecks out there.
PJ: Sunken treasure. That's really romantic. What advice would you give listeners who want to get rich quick?
FG: Basically I'd tell them not to bother. The ships carrying it often sank in bad weather. Then over the next few hundred years they move and get covered in sand.
PJ: All the same, it's just lying out there waiting for someone to pick it up!
FG: Well, treasure hunting is a bit more complicated than that. For one thing it's an incredibly expensive activity. It nearly always ends in disappointment too.
PJ: I see, but there are success stories, aren't there? I seem to remember one where lots of porcelain was found.
FG: Mm, that was the Dutch ship the 'Geldermalsen'.
PJ: The thing that amazed me was that it was in such fantastic condition.
FG: ... Yes, it looks new, doesn't it? That's because it had been packed in tea which was the rest of the cargo.
PJ: Oh, right. Have there been any other big finds?
FG: Quite a few. Mostly because of improvements in technology. One of the biggest was in 1985 off the coast of Florida. Someone called Mel Fisher found the wreck of a galleon called 'La Nuestra Señora de Atocha'.
PJ: Did he find it while he was fishing or something?
FG: Not quite. Actually he had been looking for it for fifteen years! It has been worth it because so far they have recovered over four hundred and fifty million dollars worth of silver.
PJ: But it's not the biggest?
FG: Actually no. That's the Russian treasure ship the 'Admiral Nakhimov'. It was sunk during the Russian-Japanese war at the beginning of the century. Its cargo was two billion dollars worth of gold and platinum.
PJ: Wow!

KEY

1 spent what they stole; **2** taken back; **3** not to bother; **4** bad weather; **5** in sand

• For the second part of the tape, it will be useful to have the table for completion on the board.
• Play the remaining part of the tape, several times if necessary. Students fill in the notes in the table.
• Go through answers. You can get students to complete the table on the board.

KEY

6 Dutch; **7** porcelain; **8** silver; **9** 450 million dollars; **10** 1985; **11** Fisher; **12** Russian; **13** platinum; **14** two

2 Students read the questions for themselves.
• Play the second part of the tape again. (From 'I see, but there are success stories ...')
• Discuss answers with the whole class.

KEY

1 Because it had been packed in tea (and was therefore well protected).
2 Because he had been looking for it for fifteen years.

VOCABULARY: Phrasal verbs

1 Remind students about phrasal verbs. Elicit examples.
• Get students to underline the phrasal verbs in sentences 1–4. Then students try to match them with definitions a–b below.

KEY

1 – d; 2 – c; 3 – a; 4 – b

• Get students to write further sentences using these phrasal verbs.

2 Go through the explanations and examples, slowly. Put sentences on the board and point out the features they display. Continue with examples on the board, getting students to say 'right' or 'wrong' until you are sure students have grasped the distinction between separable and inseparable phrasal verbs. Point out that students will have to make this distinction in phrasal verbs they encounter in the course from now on. (The information is of course provided by dictionaries; for example the *Longman Advanced Study Dictionary* contains the entry 'make sthg out', thus indicating separability.)

HOMEWORK SUGGESTION

Write a short summary of the interview with Francis Gosling. Use the answers to the questions on page 41 and the tapescript on page 35 (TB p 23) as the basis for your summary.

Set D

VOCABULARY: Personal treasures

• Explain 'personal treasures' = things that mean something to you, not necessarily valuable things; they can be things 'of sentimental value').

1 Students label the drawings with the words.

KEY

A radio; **B** fan; **C** record; **D** silver candlestick; **E** teddy bear; **F** sword; **G** teapot; **H** record player; **I** golf ball; **J** vase; **K** whistle; **L** sea chest; **M** tennis racket; **N** porcelain figure; **O** corkscrew

• Follow up the activity with some brief discussion of students' own personal treasures. Do students (or their families) have any of the items illustrated? Or any other items of sentimental value, perhaps preserved from childhood?

2 **Compound nouns**
• Present the explanation of compound nouns and their pronunciation. Students pick out similar words from the list.

KEY

candlestick; teapot; teddy bear; tennis racket; corkscrew; sea chest; record player
NOTE: 'Gold watch' is not a compound noun. There is equal stress on both words.

• Discuss answers. To show stress you can use the 'bubble' technique from Unit 2. Drill the pronunciation of the compound nouns.

3 **Shapes and characteristics**
• Read through the first set of adjectives. Elicit which of the adjectives relate to SHAPE (sharp, round, curved, oval, rectangular, pointed, spiral), and which relate to CONDITION (shiny, smooth, rough, heavy, light, worn).
• Read through the list of materials: wood, etc. Find items in class made of these materials.
• Get students to give one or two examples of objects corresponding to various adjectives or materials. Then get students to write down the adjectives and materials, and corresponding objects. (Students can work in pairs or groups to do this.)

KEY

shiny:	sword; silver candlestick; whistle
smooth:	radio; record; teapot; vase; sword; porcelain figure
rough:	corkscrew; teddy bear; golf ball; sea chest
heavy:	sea chest; sword; radio; record player; silver candlestick
light:	corkscrew; teddy bear; record; whistle; fan
worn:	tennis racket; sea chest; teddy bear
sharp:	sword; corkscrew
round:	golf ball; record
curved:	radio; vase; record player; teddy bear; teapot
oval:	tennis racket
rectangular:	sea chest
pointed:	sword; corkscrew
spiral:	corkscrew
made of wood:	tennis racket; sea chest; radio; record player
made of china:	porcelain figure; teapot; vase
made of metal:	corkscrew; silver candlestick; whistle; sword
made of cloth:	teddy bear; fan
made of glass:	vase

LISTENING: Treasure in our attic

1 Help students to understand the idea of 'bidding' as in an auction. Elicit students' ideas about what the different objects are worth. One figure in each column relates to the price the figure would actually fetch at auction. Discuss. Students may be able to suggest factors which would make a seemingly worthless object more valuable (the rarity value, the maker, the material, the age of the object, being an 'original', etc.).

• Play the tape. Students note down the values given to the objects, according to the speakers on the tape. Do students find any of the values surprising?

TAPESCRIPT

1

GEORGE BROWN:	Well, hello young man, and what's your name?
ROBIN:	Robin.
GEORGE BROWN:	And how old are you then?
ROBIN'S MOTHER:	He was seven last week.
GEORGE BROWN:	Seven eh! What have you brought to show us? It's a lovely old teddy bear. It's golden brown but the poor chap's fur's rather worn now and one of his eyes is loose. Where did you get it from Robin?
ROBIN:	My grandfather gave it to me. It was his when he was little.
GEORGE BROWN:	Could you tell me where he was from?
ROBIN'S MOTHER:	Actually, he was German.
GEORGE BROWN:	Just as I thought. And if we look at the bear's ear we should find a little button with the manufacturer's name. Yes, here we are. Do you know what you have here?
ROBIN'S MOTHER:	Grandad Martin's teddy, I suppose.
GEORGE BROWN:	But it's very special. You see this is a very early teddy made by Margaret Steiff in Germany. She is the lady who invented the teddy bear. Now what do you think it's worth?
ROBIN'S MOTHER:	A few pounds? I've no idea really.
GEORGE BROWN:	Well, let me tell you something. Young Robin is a lucky young man. These bears are quite valuable. This one is worth about a thousand pounds.
ROBIN'S MOTHER:	Do you know if someone would like to buy it?
ROBIN:	Come on Mummy, give me back my teddy bear. He's mine ...

2

RUPERT ANDREWS:	Yes, sir. What is it we have here? Let's have a look. Um. I have just been handed an old golf ball. It's not often you see one of these. Can I ask where you got it?
MR CROWN:	I actually came across it in the attic along with some old clubs and other things, but I just thought I'd bring this in to show you.
RUPERT ANDREWS:	Well, I'm extremely glad that you did. If I can just describe it to the listeners at home. It's not perfectly smooth like one of the plastic coated golf balls we have these days. In fact it is made of pieces of leather which have been stitched together. This is a real collector's item. A year or two ago a ball similar to this was sold for four thousand pounds! It just goes to show that you should never throw anything away; most people would take one look at this and think it was worthless. Personally, I find an antiques handbook an invaluable source of useful information.

3

GEORGE BROWN:	Now what do we have here? It is a figure of Charlie Chaplin ... um ... It looks like one which was made in England in around 1918. Oh dear.

	Unfortunately it isn't genuine. I'm afraid that it is an imitation. A real one would be worth around two thousand pounds now. Never mind. This doesn't make this entirely worthless. I would say you could probably get around fifty pounds for it. Would you mind telling me how much you paid for it?
MAN:	Not really, I suppose, it cost me ninety pounds.
GEORGE BROWN:	Pity.

4

RUPERT ANDREWS:	A young lady has just brought me something which a lot of people will be interested in. It's an early Beatles record which was issued in the mid-sixties. Where did you get this, young lady?
GIRL:	It belongs to my dad.
RUPERT ANDREWS:	Well. What makes this interesting is that it has all the Beatles' signatures on it and is signed 'All the Best, George Harrison'. Are they genuine?
GIRL:	Yeah. My dad got it from George Harrison. He was working as a waiter in a hotel and he asked them if they'd sign it for him.
RUPERT ANDREWS:	Do you know what it's worth?
GIRL:	Well, as far as my dad's concerned it's priceless, he'd never part with it.
RUPERT ANDREWS:	Well he might if you tell him it could be worth around a thousand pounds at auction.
GIRL:	A thousand pounds. Wow!

2 Give students time to look at questions 1–8. Students may already know some of the answers, but do not let them shout out answers at this point. Play the tape again (more than once if necessary).

• Obtain answers, stopping the tape and playing relevant parts in the usual way.

KEY

1 He got it from his grandfather, who was German.
2 The teddy was from Germany; it was made by Margaret Steiff.
3 In his attic.
4 It wasn't smooth.
5 Ninety pounds.
6 No; the figure is only worth about fifty pounds.
7 The record has all the signatures of the group on it.
8 He asked them to sign the record for him when he was working as a waiter.

LANGUAGE STUDY: Indirect questions

1 Go through the examples in the usual way. Try to elicit the fact that **b** and **c** contain the indirect questions *where he was from* and *what it's worth.*

2 Intonation in questions
Use the tape to demonstrate the intonation. Drill as necessary.

3 Point out the indirect questions following *I wonder* and *I'm not sure.* Use the board to underline the relevant parts of the sentences. If time allows, play the tape again while students read the tapescript. Pause the tape, focusing on the different question forms.

4 Go through the example and explanation in the usual way. Elicit the fact that the man might have said 'Yes, I would' if he had been unwilling to disclose the information. The use of 'yes' in reply to such a question is a little confusing.

5 Students do the exercise in the usual way.

KEY

1 Wrong ... what time *it is*?
2 Correct.
3 Wrong ... when *the train leaves*?
4 Wrong ... where *he works*.
5 Correct.
6 Correct.
7 Wrong. Would you mind *telling* me ...?

HOMEWORK SUGGESTION

You have taken a valuable object to the antiques expert George Brown. Write your conversation.

Set E

READING: Pirates!

1 Give students time to look at the task and find the texts about women pirates.
• Read through the 'Which one/s ...?' questions ('Which one/s' is read 'Which one or which ones'.) Check that students understand the words in the questions, e.g. *cannibal, ex-soldier*.
• Students read through the texts and write A – E in the boxes. They will need some time to work on this task.
• Go through answers.

KEY

was the most powerful: E
dressed up as men: B, C
was a cannibal: B
do we know least about: A
was an ex-soldier: C
was the most recent: E
only sailed with women: A
led a revolution: B
were active in the Caribbean: C, D
hated her fiancé: D
criticised her lover: D
was considered the best sailor: E

2 Go through the questions, briefly. If the class is weak, elicit a few ideas quickly from the class as a whole.
• Students discuss the questions in pairs or groups, then report back to the whole class.
• Finish with some brief whole-class discussion.

3 Vocabulary in context
• Students can read the questions for themselves and try to find the matching words.
• When you go through answers, try to elicit further examples of sentences containing the words.

KEY

1 **a** take to (She took to her new profession ...); **b** take up (She decided to take up a life of piracy); **c** take in (Anne was taken in by her male disguise)
2 extremely big = enormous; extremely clever = brilliant; extremely wide = vast

READING: Lost property

1 Present the task, pointing out that there are differences between a formal letter and a letter to a friend. Give students a few moments to glance through sentences a–s below, then obtain the next sentence for each letter as an example. After this students can reconstruct the complete letters as instructed.

KEY

(letter to Sue)
f; s; d; l; j; o; b; g; c
(letter to the hotel)
i; p; r; a; k; h; m; n; q; e
Accept other orders which appear logical.

2 Students make a list of informal expressions from the letter to Sue and try to work out the formal equivalents from the letter to the hotel. Group discussion will help with this task.

KEY

Just a note to say – I am writing to say
thank you for a lovely weekend – how much I enjoyed my weekend stay
I had a really lovely time – You made me most welcome
marvellous – excellent
I think I left – I believe I may have mislaid
I've looked all over ... find it – I have searched ... find it anywhere
Have a good look – I would appreciate it if you could check
Or else it could be – Failing that, it may be
If you find it – Should you discover it
can you pop it in an envelope – I would be extremely grateful ... send it
Can't wait to see you – I look forward to staying with you again
Lots of love – Yours faithfully

WRITING

Elicit some ideas about things which might have been left, where they might have been left, who the friends might be, etc. Then set students to do the writing task. This could be done as a homework task if you wish.

HOMEWORK SUGGESTION

You are a rich film star. Last night thieves broke into your house and stole lots of valuable property. Make a list of what has been taken.

5 Gods in White Coats

Aims and content

The overall aim is to provide coverage of an important topic area, and to give extensive practice in note-taking and summarising. (Students will need to draw on these skills in the guided writing part of the FCE exam.)

Set A
Aims: To launch the topic of health through a speaking activity; to teach and practise the differences in form and use of *if, unless, otherwise*; to introduce and practise reflexive pronouns; to practise the listening and reading skills.
Speaking: A monster or a saint?
Language study: If, unless and *otherwise*
Vocabulary: Reflexive verbs
Listening: A discussion of euthanasia
Reading: Guinea pigs

Set B
Aims: To deal with the topic of asking for and giving advice through listening, reading and writing; to teach phrasal verbs associated with health and illness.
Speaking: Food!
Listening: Discussing a problem/Giving advice [P]
Reading: Just puppy fat?
Vocabulary: Phrasal verbs and health
Writing: A letter of advice

Set C
Aims: To practise the reading skill, with two choices of answer (FCE Paper 1, Part 2); to practise listening and note taking (FCE Paper 4, Part 2); to teach the differences between present perfect and past simple (FCE Paper 3).
Reading: It's all in the eye
Listening: An interview with an iridologist
Language study: The present perfect and past simple

Set D
Aims: To practise the listening skill (FCE Paper 4, Part 3); to practise reading for specific information and matching information in texts (FCE Paper 1, Part 4); to practise writing an article (FCE Paper 2, Part 2).
Listening: Health care
Reading: Waiting for an operation
Speaking: Group discussion
Writing: Writing an article

Set A

SPEAKING: A monster or a saint?

1 Ask students what they see in the picture. Then ask 'Why is Dr Kevorkian in the news?' Students read the text in the usual way and answer the question.

> **KEY**
>
> He is in the news because he helped a woman who was suffering from an incurable disease to kill herself.

2 Discussion points
Allow students to discuss the questions in groups and lead into brief whole class discussion.

LANGUAGE STUDY: *If, unless* and *otherwise*

1 Go through the examples for *if not/unless* in the usual way. Then students transform sentences 1 – 5.

> **KEY**
>
> **1** You won't get better unless you rest.
> **2** If they don't get here soon, they'll miss the train.
> **3** He'll get very fat unless he eats less.
> **4** I'll report you if you don't apologise.
> **5** She won't be a dentist unless she passes her exams.

2 Use the same procedure for *otherwise*.

> **KEY**
>
> **1** You'd better rest, otherwise you won't get better.
> **2** They'd better get here soon, otherwise they'll miss the train.
> **3** He'd better eat less, otherwise he'll get very fat.
> **4** You'd better apologise, otherwise I'll report you.
> **5** She'd better pass her exam, otherwise she won't be a dentist.

VOCABULARY: Reflexive verbs

1 First, check students' knowledge of reflexive pronouns. Elicit the reflexive pronouns (*myself, yourself,* etc). Point out that reflexive pronouns are often used with verbs, as in the example: *kill herself.* Such verbs are called 'reflexive verbs'. See if students can give further examples of reflexive verbs within sentences.
• Students complete the sentences. Go through answers.

> **KEY**
>
> **1** myself; **2** yourselves; **3** himself/herself; **4** yourself;
> **5** themselves; **6** yourself

2 Make sure students understand the task. Point out that languages differ in their use of reflexive pronouns. Students will have to be alert to ways in which English differs from their own language.
•Take one or two sentences orally as examples, if necessary.

• Students do the exercise. You may want to put students of the same mother tongue together, to discuss differences they find between their mother tongue and English.
• Go through answers. You can make comparisons between different languages if students find it helpful or interesting.

KEY

The sentences containing unnecessary reflexive pronouns are: **2, 4, 5, 6, 7, 10, 11, 13** (both reflexive pronouns in 13)
Reflexive pronouns are necessary in: **1, 3, 8, 9, 12**

LISTENING

1 Remind students of the Kevorkian case, which they read about earlier. Tell them they are going to hear a discussion about it.
• Play the tape once through for general understanding. Students listen without marking in the answers. They may need help in working out which character is which among the speakers – point out that Robert is the first of the male speakers.
• Play the tape again, more than once if necessary. Students mark in their answers.
• Go through the answers, getting students to quote evidence for their answers. As you do this, you can play the tape again and pause it as necessary

TAPESCRIPT

ROBERT: So, what did you think about that article, Jasmine?
JASMINE: The one about the doctor.
ROBERT: Yeah...
JASMINE: I thought it was awful. I mean the job of a doctor is to save patients' lives not to end them. I mean, it goes against the, erm, ethics, you know, principles of their profession.
THOMAS: I don't agree. I think he did the right thing for his patient. She was in terrible pain and there was no chance of recovery. Anyway, he didn't actually kill her, she did it herself, he only helped her.
ROBERT: Mm. It amounts to the same thing, though, doesn't it? Without the doctor she wouldn't have been able to do anything.
THOMAS: So are you saying he shouldn't have helped her, Robert?
ROBERT: Not really. I think he probably did the right thing. After all, we should think about the quality of life someone has. Nowadays, it is possible to keep someone alive even though their lives are hell. Doctors don't let them pass away naturally. It's just not fair.
THOMAS: I quite agree. I mean, we ourselves wouldn't want a pet to suffer, would we? I don't really understand you, Jasmine. People should be allowed to die with dignity.
JASMINE: I see your point, but we're not animals, are we? We're human beings.
ROBERT: So we should be allowed to decide for ourselves.
JASMINE: But very often when people are ill they aren't able to think straight or make good decisions.
THOMAS: That's a good point. I suppose one thing that worries me about, erm, people being able to decide for

themselves, is what the next step might be. We could end up with doctors making these decisions themselves on behalf of patients.
ROBERT: I'm quite sure that happens anyway, Thomas... Also it could be easily abused. I don't think it was in this case...
JASMINE: Maybe not, but I don't think the doctor should be allowed to get away with it.
THOMAS: But he's not, is he? According to the article the police looked into the case, which is why he is on trial. And unless they lock him up he'll do it again.

KEY

1 – J; 2 – T; 3 – T; 4 – J; 5 – T; 6 – R; 7 – J

2 Tell students to turn to the tapescript on page 157.
• Elicit an example from the tapescript of an expression of agreement or disagreement.
• Students work in pairs and underline the expressions for agreeing and disagreeing.
• Go through answers. Write the expressions on the board.
• Get students to practise making sentences, and agreeing or disagreeing with the sentences, using the expressions they have identified. This can be done in pairs or as a whole-class activity.

KEY

Agreeing: Mm (= a certain degree of agreement – not strong agreement); I quite agree; That's a good point
Disagreeing: I don't agree; I don't really understand you; I see your point but ...

SPEAKING: Guinea pigs

1 Give students time to read the text for themselves.
• Point out the questions that follow in task 2. Tell students to try to form an opinion by themselves, first, without discussing with other students.

2 Present the task. Read through questions 1 – 3, without eliciting opinions.
• Remind students of the ways of agreeing and disagreeing they identified in the previous exercise. See if they can provide any other expressions which are useful for agreeing and disagreeing. For example:
Agreeing: Yes, I think so too.
Disagreeing: No, I don't see it that way; No, I can't go along with that.
• Put students into groups to discuss the questions. Go round and listen as they do this.
• Finish with a short session of whole-class discussion.

Set B

SPEAKING: Food!

Discuss the pictures and obtain students' reactions to them. The man is enormously fat and will probably die if he does not lose weight quickly. They may have opinions about the girl who is anorexic (thin, even to the point of starvation, but seeing herself as fat) and how to help her. (NOTE: Be careful with this topic; it may be a sensitive one for some students within the class.)

LISTENING: Discussing a problem

1 Present the situation and questions to be answered. Play the tape in the usual way.

TAPESCRIPT

FRANK: I'm so (1) *overweight*. It's (2) *making me depressed*.
ANGIE: So that's it. I thought you looked a bit (3) *fed up*.
FRANK: And the more I worry about it the more I seem to eat.
ANGIE: Frank, (4) *just between you and me*, what have you had to eat today?
FRANK: Well I didn't have breakfast so I ate (5) *a bar of chocolate* on the way to school. Then I had a (6) *packet of crisps* at breaktime.
ANGIE: And what about at lunch?
FRANK: Um ... a (7) *hamburger* and a cola.
ANGIE: It's no surprise you're getting fat. (8) *What you need* is a balanced diet.
FRANK: What (9) *are you getting at*?
ANGIE: Obviously you're taking in too many calories. You (10) *should give up* chocolate completely for a time and (11) *cut down on* all the snacks you eat. Also, (12) *have you tried one* of those slimming clubs? You get advice on nutrition and they weigh you each week. It really works.
FRANK: How (13) *come you know so much* about it?

KEY

1 He is overweight, and depressed about it.
2 Students give their opinion – perhaps Angie has been in the same situation herself.

2 Play again, stopping the tape as necessary. Students fill in the gaps.

KEY

See tapescript above – the missing words are in italics.

3 Giving advice

• Get students to pick out from the completed tapescript the expressions which Angie uses to give advice.

KEY

What you need; You should give up; Have you tried

• Organise students to work in pairs (A and B) in the usual

way. Check that each student in the pair reads through the role and understands the details.

READING: Just puppy fat?

1 Explain that 'puppy fat' is the fatness that teenagers often have. They lose it when they get older. Pre-teach the expression 'to go on a crash diet'. This means to lose weight dramatically over a very short period rather than slowly and gradually.
• Explain the task. If the class is weak you could read through one of the letters with students, and get them to suggest suitable advice. They then complete the reading and matching task on their own. Finish by discussing all the letters and replies, briefly. What do students think of the writers? Do they sympathise? What do they think of the advice given?

KEY

Letter A goes with reply B.
Letter E goes with reply C.

2 Students look at the letters again and match the headings to the letters. This can be done in pairs.
• Go through answers, getting students to read out the important sentences in the letters which allow the headings to be matched.

KEY

A 5 (Evidence: *starving myself for a week at a time*)
B 2 (Evidence: *You should never miss main meals,*)
C 1 (Evidence: *you should check with your doctor.*)
D 4 (Evidence: *I have got away with this so far ...*)
E 3 Evidence: *nothing seems to work.*)

VOCABULARY: Phrasal verbs and health

Students do the exercise in the usual way. When you go through the answers, elicit further sentences, using the phrasal verb which was correct (e.g. *look after* in number 1), then sentences showing the meaning of the wrong alternatives (e.g. *look out*, and *look into* in number 1). Encourage students to use a dictionary to check meanings.

KEY

1 – C; 2 – C; 3 – B; 4 – C; 5 – B; 6 – C

WRITING: A letter of advice

• Students look through the letters and note down the advice patterns.

KEY

Requesting advice:
Letter A: What should I do?
Letter D: Should I take any notice ...
Letter E: Please can you help me?

Giving advice:
Reply C: You should check ...; you may have to ...
Reply B: My main advice is that you should ...; You should never
...; If you ..., you'll (conditional form); Look after your
body (imperative form)

• Students look at letter B. Elicit some ideas about possible advice, using the expressions for advice in the key. Also elicit some ways in which the phrasal verbs in the previous exercise might be used (especially *look after, give up, cut down on, take up*).
• Students write a suitable letter. You may want to let students work in pairs for this. It could also be done as a homework task. Good examples of letters could be fixed to the wall of the classroom for other students to read.

HOMEWORK SUGGESTION

Your friend weighs 100kgs, smokes forty cigarettes a day, eats 'junk food' (e.g. crisps, chips, cakes, etc.), takes no exercise and has a stressful job. Write him/her a letter of advice which begins like this ...
Dear Nicky,
I was quite shocked to see you last week; you looked really awful ...

Set C

READING: It's all in the eye

1 Make sure students understand *owl*. They then read the text and find out the connection between an owl and medicine.

KEY

The relationship between the health of the body and iris was rediscovered through observation of an owl with a broken leg. When the owl hurt itself, a mark appeared in the iris which disappeared as it got better.

2 Students read the text again in order to choose the best answers.

KEY

1 – B; 2 – B; 3 – A; 4 – A

LISTENING

NOTE: Students should be advised not to take all the claims for any form of medical treatment as absolutely true. All medical claims should be looked at critically.

1 Key vocabulary
Students work in pairs or groups and try to work out the parts of the body from the jumbled italic letters. When you go through the answers, check that they understand all the parts of the body listed. Translations into the mother tongue can be used here.

KEY

face; skin; stomach; brain

2 Give students time to have a look at the notes for completion, and to think of the kinds of words which might go in the blanks.
• Play the tape once through for general understanding.
• Play the tape again, several times if necessary. Students complete the notes.
• Go through answers, pausing the tape at relevant sections.

TAPESCRIPT

ANNIE: So how long have you been an iridologist?
PAOLA: Oh, I've been practising for about seven years now.
ANNIE: And do you have an ordinary medical background too?
PAOLA: Actually, yes, I have been a pharmacist, I trained as one and practised for a few years.
ANNIE: Really? Why did you give up?
PAOLA: I decided to stop when I noticed how many people are made sick by the medicines they are prescribed.
ANNIE: What, from the side effects?
PAOLA: Not just that. Fortunately, I have never taken sleeping pills in my life but lots of people get addicted to them.
ANNIE: How come this happens?
PAOLA: Quite simply, the doctor often makes the wrong diagnosis. The wrong medicine is prescribed to people who are already ill, and weak.
ANNIE: So that explains why you're fed up with conventional medicine; but why iridology?
PAOLA: Because it gives an accurate diagnosis and cares about prevention as much as cure. Conventional medicine is only interested in you once you get sick.
ANNIE: Mm, I'm not sure that's always true. But anyway, how can you tell someone's health by looking at their eyes?
PAOLA: We start with the colour which tells us about your basic constitution. Erm ... people with blue eyes tend to have allergies and rheumatism, things like that. Those with brown eyes have problems with circulation and their digestion.
ANNIE: Huh, huh. And what about hazel eyes like yours?
PAOLA: Well, hazel and green eyes are actually false colours. Hazel is a mixture of brown on blue. Green eyes are also basically blue but liver problems give them a yellow overlay.
ANNIE: And what can you tell from my eyes?
PAOLA: OK then ... Mm ... Now, eyes wide open, look straight in front. Good. Well, you've got a good constitution. There's something wrong with your left knee though. I can see that you have hurt it at some time.
ANNIE: Goodness! That's right. I had quite a bad skiing accident two years ago; I had an operation but it has bothered me ever since. How on earth did you see that?
PAOLA: Well, there's a mark on the iris here at about six o'clock ... let me show you on the chart.
ANNIE: Well, that's quite incredible, I'll have to come to you for a consultation. And can you see ...

LANGUAGE STUDY: The present perfect and past simple

1 Some time in the past

• Go through the explanations and examples, eliciting and writing on the board further examples in the usual way. Make sure students associate the 'indefinite' past (= occurring at an indefinite period between past and present, hence 'shading into' the present) with the present perfect, and the 'definite past' (= past that is definitely over and done with) with the past simple.
• Students do the exercise in the usual way.

KEY

1 has been; **2** has lived; **3** left; **4** studied; **5** worked; **6** was;
7 died; **8** has had; **9** has saved; **10** has performed; **11** has given;
12 won; **13** has written; **14** published; **15** has not become;
16 has never believed; **17** has always worked

2 The unfinished past

Go over the explanations of the 'unfinished past' in the usual way. Students may realise that the basic idea behind the 'indefinite past' and the 'unfinished past' is the same – that the past is in a way part of the present in each case. Then students make decisions for sentences 1 – 5.

KEY

1 unfinished (he is still a smoker)
2 indefinite (no specific time in the past mentioned)
3 unfinished (he is still at work in the same hospital)
4 indefinite (his travels are not given times or dates)
5 unfinished (they are still in the same place)

3 Talking about an activity

Go through the explanations in the usual way. Elicit the fact that if Paola had used *since* she would have said: 'I've been practising *since (a certain year)*' (e.g. 'since 1986').

4 This exercise relates to FCE Paper 3, Part 3. Students do the exercise in the usual way. Notice that the answers include both present perfect simple and continuous forms.

KEY

1 He has been a dentist for ten years.
2 They started dieting three months ago.
3 How long have you been training to be a doctor?
4 She has been sleeping/been asleep since the doctor left.
5 The children's ward opened nine months ago.

Set D

LISTENING

1 Read through questions 1 and 2. You can elicit a few preliminary ideas from students, but then put them into groups to discuss the questions. If you can form groups of the same nationality, do so.

• Students report back to the class on what the groups discussed. You can appoint a spokesperson for each group if you wish. Find out if any students are particularly dissatisfied with medical treatment in their country, and why.

2 Go through the instructions. Give students time to read through the summarising sentences A – E. Point out that the tape does not consist of a conversation, but of a series of spoken paragraphs.

• Play the tape once through for general understanding.
• Play the tape several times if necessary. Students match the speakers 1 – 5 with the summarising sentences A – E.
• Go through answers, pausing the tape as necessary, and getting students to pick out important sentences which indicate answers.

TAPESCRIPT

Medical treatment

1 Well, it was terrible. My sister, she's seventy seven, she fell down the stairs at home and we had to wait two hours for the ambulance. And when we got to the hospital this young doctor examined her. She was really **inexperienced**, she can't have been more than twenty-three. We were really **dissatisfied**... after all, we both worked for almost fifty years and paid a lot in taxes. It is a scandal, it really is. I think it is so **unfair**, I mean people with money they don't have to queue, do they? They can just go to an expensive clinic straightaway.

2 When I asked if my daughter could see a specialist that week they told me it was **impossible**. You see there is a waiting list which means we'll have to wait at least four months for a minor operation. The doctor was sorry but said the delay was **unavoidable**. I just don't know what she is going to do at school; if she can't hear properly she won't be able to follow the lessons. She might never catch up again.

3 I think it is **unforgiveable**... she'd been waiting six months for the operation but it was cancelled at the last minute. Poor mum, she's been in terrible pain with her hip but they said there was an emergency and they needed to operate on someone immediately. This is the second time it's happened. There should be more surgeons and facilities so people don't have to wait. She was so looking forward to walking properly again.

4 I think it's a scandal that we **misspend** so much money on weapons and bombs but that there's never enough for things like hospitals and education. It's completely **immoral**. The government has got completely the wrong priorities. It should be **illegal** to cancel operations and send people away.

5 As your local Member of Parliament I am fully aware of the problems affecting the City Hospital and can fully sympathise with your **dissatisfaction** at the **inefficient** running of the hospital. However, I would like to remind your readers that this **unsatisfactory** state of affairs is largely the result of the **irresponsible** behaviour of members of Trade Unions. The last strike was totally **unnecessary** and could have been avoided but they didn't want to talk.

KEY

A – 4; B – 3; C – 2; D – 5; E –1

3 Go through the instructions. See if students can remember any examples of words with negative prefixes, in addition to the example given.
• Play the tape. Students call on you to stop where appropriate. Make sure everyone hears or understands the word with the negative prefix. You can get students to write the words on the board as they are identified.

KEY

1 inexperienced; dissatisfied; unfair
2 impossible; unavoidable
3 unforgivable
4 misspend; immoral; illegal
5 dissatisfaction; inefficient; unsatisfactory; irresponsible; unnecessary.

• Students should be able to group the words with negative prefixes under a series of main headings, as follows:
un- unfair; unavoidable; unforgiveable; unsatisfactory; unnecessary
in / im / ir / il- inexperienced; impossible; immoral; illegal; inefficient; irresponsible
dis- dissatisfied; dissatisfaction
mis- misspend

4 Go through the instructions and give students a few moments to look at the article. Take the first item as an example if necessary.
• Students complete the article. They can check their answers in pairs.
• Go through answers, getting students to write the correct form of the word on the board.

KEY

0 dissatisfied; **1** inefficient; **2** inexperienced; **3** unsatisfactory; **4** impossible; **5** unavoidable; **6** unforgivable; **7** immoral; **8** misspend; **9** illegal; **10** unfair; **11** dissatisfaction; **12** irresponsible; **13** unnecessary

5 Read through the explanation of the structure of the text.
• Elicit the main summarising sentence (the first one: *Local people ...*), some examples in the second paragraph, and a sentence from the third paragraph which expresses the newspaper's opinion (*This paper believes ...*).

READING

Present the task. Help students to understand the essentials of the situation: that there are a number of people waiting for operations, that the hospital cannot do all the operations immediately, and that there will have to be decisions about which patient(s) should have priority.
• Read through the 'Who ...' questions that follow the texts, so that students understand the kinds of things to look out for in reading the texts.
• Students read the texts and mark in answers to the questions.
• Go through the answers quickly. Do not discuss the texts in detail at this point, as there are further tasks to follow.

KEY

1 – C; 2 – D, F; 3 – A, F; 4 – B; 5 – A; 6 – E; 7 – A, B; 8 – E

SPEAKING

The background information here explains the task more precisely. Read out or get a student to read out the scene-setting paragraph. Make sure the details of what the hospital can and cannot do are understood.
• Get students to read the text, write notes and then compare their answers with a partner. Go round quickly and check on the notes students are producing. (See page 34 for example notes.)
• Form students into groups to decide who should receive the operation. Elicit ways of giving opinions, agreeing and disagreeing before students start on the discussion.
• Groups report back to the whole class about what they decided.

WRITING

• Read through the task. Make sure students find the original article on page 52.
• Elicit ways of beginning the article, and also a suitable title, e.g.:
The Patients Who Must Wait
Several seriously ill patients are having to wait for operations at the City Hospital ...
• Students write articles. You can allow students to work in pairs if you wish. The task could also be done as a homework task.

Example notes

NAMES	FOR	AGAINST
Lorna Dobson	Needs operation now/Young.	Why can't family pay? Long operation.
Richard Bloom	Needs operation now. Kidneys available. Society owes him a debt – an old soldier.	Quite old. A tramp. A useful person?
Carlos Rodriguez	Young. Good chances of recovery. Will be grateful and could be a friend to Britain in the future. Short op.	Life not in danger. Not British.
Prof. Greene	Op. already cancelled twice. Low quality of Life. Life for daughter difficult.	Old. Has already had a long life.
Pauline Bolton	Depressed. Op. will change life for her and entire family. Has a lot of responsibilities.	Life not in danger. Long op. (3 hrs.)
Arthur Griffiths	An important member of society. Will give him more years of active life. Ill because of job.	Long term prospects poor. Better to give time to someone with a better future.

HOMEWORK SUGGESTION

Using the letter of complaint in Set A as a guide, write to the hospital on behalf of one of the people who was not accepted for an operation.

6 Genius

Aims and content

The overall aims are to challenge the student with more demanding listening and reading material, to continue work on the writing sub-skill of ordering events, and to revise past simple passive, basic reported speech, and the expression of ability. (These areas are extended in *Think First Certificate.*)

Set A

Aims: To teach vocabulary for professions and the suffixes used to form them; to revise and practise the past simple passive; to provide speaking practice via a discussion activity.
Speaking: Famous faces
Listening: The impersonators (FCE Paper 4, Part 2)
Vocabulary: Professions
Language study: The past simple passive
Speaking: A party for all time

Set B

Aims: To practise the listening skill and emphatic stress and intonation; to teach a set of 'extreme' (non-gradable) adjectives; to revise and teach reported speech (FCE Paper 3, Part 3.)
Listening: In an art gallery – emphasising what you think
Language study: Reported speech
Writing: A description of a painting
Speaking: Two paintings [P]

Set C

Aims: To practise the intensive reading skill through a challenging text and a demanding comprehension task; to build skills for FCE Paper 1, Part 2.
Reading: A tragic genius – the life of Vincent van Gogh (FCE Paper 1, Part 2)
Language study: Time expressions
Listening: Vincent

Set D

Aims: To practise the listening skill (monologue); to revise ways of talking about ability; to practise the pronunciation of separable phrasal verbs; to practise guided writing (a biography from notes).
Listening: The sad geniuses
Language study: Expressing ability; How to say separable phrasal verbs
Writing: The life of Mozart

Set A

SPEAKING: Famous faces

Students can work in groups to try to identify the famous faces. This could be a competition: you could go round groups and see which group identifies the most faces and professions in a limited time. Then conduct feedback with the class as a whole.

LISTENING

1 Present the task. Make sure students understand *impersonate*. Ask students why they think anyone might want to impersonate a famous person.
• Spend a few moments on the table to be filled in. Elicit the meaning of 'real job' and 'ex-job' (= former job). Make sure students know who the various people in the table are. (John Major replaced Margaret Thatcher as Prime Minister of the United Kingdom. Queen Elizabeth I was a famous queen of England in the 16th century.)
• You may find it useful to copy the table onto the board before the lesson.
• Play the tape once through for general understanding.
• Play the tape again, several times if necessary. Students complete the table.
• Go through answers. These can be written on the board.

TAPESCRIPT

CORINNE JAMES:	Now it's quite remarkable how closely you resemble John Major, the British Prime Minister. When were you first aware of it?
DOUGLAS ROYALE:	About four years ago. It happened by accident really... We were watching TV when my wife said ' You look exactly like John Major'. I was a bit upset at first; he's not the most attractive man in the world. Anyway, it started from there.
CORINNE JAMES:	Ha ha... I suppose not. And, erm, why did you start impersonating him?
DOUGLAS ROYALE:	Well, we wanted someone to present the prizes at our local tennis club and we thought it would be fun for me to pretend to be Mr Major.
CORINNE JAMES:	Do you have to dress up?
DOUGLAS ROYALE:	Not at all. I just wear one of the suits I have for work... The only thing I have to do is put on a pair of glasses with a, erm, black frame, 'cos I wear contact lenses normally.
CORINNE JAMES:	Right. And has it led to other things?
DOUGLAS ROYALE:	Well, I've opened a couple of supermarkets and been on a TV show...
CORINNE JAMES:	And is there any money in it?
DOUGLAS ROYALE:	A little bit. I charge £50 for an appearance, which I donate to charity.
CORINNE JAMES:	So what do you actually do for a living?
DOUGLAS ROYALE:	I'm an accountant.
CORINNE JAMES:	Ever thought of being a full-time John Major?
DOUGLAS ROYALE:	Not really. I think he'll be out of work very soon!

CORINNE JAMES:	So, Janet, or should I call you Marilyn?
JANET KLEIN:	Janet will do.
CORINNE JAMES:	How did you become Marilyn?
JANET KLEIN:	Well, I knew I looked a bit like her but then, when I was 19, some of the of girls at work sent my photo off to an agency. They called me in and that was that. I became a full time Marilyn.
CORINNE JAMES:	And what about your old job?
JANET KLEIN:	Well, I was training to be a hairdresser but I'd always wanted to be an actress.
CORINNE JAMES:	And does it take you a long time to turn into Marilyn?
JANET KLEIN:	Oh yes... It takes about three hours to dress up and put on my make-up. I also have to dye my roots 'cos I'm not naturally blonde.
CORINNE JAMES:	I see. And do you make a living at it?
JANET KLEIN:	Oh yes, quite a good one too. I charge five hundred pounds to do something like open a new supermarket or car showroom. The most I've ever made was six thousand pounds for a TV advert.
CORINNE JAMES:	Wow! What just for being there and looking like Marilyn?
JANET KLEIN:	There's a bit more to it. I've managed to copy her walk too, and her look and her smile, of course. That was really difficult... I sing a couple of her songs too, you know 'I want to be loved by you."
CORINNE JAMES:	Ha ha... And are there many of you around? Marilyns, I mean.
JANET KLEIN:	Oh yeah... but me and another girl are the best so we get all the big jobs.
CORINNE JAMES:	Now, Marilyn died about 35 years ago, why is she still so popular?
JANET KLEIN:	She was just so beautiful and everything, she'll never go out of fashion.
CORINNE JAMES:	Now, Elvis. Can I call you that?
ELVIS O'NEILL:	You can, 'cos it's my real name.
CORINNE JAMES:	You're kidding.
ELVIS O'NEILL:	No, my mum and dad have always been Elvis fans so they named me after their favourite musician.
CORINNE JAMES:	I see... and when did you start to impersonate him?
ELVIS O'NEILL:	Oh, when I was a kid... There are pictures of me dressed up like Elvis when I was five. It was expected of me...
CORINNE JAMES:	Goodness. And, er, do you take off Elvis full time?
ELVIS O'NEILL:	No, I wish I could... but even though I look like him my voice isn't that good...
CORINNE JAMES:	So what do you do?
ELVIS O'NEILL:	I'm an electrician and plumber.
CORINNE JAMES:	Right... And do you get fed up with people saying you look like the king of rock and roll?
ELVIS O'NEILL:	Yeah. I only grease back my hair and wear the, erm, clothes at the weekends.
CORINNE JAMES:	And does it take a long time to get ready?
ELVIS O'NEILL:	It depends what I'm wearing. A T shirt and jeans takes about ten minutes but if I want to put my full Elvis costume on it takes a lot

	longer, maybe an hour. I've got hundreds of pounds' worth of costumes.
CORINNE JAMES:	Wow... And have you made any money at it?
ELVIS O'NEILL:	Not a penny.
CORINNE JAMES:	So Juliet, you, erm, you impersonate Queen Elizabeth the first. Is that right?
JULIET ASHE:	Yes, that's right.
CORINNE JAMES:	Forgive me for saying this, but you don't actually look much like her.
JULIET ASHE:	This is true, but it is a case of putting on loads of make up and then the costume and I think you'd be quite surprised at the transformation.
CORINNE JAMES:	It must take ages.
JULIET ASHE:	Only about half an hour. It's basically lots of white make up and a wig.
CORINNE JAMES:	And, er, why do you do it?
JULIET ASHE:	Well, it's great to be Queen for a day or just for the evening. You get to order everyone around..
CORINNE JAMES:	I see.. And what do you do normally, then?
JULIET ASHE:	I'm a history teacher.
CORINNE JAMES:	Really! And is this why you chose Elizabeth?
JULIET ASHE:	Yes.. I've always been fascinated by her... She's always been a heroine of mine.
CORINNE JAMES:	And what does your family think about this?
JULIET ASHE:	Well, they think it's great. My husband, who's a doctor, looks a bit like Shakespeare so we make a wonderful couple. It's marvellous for going to fancy dress parties.
CORINNE JAMES:	And would you ever do it professionally?
JULIET ASHE:	Well, we've gone along to historical evenings for tourists. They love us! We get a meal and about twenty pounds and that's fine. We want to keep it as a hobby; that way it stays fun.

KEY

1 accountant; **2** four; **3** for fun; **4** £50 for an appearance; **5** glasses; **6** hairdresser; **7** 19; **8** always wanted to be an actress; **9** £6000; **10** dye, make-up ('three hours' and 'dress up' could also be included); **11** plumber; **12** at; **13** expected of him (by parents); **14** none; **15** tee shirt, jeans; 1 hour – full costume; **16** history; **17** all her life; **18** get to order everyone around; **19** £20 per evening (+ meal); **20** wig

2 Read out the discussion questions. Let students discuss briefly in pairs or groups, then have some brief whole-class discussion.

VOCABULARY: Professions

Write examples of professions formed from words + suffixes on the board. Elicit further examples as necessary. Students do the exercise.

KEY

1 politician; **2** actor, actress; **3** writer/novelist; **4** opera singer; **5** tennis player; **6** explorer; **7** inventor; **8** scientist; **9** philosopher; **10** artist/sculptor; **11** composer; **12** musician; **13** (film) director

LANGUAGE STUDY: The past simple passive

1 Active to passive

Use the board to go through examples and point out features in the normal way. Elicit further examples as necessary.

2 Practice: quiz time

Elicit questions to demonstrate the activity. Before students ask questions you may want to check to make sure that the questions are fair and correctly formed.

SPEAKING: A party for all time

Students decide on their guest list and questions in groups or pairs, followed by whole class discussion.

Set B

LISTENING: In an art gallery

1 Present the task, obtaining some comments about the pictures. Read out 'main point' questions 1 and 2. Continue in the normal way for listening.

TAPESCRIPT

PHIL: What do you think of this, Jane?

JANE: Ugh! I think it's awful, I don't like it at all.

PHIL: Why on earth not? I think it's fascinating.

JANE: It's just a lot of funny black lines. It does nothing for me. Ah, but look! What a marvellous picture! All those gorgeous colours.

PHIL: Do you really think so? You have never seen grass that colour. It's terrible.

JANE: But it's not supposed to be realistic. Anyway, let's not argue. Do you like this one over here?

PHIL: Oh yes, fantastic. That's what I call a painting.

KEY

1 They have completely opposite tastes.
2 Jane likes Painting 2. Phil likes Paintings 1 and 3. (It's not clear if Jane likes Painting 3 but her tone of voice suggests she does.)

2 Say and get students to repeat the adjectives listed. Play the tape again. Students put the words in order as they occur on the tape, and pick out the adjectives which express different ideas.

KEY

awful – fascinating – marvellous – gorgeous – terrible – fantastic
very good = marvellous/fantastic
very bad = awful
extremely beautiful = gorgeous
very interesting = fascinating

3 Stress for emphasis

Use normal procedures for pronunciation practice.

4 Practice

Use normal pairwork procedures.

LANGUAGE STUDY: Reported speech

1 Use the board to go through the examples. Point out features and give or elicit further examples.

2 Students try to work out the changes in tense, etc.

KEY

Changes in tense: present simple –> past simple; past simple –> past perfect; present perfect – > past perfect; *will* – > *would*; *would* – > *would* (no change)
Changes to pronouns: *my –> her, I –> she*; etc. Also changes in indirect questions: *Will I win? –> if she would win; What would you give? –> what he would give.*

3 Students finish each sentence so that it means the same as the one above it.

KEY

1 The expert said that true genius was very rare.
2 Frank said, 'I have bought a new computer'.
3 Sally asked me if (I thought) she would fail her driving test.
4 She said that Mozart wrote/had written music at the age of four.
5 Tom told Alice that he was leaving/he would be leaving soon.
6 Mary asked how much the painting was.

WRITING: A description of a painting

First get students to look at the paintings for themselves. Elicit ways of describing each painting. Students answer the question. Then set students to rewrite the description so that it applies to the other painting. Students may need time for this, and it could be done as a homework task.

KEY

1 The text describes the first painting.
2 The second painting is called 'Path in the Long Grass' by Renoir. It is a scene of a stroll through a field full of wild flowers and trees on a summer's day. We can see a woman and small child, wearing a hat, and behind them, another couple.

SPEAKING: Work in pairs

Use normal procedures for information gap activities.

Set C

READING: A tragic genius

1 Introduce the topic of Van Gogh. Remind students that he is probably most famous for his painting of sunflowers. Refer students to the self-portrait, and ask for their opinions about the sort of person it seems to portray (e.g. a person who is unhappy and unsure of himself). The picture shows Van Gogh shortly before he killed himself. His face is lined and haunted. He looks anxious and unhappy. The swirls in the background symbolise his inner torment and unhappiness. Students then say what they know about Van Gogh. This could be a brief discussion in pairs or groups, followed by whole class discussion.

2 Students read the text and do the multiple-choice exercise. The text is intended to be quite demanding and you may want to give students a little help, depending on the level of the class. Point out that the text contains blanks which will have to be filled in later.
• When you go through answers, make sure students can justify their choices by referring to sentences in the text.

KEY

1 – B; 2 – A; 3 – A; 4 – B; 5 – C; 6 – B; 7 – B; 8 – B

LANGUAGE STUDY: Time expressions

1 and **2** Tell students to look at the gaps in the text. Elicit the fact that the gaps all contain time expressions.

KEY

1 When; **2** After; **3** this time; **4** for; **5** Until; **6** During; **7** As; **8** after; **9** By now; **10** during

LISTENING

• Ask students if they are familiar with the song 'Vincent', which is about Van Gogh. You can play the beginning of the song to remind them of it.
• Give students time to have a look at the text of the song, and to think which words might best fill the blanks.
• Play the song through, several times if necessary. Students listen for words to fill the blanks.
• Discuss answers.

TAPESCRIPT

Starry starry night
Paint your palette blue and grey
Look out on a summer's day
With eyes that know the darkness in my soul.
Shadows on the hills
Sketch the trees and the daffodils
Catch the breeze and the winter chills
In colours on the snowy linen land.

Now I understand
What you tried to say to me
And how you suffered for your sanity.
And how you tried to set them free
They would not listen, they did not know how
Perhaps they'll listen now.

Starry starry night
Flaming flowers that brightly blaze.
Swirling clouds in violet haze
Reflect in Vincent's eyes of china blue
Colours changing hue.
Morning fields of amber grain
Weathered faces lined in pain
Are smoothed beneath the artist's loving hand

For they could not love you
But still your love was true
And when no hope was left in sight
On that starry starry night
You took your life as lovers often do.
But I could have told you, Vincent
This world was never meant for one as beautiful as you.

KEY

eyes
breeze
sanity
flaming
hue
smoothed
could
life

Set D

LISTENING: The sad geniuses

1 Introduce the topic. Students may already want to give some examples of 'idiot-savants' from their own knowledge (but notice that 1.2 below also deals with this). Some students may also have seen the film *Rain Man* in which Dustin Hoffman plays such a character. Play the tape in the usual way.

TAPESCRIPT

Unfortunately, some children will never be able to lead ordinary lives because they have serious mental and physical disabilities. However, a tiny few are able to do things that ordinary people would find quite impossible. Take the case of Ellen Boudreaux. When she was four months old doctors realized she was completely blind. Yet two months later her parents noticed something extraordinary. Above her bed she had one of those musical toys which plays a tune. Ellen could copy it exactly by humming the tune. Other incredible things followed. Little Ellen couldn't walk until she was four. However, when she finally started she managed to get around without knocking into anything even though she was blind. Even outside in woods and forests she just knows where all the trees are and can avoid them. When she walks about she makes a little noise. Some doctors believe it is her own personal kind of radar. But let's go back to her remarkable musical ability. Ellen learned how to play the piano and the guitar like an expert. But what is amazing is her musical memory. She only has to hear a piece of music once and she can reproduce it exactly. What's more, she never forgets anything and can play and sing all the songs she has ever heard. These abilities are extraordinary, particularly if we remember that she can't hold a simple conversation, she can only echo and repeat questions. All doctors also agree that she has a very low intelligence. Yet she has one more miraculous gift I would like to tell you about. Ellen has an incredible 'internal clock' inside her brain which tells her to the second what the time is. This means she knows exactly when to turn the radio on for one of her favourite programmes.

KEY *(Correct answers should show a tick.)*

1 Correct.
2 Incorrect. (She couldn't walk till she was four.)
3 Correct.
4 Incorrect. (She seems to have a 'personal' sort of radar, within her.)
5 Correct.
6 Incorrect. (She cannot hold a simple conversation.)
7 Incorrect. (She can only echo and repeat questions.)
8 Incorrect. (She has an incredible 'internal clock'.)

2 This can be done as a whole-class discussion.

LANGUAGE STUDY

1 Play the tape again, stopping it and repeating as necessary. Students note down phrases relating to ability.

KEY

... are able to do things ... find quite impossible
Ellen could copy it
Little Ellen couldn't walk until she was four
... she managed to get around ...
... and can avoid them (plus many further uses of *can*)
... her remarkable musical ability
Ellen learned how to play the piano and the guitar like an expert.
... she can't hold a simple conversation
... she has one more miraculous gift
... she knows exactly when to ...

2 Students can work in pairs or groups for this. Follow up with some brief whole-class discussion. Were any students particularly advanced for their age?

3 You can elicit ways of beginning the expansion of the notes and write them on the board. Students continue the expansion, working individually or in pairs.

KEY *(example paragraph)*

Alonzo Clemons was a normal baby until the age of three. At that age he had a bad fall and suffered brain damage. He has poor speech and very low intelligence – even now, at the age of

25, he can only count to ten. However, he sculpts constantly, and only needs to see something once to be able to reproduce it. Even more astonishingly, he sculpts in the dark. He can sculpt a complete horse in twenty minutes. During his sculpting career he has sold over 500 pieces.

4 **Separable phrasal verbs**
Go through the explanation, using the board to point out examples of object, verb, particle, and stressed word. Students listen to the sentences and repeat, paying particular attention to the stress on the particle.

WRITING

1 Introduce the topic of Mozart. Elicit a few facts about Mozart (when and where he lived), and perhaps the names of some of his compositions. Are students familiar with his music? Do they like it?
• Read out the task. Students read the text and find when Mozart's life was happiest and most successful.

KEY

He was happiest and most successful when he was a child.

2 Present the task of finding the words which should not be there. Make sure students find the first example (*been* learned). This is good practice for Part 4 of Paper 3 (Use of English).
• Students find the remaining words which should not be there. They could do this task in pairs.
• Discuss answers.

KEY

been learned
the Europe
for to prove himself
could not *to* find
because *of* he argued
like as a freelance composer
despite *of* being known
another *one* court composer
to relax *himself*
and *was* died
he was buried
and *was* composed

3 Elicit some suggestions for famous people who might be written about. Also elicit possible sentences which might go in a short biography. Students should pay particular attention to (1) early life: place of birth, year of birth, parentage, childhood; (2) how success came; (3) greatest achievements.
• Students write the biography. This could also be done as a homework task.

HOMEWORK SUGGESTION

Write sentences putting each of the phrasal verbs in Language study 4 into a clear and memorable context.

Aims and content

The overall aims are to provide coverage of an important topic (education), with opportunity for writing practice (descriptions of people, learning experiences); to give speaking practice via a role play and problem-solving activities; to revise key structural and functional areas: indefinite pronouns, adverbs of manner, comparison, regrets and wishes.

Set A

Aims: To launch the theme of education; to deal with phrasal verbs in context; to practise speaking through a ranking and discussion task (FCE Paper 5, Part 3); to practise the listening skill; to teach vocabulary for faces; to practise freer writing.
Speaking: Predicting from a photograph
Reading: The last school to cane its girls
Listening: Crime and punishment in the classroom
Language study: Describing physical appearance
Writing: 'I shall never forget what happened …'

Set B

Aims: To teach vocabulary for educational institutions; to practise reading; to revise indefinite pronouns; to teach vocabulary to do with people and learning.
Vocabulary: Education
Reading: All I really need to know …
Speaking: Lost lessons
Language study: Indefinite pronouns

Set C

Aims: To practise reading and processing information; to practise comparative and superlative forms; to teach adjective + preposition combinations; to practise speaking through role play.
Reading: Interpreting information (FCE Paper 1, Part 4)
Language study: Comparatives and Superlatives;
Vocabulary: Adjective + preposition
Speaking: Role play

Set D

Aims: To practise listening; to revise adverbs of manner; to practise punctuation and writing about a learning experience (FCE Paper 2, Writing); to practise listening and the expression of wishes and regrets.
Listening: A miraculous way to learn?
Language study: Revision of adverbs
Writing: Learning to swim

Set A

SPEAKING

Students look at the photograph and give their opinions. Get students to give reasons for their opinions, but do not say whether they are right or wrong. They should be able to say that it looks as thought it's a girls only school. The girls look relaxed and happy and are wearing a smart uniform.

READING: The last school to cane its girls

1 Exploit the headline of the article. Ask the students if they can explain what it's about. Students read the text in the normal way. Briefly discuss whether students' assumptions were correct or not.

2 **Phrasal verbs in context**
Remind students about phrasal verbs, using examples from previous units as necessary. Students then do the matching activity.

KEY

to criticise – to tell off; to be in the act of doing – be up to; to escape punishment for – to get away with; to support – to back up

3 Use normal procedures for discussion. Groups should not spend too much time on each question, though you may take one question as a focal point for more prolonged discussion if you wish. End with brief whole class discussion.

4 This could work well as a 'pyramid discussion' task (see Introduction). Check carefully that students understand the 'crimes' on the board. You may find these examples useful:
Cheating is when you copy another student's answer.
If you play truant it means you stay away from school without permission.
A bully hurts or frightens weaker or smaller children.

LISTENING

• Introduce the listening passage briefly, with a few words about the main 'characters' in the story. Play the tape through, one or more times, so that students can write down the descriptions of Angela and Mr Gilbert.

TAPESCRIPT

I don't think I'll ever forget what happened that day in 1975. I was just seven years old and had fallen deeply in love for the first time. Angela had beautiful blue eyes, long red hair, pale skin and freckles. While the teacher's back was turned, I passed her a note which said 'Angela. I love you – Tim.' She looked at it and at once put up her hand. 'Mr Gilbert,' she shouted, 'Tim has been naughty, he wrote this.' Mr Gilbert, a big man with a bald head and glasses took the note and looked at it. He smiled and I thought he was going to let the incident pass. Instead, he called me to the front of the class and told me to read the note aloud. As I said the words I felt so ashamed that my face turned a deep shade of red. All the other children laughed and I returned to my desk. However, this was not the end of it; each time he turned away from the class to write something on the board Angela turned towards me and stuck out her tongue. After the seventh or eighth time I stood up, picked up a heavy dictionary and did something which would have the most terrible consequences ...

KEY *(Tim's description)*

ANGELA: She had beautiful blue eyes, long red hair, pale skin and freckles.
MR GILBERT: a big man with a bald head and glasses

• Play the tape again if necessary. Students give their opinion of the three characters. They may express the idea that Tim was a nervous, romantic boy, Angela was horrible, and Mr Gilbert was a sadistic man who should probably not have been a teacher.

• Students could work in groups briefly and talk about what might have happened next. Elicit their ideas. We don't know for sure what happened, but probably Tim hit Angela over the head with the dictionary.

LANGUAGE STUDY: Describing physical appearance

1 This follows on from the Listening. Elicit the main patterns from the sentences students wrote down and write them on the board.
She has/had ... (eyes), (hair), (skin) and (freckles, etc.)
He was/is ... (height) with (facial characteristics) and (glasses, etc.)
NOTE: We generally use *to have* to talk about eyes and hair, *to be* for height, age and weight, and *with* for extra things like beards, moustaches, glasses, wrinkles and gold teeth!

2 Read out the items in the box, making sure that students know what the words refer to. (NOTE: We usually say where wrinkles and a scar are, e.g. 'wrinkles on his forehead', 'a scar on his cheek').
• Elicit as necessary example sentences describing one of the pictures. Then get students to continue with written description themselves.

KEY

An old lady with glasses, curly hair and wrinkles.
The man had dark hair, dark eyebrows, a moustache and a scar on his cheek.
A young girl with fair curly hair.

WRITING: 'I shall never forget what happened ...'

• Go through the task, pointing out the stages to be covered in the story. Students may be willing to volunteer experiences they remember to provide examples leading into the writing task.
• If the students concerned agree, the written paragraphs could lead to an amusing game in a later lesson. The

teacher reads out a paragraph. Other students in the class guess which student wrote it.

HOMEWORK SUGGESTION

Finish the writing activity 'I shall never forget what happened ...'

Set B

VOCABULARY: Education

1 To lead into the task you could get students to say what they understand by the words in the box, before they complete the sentences. Then they try to fill in the blanks.

KEY

1 nursery school; kindergarten
2 primary school
3 secondary school
4 university; college

• Follow up the previous task with some brief discussion of educational institutions in the students' own country. How far do they correspond to the English system?

2 Read out the words in the box. How many students think they know what all the words mean? (Do not elicit answers at this point.) Then students try to match the words with the definitions which follow. When you go through answers, check whether students changed their ideas about meanings (e.g. about the word *coach*) as a result of the exercise.

KEY

1 a coach; **2** an instructor; **3** a lecturer; **4** an apprentice; **5** a professor

FIRST EXTRACT: a driving instructor *(mirror, signal, traffic lights, etc.)*
SECOND EXTRACT: a carpenter or a craft instructor/carpentry instructor *(measure, cut)*
THIRD EXTRACT: a professor *(results, degree, course)*
FOURTH EXTRACT: a football coach *(goal down, game)*

READING: All I really need to know ...

1 Students look at the pictures and put forward their ideas.

KEY

The children are painting; playing in the sand; having a snack during a break; watching the goldfish; looking at a plant

2 Students discuss, briefly exchanging ideas with a partner. After this you can get students to report to the class what their partner told them.

3 Present the text, drawing students' attention to the

ranking question set at the beginning. Students then read the text and discuss the ranking in pairs or groups. This could be set up as a pyramid discussion.

KEY

Opinions may differ. Students may agree that lessons like 'share everything' and 'play fair' are more fundamental than 'warm cookies and cold milk are good for you' – but even that can be argued!

• At the end of the discussion, find out what students think of the text as a whole. Is it humorous? If so, what provides the humour? Does it have a serious message?

SPEAKING: Lost lessons

This can be done fairly quickly, with students working individually or in pairs.

KEY

1 Clean up your own mess.
2 Share everything.
3 When you go out into the world, watch out for traffic, hold hands, and stick together.
4 Live a balanced life ...
5 Play fair.
6 Goldfish and hamsters ... all die. So do we.

LANGUAGE STUDY: Indefinite pronouns

1 Go through the example sentences in the usual way. Try to elicit from students any rules they already know about the use of the *some-/any-* forms.
• Students work out answers to questions 1 – 4. Get students to formulate the answers as 'rules'.

KEY

1 any-; 2 some-; 3 no-; 4 any-

2 Students decide on *every-* forms to match the words in italics.

KEY

1 everyone/everybody
2 everything
3 everywhere

3 Students fill in the blanks.

KEY

1 something; 2 anyone/anybody; 3 Nobody/No-one;
4 everywhere; 5 someone/somebody/something; 6 something;
7 nothing; 8 everything

HOMEWORK SUGGESTION

Write a short 'article' in which you explain the educational system of your country to a foreign visitor.

Set C

READING: Interpreting information

• Introduce the task. To 'prime' students, ask them a few questions, e.g. 'How long does compulsory education last in your country?' 'Do you get end-of-term reports in your country? What kind of information do they give?' 'Do pupils do both optional and compulsory subjects in your country?'
• Give students time to look at the task for themselves, and questions 1 – 7.
• Although reading aloud in class is not a standard procedure, you might get students to read aloud some of the Class tutor's comments, to vary the procedure, and to deal with the kind of language that occurs in these comments.
• Students look at the results for each pupil, read the texts, and answer the questions. They can check their answers in pairs or groups.

KEY

1 AR, AD
2 AR
3 RP, AD
4 BG
5 AD
6 BG
7 RP

LANGUAGE STUDY

1 Go through the structures for comparatives and superlatives in the normal way. Elicit further examples as necessary.
• Students write sentences. Go round as students write and check that the sentences they write are both true and correctly formed. Finally elicit sentences from the class as a whole and discuss any problems.

KEY *(examples)*

Ratan is good at English. Alison is good, but not as good as Ratan.
Ratan is as good at Mathematics as Alison.
Alison is as good at French as Ratan.
Ratan is much better at History than Alison.
Ratan is good at Geography, and slightly better than Alison.
Alison is much better at Art than Ratan.

2 Students write sentences as for the previous exercise.

KEY *(examples)*

1 Ratan and Alison are better at French than Arnold, and much better than Belinda.
2 Ratan is the best pupil at History. Alison is the worst. Belinda is better than Arnold.
3 Belinda is as good at Science as Arnold, and better than Ratan or Alison.
etc.

VOCABULARY: Adjective + preposition

1 Write the example sentence on the board. Point out the adjective + preposition. Point out that other adjective + preposition combinations occur (students will identify some of these in this exercise). Then students do the matching task. When they have done the task, elicit examples of sentences containing the adjectives + prepositions.

KEY

1 – D good/bad at; **2 – E** keen on; **3 – A** interested in;
4 – B tired of; **5 – C/D** disappointed with/at (also *in* a person)

2 Students do the exercise in the normal way.

KEY

1 bad at; **2** good at/interested in/keen on; **3** disappointed with/at; **4** interested in/keen on; **5** best at, worst at; **6** interested in; **7** tired of

SPEAKING: Role play

• Present the topic of a parent-pupil-teacher meeting. Point out that the pupils in question are listed below, together with notes on their family/study situation. You can go through the notes on pupils if you wish.
• Allocate roles. Students carry out the role-play task in the normal way. (See the Introduction.) Go round and listen as students role play and note down any interesting points for later whole class discussion.

HOMEWORK SUGGESTION

Write a report on how good you are/were at different subjects at school.
e.g. I was good at History. I enjoyed it a lot.
I was bored by Latin. We had to learn stupid rules.

Set D

LISTENING: A miraculous way to learn?

1 Part A
• Introduce the situation. Get students to look at and comment on the diagram of the human brain. Tell them that they should label the diagram considering right and left looking at the page, i.e. ⇐ left; ⇒ right.

• Play the tape of the interview (Part A) in the normal way. Students label the diagram.

TAPESCRIPT

Part A
KAY ABLE: What is this fast method for learning languages, doctor?
DR GREEN: Basically, it gets us to use all our brain. The brain is divided into two halves. Each half has different jobs. The left half is the logical side. This is where language is stored. The right side deals with space, artistic ability and music.

KEY

Left side: logic + language
Right side: space + music + artistic ability

2 Part B
Read out questions 1 – 3. Then play the tape of Part B. Elicit answers.

TAPESCRIPT

Part B
KAY ABLE: So artists and musicians use the powers in the right half.
DR GREEN: ... that's correct. Now, most teaching methods depend on studying grammar and doing exercises. There is also a lot of repetition. This is all logical left brain activity.
KAY ABLE: But what's wrong with that?
DR GREEN: Well, what happens is that students work hard but often don't learn a lot. By the next lesson they can hardly remember anything. It's slow. What they need to do is use all of their brain.
KAY ABLE: How exactly can you do this?
DR GREEN: Well, you know how we can remember rhymes and songs from childhood ...
KAY ABLE: Mm, yes. The other day I sang a song to a child which I last heard, it must have been twenty years ago. I was surprised I could still remember it.
DR GREEN: Well, it doesn't surprise me. The two halves of your brain were working together. The words were kept in the left part but you were able to remember them because the music from the right side helped to fix them there.

KEY

1 The left side.
2 They rely too much on repetition and students quickly forget what they have learnt.
3 Because songs and rhymes help the two sides of the brain to work together, and are therefore very easily remembered. The interviewer agrees with him.

3 Part C
• Read out the sentences to be ticked or left alone. Then play the tape for Part C.

TAPESCRIPT

Part C

KAY ABLE: So we should learn languages through singing?

DR GREEN: Not exactly, but let me quickly say something about the method which was invented by a Bulgarian professor called Lozanov. His method has lately been developed in the United States. The teacher speaks to the students using special rhythm and intonation which helps us to remember the language longer. The lesson is also accompanied by slow music. All these things make the brain work more efficiently and the language learning process faster, easier and much less stressful.

KAY ABLE: So the two halves work together. It sounds fantastic. I think I'll take up German again.

DR GREEN: It's never too late to learn, Kay.

KEY

The ticks should be put at these points:
3 The teacher speaks in an unnatural way.
5 The students listen to music while they study.

• Finally have whole class discussion. Is the method of learning described on the tape a good one? Would it work? How do students remember new words?

LANGUAGE STUDY: Revision of adverbs

1 Elicit examples of adverbs. Point out that not all adverbs end in *-ly*.
• You can take the first item in the exercise as an example. Then students to the rest on their own.

KEY

1 badly; **2** slowly; **3** hard; **4** beautifully; **5** fast; **6** quickly; **7** well
The irregular adverbs are *hard, fast, well*.

2 Important differences
Go through the example sentences. Get students to say in their own words what the words in bold type mean.

3 Student match the sentences with comments a – f which bring out the meaning of the adverbs.

KEY

a – 2b; b – 1b; c – 3a; d – 2a; e – 3b; f – 1a

4 Students work out the meaning-equivalents. They can work in pairs for this.

KEY

not on time = late; not much/only just = hardly; close = near; almost = nearly; recently = lately; a lot = hard

• Get students to provide more examples of sentences containing the adverbs in this exercise.

WRITING: Learning to swim

1 Students say what is happening in the picture (a swimming lesson). They say how they think the child feels and recall their own efforts at learning to swim. (But be aware that not all students may be able to swim even now.)

2 Students read quickly through the text and pick out the main stages the writer went through.

KEY (different stages)

splashing about in the shallow end of the pool
using a board when moving up and down the pool
swimming holding onto a cotton reel

3 Students punctuate the text and put it in paragraphs.

KEY (some variations in punctuation may be possible)

I shall never forget how I learned to swim. I was nine years old, and like many other children I was terrified of the water. However, my teacher, Miss Townsend, had a wonderful system for teaching swimming. It worked with nine children out of ten. Once a week we all went to the swimming pool. The first couple of times we got used to the water and splashed about in the shallow end. After that we had a kind of board, which helped us to float when we moved up and down the pool by kicking our legs.
By now, most of us knew how to float, but we did not have the confidence to swim on our own. Our teacher had a brilliant idea. She took two ordinary cotton reels and tied a long piece of string between them. I held one of them and Miss Townsend held the other and I swam for the very first time, supported by my belief in the power of the tiny cotton reel!

4 Discuss ideas before getting students to start on the writing task. Obtain examples of different things that students found difficult to learn, and the stages they went through in their learning. Was there any special method, or any 'trick' which made all the difference? Then students do the task.

HOMEWORK SUGGESTION

Write a paragraph explaining what you think the best way is of learning a foreign language.

8 City Life

Aims and content

The overall aims are to develop the learner's awareness of discourse features (essential for FCE Writing paper); to practise guided writing (written directions, description of one's home town) and summary writing; also the structural/functional areas of question making, first and second conditionals, asking for and giving directions.

Set A
Aims: To launch the theme of the unit with speaking practice based around photographs (FCE Paper 5, Part 2); to teach vocabulary round the theme of city life (FCE Paper 1, Part 2).
Speaking: Describing photographs
Listening: City thoughts
Vocabulary: City Life (FCE Paper 1, Part 2)
Speaking: Describing photographs (FCE Paper 5, Part 2)

Set B
Aims: To practise the reading skills through re-assembling jumbled paragraphs; to practise question making; to practise written directions according to a reconstructed model; to practise listening, note-taking and summary writing (FCE Paper 4, Part 2).
Reading: Ordering paragraphs
Writing: Giving written directions
Listening: Two cities
Writing: Summary writing

Set C
Aims: To practise reading for gist; to revise and contrast first and second conditionals; to practise listening and note-taking; to revise basic punctuation.
Reading: Rome the transformer (FCE Paper 1, Part 1)
Language study: The first and second conditional
Speaking: Cultural exchanges
Writing: Just like you!

Set D
Aims: To practise intensive reading (matching texts to pictures); to develop sensitivity to cohesion and logic within a text (re-positioning misplaced sentences); to practise describing one's own town or capital city; to practise listening to, following and giving directions.
Reading: London then and now (FCE Paper 1, Part 3)
Writing: Guided writing – My Own Town
Listening: Finding the way (FCE Paper 4, Part 2)
Speaking: Giving directions

Set A

SPEAKING

Students look at the photographs and briefly put forward their ideas.

LISTENING: City thoughts

Play the tape in the normal way. Students associate what they hear with people in the photographs. They should be able to quote sentences from the tape to back up their ideas.

TAPESCRIPT

1 Oh no! This looks like trouble ... He's coming towards us. What's *that* in his hand? ... we should have taken a cab.
2 Either you don't exist or they treat you like an animal in a zoo. Tourists! What do you expect – a big smile? You've got your photo – now how about some change?
3 What a jam! I'll never get my flight. The only thing that's moving is the meter in this funny old taxi.
4 Whee, this is great. What a neat birthday gift!
5 Drivers. Think they own the road; and all the pollution. I'm glad I've got this mask ... The lights are going to change! Just watch me beat this guy!

KEY

1 – photo **E**; **2** – photo **A**; **3** – photo **D**; **4** – photo **B**;
5 – photo **C**

VOCABULARY: City life

• Introduce the passage about London. Quickly find out which students in your class have been to London. Elicit an example of something any student liked or disliked about London.
• Give students time to have a general look at the passage.
• Students choose words to fill in the gaps. They can check their answers in pairs.

KEY

1 – B; **2** – C; **3** – B; **4** – B; **5** – B; **6** – B; **7** – C; **8** – C; **9** – B;
10 – B; **11** – A; **12** – A; **13** – A; **14** – B; **15** – B; **16** – C; **17** – B;
18 – C; **19** – C; **20** – C

• In feedback, briefly elicit/explain why the other choices are incorrect. Provide controlled practice of the items for pronunciation.

SPEAKING

1 Students can first describe the photographs to each other (pairs or groups). Then you can elicit descriptions from the class as a whole.
• Monitor them to see how much of the vocabulary from the previous exercise they are able to use.

2 Obtain students' ideas. Elicit adjectives which express feelings as precisely as possible.

HOMEWORK SUGGESTION

Choose fifteen of the words from the vocabulary exercise. Either write sentences for each of the words or else put them into a story.

Set B

READING

1 Go through the situation – who Poppy is, what she wants to do, who sends her a letter. Give students time to read the paragraphs and think of a suitable order. Discuss. (You can try out some wrong orders on students and see what they find wrong in them.)

KEY

1; 4; 6; 3; 5; 2; 7

2 Students work out and trace the route on the map (with finger only, or marking with a pencil). Go round and check.

3 Question making
Make the situation clear (Poppy's friend is asking the questions; Poppy is answering). Point out that the questions are based on the paragraphs students have read.

KEY *(examples; variations are possible)*

1 How old is Mrs Hallam?
2 Is she married?
3 How much is the rent? What/How much do you (have to) pay each week?
4 Can you/Are you allowed to cook?
5 Which airport did you arrive at?
6 Is it direct on the underground?
7 How long does it take (on the underground)?
8 How far is the house from the station? (NOTE: In the text it says it's a ten-minute walk, i.e. about a kilometre.)
9 Is it the first/etc. turning?

WRITING

Students write directions using as a general model the letter they have reconstructed.

LISTENING: Two cities

Briefly discuss the situation, getting students to say what they see in the picture. Ask about the atmosphere and if they can guess how old the house might be.

1 Part A
Read out questions 1 – 3. Play the tape in the usual way and obtain answers.

TAPESCRIPT

Part A
POPPY:	This is a lovely house, Mrs Hallam. Is it very old?
MRS HALLAM:	Quite old. It's Victorian, you know, it was built about a hundred years ago. There are thousands like it. You see, in the last century London grew enormously.
POPPY:	But how did people get to work?
MRS HALLAM:	By train. People have moved further and further out. Loads of people commute. The quality of life is often much better. They can live in the countryside and maybe have a bigger house. You escape all of the social problems we have here.
POPPY:	Social problems. What do you mean?
MRS HALLAM:	Well, during my childhood it was lovely round here. Nowadays there's quite a bit of crime.
POPPY:	Crime! Goodness! What kind of thing?
MRS HALLAM:	Burglaries, and muggings too. You see, you've got people like me who are reasonably well-off, then unemployed and homeless people. You have to be careful at night.
POPPY:	Oh dear. And what else?
MRS HALLAM:	There's all the litter and the dirty streets.
POPPY:	You make it sound terrible! Why on earth do you stay?
MRS HALLAM:	Because I love it really. You've got the theatre here, all of the cinemas and museums and things. It's interesting too, just wandering around the streets. There are lots of lovely parks as well. We moved out into the country for a while but we were bored. It was green and beautiful and everything but it was just too quiet I suppose.
NOTE: *Mugging* means attacking people in the street in order to rob them.

KEY

1 She loves it, but she is aware of the serious problems there are.
2 She sounds rather shocked, and also rather worried.
3 She is lively and straightforward, but perhaps she enjoys looking on the dark side of things.
(Students give their own opinion.)

2 Give students time to look at questions 1–6. You may already be able to obtain an answer to the first question as an example. Then play the tape again and obtain answers in the usual way.

KEY

1 In Victorian times, about a hundred years ago.
2 There was a boom in its population about a hundred years ago; also, public transport meant that people could live further away.
3 Because the quality of life is better in the countryside: people can escape London's social problems and perhaps get a bigger house.
4 During her childhood it was lovely, but now it isn't as safe as it used to be because of all the social problems.
5 The social problems she mentions are burglary, mugging, drugs and homelessness.
6 Because the country was too quiet for her. She finds the city more interesting.

3 Part B
Read out the questions and play the tape. Go over answers in the usual way.

TAPESCRIPT

Part B

MRS HALLAM: Anyway, tell me about Athens. I went when I was a girl. I had a marvellous time sightseeing. It was marvellous – I'll always remember it.

POPPY: Well, I think it must have changed since you were there. We've got our problems too. Pollution mainly. There are too many cars. Sometimes Athens is just one big traffic jam. Sometimes we're covered by a yellow cloud we call the 'nefos'.

MRS HALLAM: ... sounds like London in the fifties with our smog.

POPPY: It's terrible for the buildings like the Parthenon. The stone is just being eaten away.

MRS HALLAM: Oh dear. Can't the government do something?

POPPY: Well, it tried to cut down traffic in the centre. You can only go in every other day; according to whether your number plate is odd or even.

MRS HALLAM: Has it worked?

POPPY: It has helped a bit.

MRS HALLAM: What would you do if you were in charge?

POPPY: First of all I'd try to improve public transport, then ...

KEY

1 Yes, she went there when she was a girl.
2 Pollution

4 Play the tape again. Check if students understand the solution that has been tried. Ask students what they think of the solution.

KEY

The government has tried to cut down traffic in the city centre by allowing cars with odd number plates in the centre on one day, and cars with even number plates the next.

WRITING: Summary writing

1 Students complete the grid. You may have to play the tape again for this. Copy the grid and answers onto the board.

KEY *(example of points to go in grid)*

LONDON: Advantages: beautiful parks and buildings, museums, cultural life
Disadvantages: social problems; litter; dirty streets
ATHENS: Advantages: places for sightseeing; good food
Disadvantages: traffic; pollution

2 Students compare their grids as instructed. At this point, instead of dealing purely with London and Athens, you might get students to decide on the points which could go in a similar grid for their own capital city.

3 Students write a summary comparing London and Athens, or comparing London with their own capital city.

HOMEWORK SUGGESTION

Using the conversation between Mrs Hallam and Poppy as a guide, write a short conversation between yourself and a foreigner about your own city or town.

Set C

READING: Rome the transformer

Generate interest in the text through the title and the pictures. Get the students to imagine what it would be like to live in Rome. Pre-teach *genetic* i.e. the physical and emotional things we inherit from our parents; and *take for granted* i.e. accept without thinking.

1 Students read the text quickly and answer the questions.

KEY

1 She was calm, quiet, always obeyed the rules and was probably afraid of expressing her emotions.
2 In Rome she learned how to 'loosen up' and express herself more. She got a lot more fun from life.
3 Her theory is that anyone who went to Rome from a northern country would rapidly become a Roman in their behaviour. Of course, students may agree or disagree with this!

2 By now, the task of matching headings with paragraphs should be familiar to students. When you go through answers, get students to quote sentences which helped them to do the task.

KEY

1 F (Evidence: *The years I spent in Rome changed me.*)
2 B (Evidence: *I had probably never really enjoyed myself ...*)
3 D (Evidence: *I no longer felt like a stranger – I belonged there.*)
4 A (Evidence: The whole paragraph is a list of skills and customs.)
5 E (Evidence: *You would belong there.*)
6 C (Evidence: *Actually, the real test is this ...*)

3 Students do the true/false exercise.

KEY

1 True. 2 True. 3 True. 4 True. 5 False – You argue heatedly without any fear of physical violence. 6 False – The best way is to walk across and allow the traffic to steer round you.

4 Word search
• For this task it will help if you have the words (*behave, grateful, proud,* etc.) listed on the board.
• Take 'grateful' as an example, and elicit 'gratitude' from paragraph 1. Then students find the nouns formed from the other words.

• Go through answers, getting students to write answers on the board.

KEY

grateful – gratitude; frustrated – frustration
proud – pride; appear – appearance
violent – violence; speak – speech
embarrasses – embarrassment; please – pleasure
confident – confidence; recognise – recognition

LANGUAGE STUDY: The first and second conditional

1 Go through the explanations, examples and questions in the usual way.

KEY

The speaker believes you may possibly move to Rome in (a).
The speaker believes this is unlikely or impossible in (b).

2 Go through the explanations and elicit further examples as necessary.

3 Present the task, the 'probability meter' and the example. Refer to the first sentence or two in the task and use them as further examples if necessary. Then students to the exercise in the usual way.

KEY

1 If I eat less pasta, I'll lose a lot of weight.
2 If Rome were less polluted, life would be more pleasant.
3 If you cross the road now, you'll get run over.
4 If you crossed the road now, you'd get run over.
5 If the underground were more efficient, I'd use it more often.
6 If you enjoy ice cream, you'll be in heaven in Italy.
7 What would you do if I gave you a plane ticket?

SPEAKING: Cultural exchanges

Students work in pairs or groups to discuss different aspects of life in their different countries. With monolingual classes, ask them to imagine what they could learn from a completely different culture.

WRITING: Just like you!

Students will give individual responses. Make sure that they include examples of the second conditional in their answers.

HOMEWORK SUGGESTION

Write a short text (maximum 150 words) explaining 'How to be someone from your own town or city'. If you can, try to include natural examples of the second conditional.

Set D

READING: London then and now

1 Students match pictures with pieces of text.

KEY

Picture A (Regent's Park): *Paragraph 1:*... relax in one of London's beautiful parks
Picture B (Canary Wharf – London's highest building): *Paragraph 3:* Docklands ... smart residential areas
Picture C (Painting of the Great fire of London): *Paragraph 3:* In 1666, the Great Fire destroyed ... old city
Picture D (The Changing of the Guard at Buckingham Palace): *Paragraph 2:* ... timeless traditions
Picture E (West End theatreland): *Paragraph 4:* ... the theatres offer ...
Picture F (Oxford Street): *Paragraph 4:* ... best department stores

2 If necessary, take one of the sentences A – F orally, as an example. However, students may be able to work on this task without any special lead-in being required. When you go through answers, get students to say what words or phrases in the text helped them.

KEY

1 – C; 2 – B; 3 – D; 4 – F; 5 – A; 6 – E

WRITING

• Students read the questions and produce written answers.

KEY

1 See first paragraph; **2** See first paragraph; **3** See second and third paragraphs; **4** See fourth paragraph

• Students work out answers to similar questions about their own town or capital city and use the answers to write an article about it. Ask students to work in pairs or groups to help each other with ideas and planning. Monitor closely.

LISTENING: Finding the way

Generate interest in the topic through the Underground map.

1 Play the tape, several times if necessary. Students fill in the missing words.

TAPESCRIPT

POPPY: I was (1) *wondering if you could* help me, Mrs Hallam. I want to get to Covent Garden.

MRS HALLAM: Oh yes. That's easy. Let's look at the Underground map. Right, we're in West London, so you (2) *take the brown line* – that's the Bakerloo line – to Piccadilly Circus. Then (3) *change* to the Piccadilly line, and (4) *take the* eastbound tube to Covent

	Garden.
POPPY:	Thank you. How (5) *long do you think it will take*?
MRS HALLAM:	About half an hour.
POPPY:	Excuse me. (6) *Could you* tell me (7) *the way to* Garrick Street?
PASSER-BY 1:	Sorry, (8) *I'm a stranger here myself*.
POPPY:	Oh dear. Excuse me, (9) *can you tell me where* Garrick Street is?
PASSER-BY 2:	Yes but you're walking the wrong way. (10) *Go back down this road past* the tube station, (11) *take the third or* fourth turning (12) *on the left* and cut through into Garrick Street. It's only a couple of minutes walk.
POPPY:	Thanks a lot. (13) *Do you happen to know the* time, please?
PASSER-BY 2:	Yes, it's 9.15.

KEY

See tapescript above – the missing words are in italics.

2 Ways Poppy makes requests:
I was wondering if you could ...
Could you ...?
Can you ...?
Do you happen to ...?

Giving directions:

MRS HALLAM:	Let's look at ... you take ... change to .... take the ...
PASSER-BY 2:	Go back down ... take the ... cut through ...

SPEAKING: Giving directions

Check that students understood the points of the compass, North, South, East and West, and the idea of *-bound* which means 'going in that direction'.

KEY

- *Notting Hill Gate to Charing Cross:* Central line eastbound to Bond Street. Jubilee line southbound to Charing Cross.
- *Knightsbridge to Covent Garden:* Piccadilly line northbound.
- *The Elephant and Castle to Euston:* Bakerloo line northbound to Waterloo. Northern line northbound to Euston.
- *Piccadilly Circus to High Street Kensington:* Piccadilly line southbound to Gloucester Road. District line northbound to High Street Kensington.

HOMEWORK SUGGESTION

Using Poppy's conversations as a guide, write a conversation where you help a foreigner find his/her way around your own town or city.

9 As Others See Us

Aims and content

The overall aims are to provide opportunities for writing (text improvement, levels of formality in letter writing); to examine national stereotypes; to teach/revise a set of adjectives for describing personality; to develop reading and listening skills through a variety of tasks.

Set A

Aims: To launch the theme through reading and discussion; to teach and practise colour idioms
Reading: A case of prejudice?
Vocabulary: Expressions associated with colours
Speaking: Versions of the truth

Set B

Aims: To teach and practise a set of adjectives to describe personality; to revise questions using *like*; to develop the above through a role-play speaking activity.
Vocabulary: Adjectives of personality
Speaking: Who are you? (FCE Paper 5, Part 3)
Language study: Different types of description
Listening: Describing someone
Speaking: Describing someone

Set C

Aims: To practise letter writing (FCE Paper 2, Part 1) through correcting errors, comparing a formal and informal letter, redrafting, writing a letter of application.
Writing: The nanny hunt – replying to an advertisement

Set D

Aims: To practise speaking based on a photograph (FCE Paper 5, Part 2); to practise reading and listening around the theme of national stereotypes; to teach ways of expressing agreement.
Speaking: Describing a photograph (FCE Paper 5, Part 2)
Reading: The typical Englishman
Writing: National stereotypes (FCE Paper 2, Part 2)
Listening: Agreeing and disagreeing
Speaking: We're all different!

Set E

Aims: To practise speaking around a discussion activity; to practise intensive reading; to revise ways of expressing regrets and wishes about the past.
Reading: It's a woman's world – Arnie the Au Pair (FCE Paper 1, Part 3)
Language study: The third conditional and *wish*
Speaking: A woman's place

Set A

READING: A case of prejudice?

1 Give students time to read the definitions. Then go through the definitions with them, asking questions to check that they understand the definitions.

2 Generate interest in the text through the headline and photograph. Pre-teach the word *nickname:* a name used informally instead of someone's real name, e.g. 'My name's Paul Miller but my friends call me "Dusty".' Then ask students to read the text and answer the questions.

> ### KEY
>
> Nigel Benn is a black British boxer.
> He was stopped by the police.
> They had used his photograph in a 'wanted' poster.

3 Discussion
Students discuss the questions among themselves in the usual way. Finally discuss with the class as a whole.

VOCABULARY: Expressions associated with colours

Elicit examples of colour idioms. Then students work through the exercise individually or in pairs.

> ### KEY
>
> **1** blue; **2** red; **3** green; **4** yellow; **5** blue; **6** black; **7** black and white; **8** green; **9** white; **10** black, red

SPEAKING: Versions of the truth

Instructions for role play
• Chief Inspector Hunter
• Nigel Benn
• Ambrose Mendy
• The policeman who arrested Nigel Benn
• Witness 1: A lorry driver
• Witness 2: A motorist
There are potentially six characters. The role play can work with fewer. For five characters eliminate Ambrose Mendy, for four, Ambrose Mendy and a witness.
Suggested procedure: Allocate students roles then get them to work together according to their role, i.e. all 'Chief Inspector Hunt' characters discuss what they are going to say, etc. Meanwhile you go round helping students with ideas and vocabulary. You could suggest when they can use some of the colour idioms.
• Chief Inspector Hunter has the main role so you should choose good students who will help to keep the discussion going without being too dominant. This role needs someone who is ready to ask questions and 'chair' the discussion.
• Explain that the inspector has to open the meeting and say why it is being held. He should then ask each of the characters in turn for their side of the story. He could

perhaps end it by stating his conclusions and saying that it's very difficult to see things in black and white. There is plenty of information in the text for ideas for Benn, Mendy and the policeman. Obviously Benn and Mendy should be angry and the policeman should deny their accusations.

• Benn could perhaps say that the arrest 'came out of the blue'. That when the policeman hit the car 'He saw red'.

• Choose good students for the witnesses. One of the witnesses should appear to support Benn and the other should support the policeman's side of the story. One could say how 'green with envy' they were when they saw Benn's Porsche.

• When you think they are ready, allocate students to their role-play groups and tell them to begin. In classrooms with two or even three groups, it can be a good idea to play some fairly loud music which will help students to concentrate on what's going on in their group by blocking out the others.

• Keep correction to a minimum after the role play has finished. Only interrupt if errors stop communication.

HOMEWORK SUGGESTION

Imagine you are Chief Inspector Hunter. Write a short (100 word) report about the discussion you had with the people in the Nigel Benn case and what should happen next.

Set B

VOCABULARY: Adjectives of personality

1   Elicit meanings for one or two of the adjectives of personality. Then students do the joining task.

KEY

1 – k; 2 – j; 3 – g; 4 – c; 5 – i; 6 – a; 7 – b; 8 – l; 9 – d; 10 – e; 11 – f; 12 – h

2   Students work individually or in pairs to work out the words meaning the opposite or the same.

KEY

a The opposite of *generous* is *mean*.
b The opposite of *trusting* is *suspicious*.
c courageous, unafraid of danger = *brave*
d intelligent and lively = *bright*
e nervous in the company of others = *shy*
f extremely unkind = *cruel*
g boring = *dull*
h proud and self-important = *arrogant*
i *Sensible* is often confused with *sensitive*.
      (*Sensible* is a 'false friend' for e.g. French speakers.)
j *Nice* is often confused with *sympathetic*.
      (*Sympathetic* is another 'false friend'.)

• If there is a good atmosphere in the class, you could follow up with a guessing activity. Students think of someone and describe them using adjectives of personality. Other students guess who the person is.

SPEAKING: Who are you?

1   Go through the task. You may have to elicit examples of preferences to show how the 'colour test' works.

2   Students look at the table which is printed upside down on page 81 and which explains the personality associations. Discuss how valid the 'test' is. Do students believe in it?

LANGUAGE STUDY: Different types of description

1   Introduce the areas involved in the language study section, pointing out that different questions can apply to different kinds of description, concerned with health, appearance, personality, etc. (You may be able to use or elicit examples from the mother tongue to demonstrate this.) Then students do the matching task.

KEY

1 – **d** (kind); **2** – **a** (much better); **3** – **b** (reading and playing tennis); **4** – **c** (tall and slim)

2   Students match questions with areas of description.

KEY

a – question 4; **b** – question 3; **c** – question 1; **d** – question 2
Questions 1 and 4 can sometimes mean the same (i.e. both sometimes refer to appearance).

LISTENING

1   Go through the situation and make sure students understand who is who. Play the tape in the normal way. Students note down the things Roger wants to know. Do the next part before you check the answers.

2   Play the tape of both sides of the conversation. Students check their answers.

TAPESCRIPT

CARMEN: It's really kind of you to offer to meet my aunt.
ROGER: No problem. It's a pity you don't have a photo of her. What does she look like?
CARMEN: Well, she's quite short and plump. She's about fifty-five and has got curly grey hair. She wears glasses and loves bright clothes.
ROGER: I see. And what's she like? I mean, what kind of person is she?
CARMEN: Really nice. Very lively. I haven't seen her since my Uncle Pablo died.
ROGER: Oh right. How is she now? Has she got over it?
CARMEN: Oh yes. She was very sad at first but she's OK now.
ROGER: And what's her English like?
CARMEN: She doesn't speak a word. You'll be able to practise your Spanish.
ROGER: Great. And what does she like doing?
CARMEN: She adores shopping. The last time she came to

England we went to Harrods. I'm sure she'd love to go again.

KEY

Roger wants to know:
1 what Carmen's aunt looks like.
2 what she is like as a person (i.e. her character).
3 how she is now (since her husband's death).
4 what her English is like.
5 what she likes doing.

SPEAKING

Set students to work in pairs in the normal way. Get a pair to demonstrate the task if necessary.

HOMEWORK SUGGESTION

Write a description of a friend or member of your family. Remember to cover looks, dress and character.

Set C

WRITING: The nanny hunt

1 Introduce the task. See if any student knows the word *nanny*. Set the pre-questions and get students to read the text and answer in the normal way.

KEY

They are looking for a live-in nanny, i.e. a woman who would live in their house and look after their children. Students discuss the qualities required in a nanny, e.g. good-humour, reliability, common sense, efficiency, etc.

2 Students discuss the photographs in pairs or groups. Then obtain ideas from the class as a whole.

3 Students correct the letter in pairs or groups. When you go through the letter, try to explain *why* the words are wrong, not just give the correct version.

KEY

57 Richmount St
Churchington
(+ date)

Dear Professor and Mr Wallace,
I am writing to apply for the job which was advertised in last week's 'Nanny' magazine. I am twenty-three (years old) and I come from Andorra. I have been in England for six months; I am here to improve my English. I am working as an au pair with an English family. They are very nice but the husband has got a job in Germany so (all) the family is going there. The order of my favourite colours is: blue, yellow, red, black and green.
Yours sincerely,
Nadia Ivanovic

4 Students say which letter is more appropriate, and why.

KEY

Letter C is much more appropriate; a formal style is needed for any letter applying for a job.

• Students briefly discuss general advice to Sally Fairclough (the name rhymes with 'hair-stuff'). Obtain some ways of making the letter more formal and respectful. (Students can make a more complete 'corrected' version after the step below.)
• Students list formal and informal language.

KEY *(examples)*

Informal language (letter B)
Hello there; ad; really; just to fill in; kids; what's more; I could do with; photo of me; great; have a chat; bye for now; all the best

Formal language (letter C)
I am writing in reply to; I can supply; if you should require; currently employed; coming to an end; I am available; at your convenience; commence; position; as requested; I look forward to your reply

• Point out that parts of Lucy's letter could be written in a more neutral style without any real impoliteness. For example, paragraph 2:
I can give references if you need them. At the moment I am working for an American family and am looking after three children. My contract is finishing and I would be ready to see you whenever it is convenient. I could start a new job almost immediately.
NOTE: If students are in doubt about 'tone' to adopt in a letter, it is better to err on the side of being too formal rather than not formal enough.
• Now students can correct Sally's letter, perhaps writing out a better version of it.

KEY *(Sally's letter, with some of the most serious faults corrected)*

Dear Professor and Mr Wallace,
I saw your advertisement in the paper and decided to apply for it. I am nineteen years old and left school last year. I am currently working in a clothes shop. Although I have not had any training as a nanny, I love children and come from a large family. I could begin immediately. I have enclosed a photograph of myself. I would be available for an interview next Friday evening as I am planning to be in London then. I look forward to hearing from you soon.
Your sincerely,
Sally Fairclough
PS My favourite colours are yellow, green, red, blue and black.

5 Students discuss the colour choices in the light of the colour-personality table in Set B. They should realise that Lucy Clinton-Roger's colour choices are worrying!

6 Point out that students have the choice of applying for a job as nanny, au pair or butler (explain *butler*). Elicit examples of points which might be included in the letter, based on students' real-life circumstances. Then students do the task in the usual way for written work.

HOMEWORK SUGGESTION

Finish writing exercise 6.

Set D

SPEAKING

Obtain comments on the picture. Find out what stereotype students have of the 'typical' Englishman or English woman. The picture probably does fit a stereotype. The man is wearing a formal suit and a bowler hat and holding an umbrella. He clearly dislikes foreigners. The picture shows him kneeling on a map of England waving his umbrella aggressively at the rest of the continent of Europe.

READING: The typical Englishman

Students read the passage. Discuss the passage briefly with them. Is it accurate? Do students find it amusing?

WRITING: National stereotypes

Students could first discuss ideas among themselves before you elicit some ideas from the class as a whole. Then students write their description (this could be a pair or group activity). If you have different nationalities in your class you could make use of this fact (a) for students to write stereotypes of other nationalities in the class (but make sure no offence is taken), or (b) for students to swap paragraphs around at the end and compare.

LISTENING: Agreeing and disagreeing

1 Present the questions to be answered in the usual way, and continue in the usual way, playing the tape several times if necessary.

TAPESCRIPT

SIMON: Mm ... he is just one kind of Englishman. Lots of black people are English too. Another thing, nobody dresses like him these days.

SHIRLEY: That's just not true. What about on the tube every morning. All those businessmen and civil servants?

SIMON: All right, but the other day I went to the post office and there was this guy – you know, behind the counter – a civil servant – and he had punkish hair and an earring.

SHIRLEY: Did it bother you, the hair and that?

SIMON: Not really. Surprised that's all ...

SHIRLEY: Mm. You might be right. Anyway, that bit about the typical English family, you know, dad at work, mum at home, I thought that was wrong.

SIMON: Why's that?

SHIRLEY: Well, a lot of kids are only brought up by one parent. Dad's living with someone else ...

SIMON: ... he's not in the garden with the roses.

SHIRLEY: Right, that bit about the daughter living with a punk was realistic ... It always seems to happen with middle class families, doesn't it?

SIMON: Yeah, you're right. For me the best thing about the article was that it made me wonder what foreigners think of us. I'm sure if you spoke to them about the English gentleman they'd laugh.

SHIRLEY: Absolutely, all those awful English holidaymakers. Mm, they probably think the typical Englishman is a drunk football fan ...

SIMON: That's right, wearing union jack swimming trunks and reading a copy of *The Sun*.

KEY

1 Simon.
2 Because the man behind the counter had 'punkish' (= in the style of a punk) hair and an earring.
3 They think that in the typical family only the mother brings up the children – the father is living with someone else; however, the idea of the daughter living with a punk seems realistic to them.
4 Because of the behaviour of English holidaymakers and drunken football fans.

2 Read through the task. Students can probably match the phrases with full agreement/partial agreement/disagreement without actually having to listen to the tape again.
• Now play the tape again. Students put the phrases in order. You may have to pause during the playing to allow students to catch the phrases as they occur.

KEY

Order of phrases
d – b – e – a – c
Categories of agreement
Full agreement: Absolutely ... You're right, That's right
Partial agreement: All right but ...
Disagreement: That's just not true ...

SPEAKING: We're all different!

1 Students do the task as instructed, drawing the map, and writing adjectives to match areas (stereotypes such as *mean, foolish, humorous* are attached to localities in most countries).

2 Students discuss with partners the attributions of qualities given to different places, agreeing or disagreeing according to their beliefs. If the class is of mixed nationalities you may have to adapt this part of the task so that it deals with opinions about countries rather than regions within a country.

Write short stereotypical descriptions of five nationalities other than the English and your own, e.g. 'This nationality is supposed to be very proud and hot blooded. Its people spend a lot of money on clothes and care about the way they look.' Then bring them to class and see if anyone else can guess.

Set E

READING: It's a woman's world – Arnie the au pair

NOTE: The law concerning au pairs has now changed to allow male as well as female au pairs to be employed in England.

1 Students look at the photo and the headline and discuss briefly what they think the article will be about. You may have to explain the meaning of *trap* and *gender* to them. Then students read the article and check their predictions.

2 Students read the text closely and match sentences A – E with the gaps in the text. When you go through answers, get students to say what words or phrases helped them.

KEY

1 – D; 2 – F; 3 – B; 4 – A; 5 – C; 6 – E

• As usual, you can continue with classroom discussion about the case (pairs followed by whole class). Is there any justification for the discrimination against male au pairs? Do students agree with the views of Maria Mirkova?

3 Students read the article closely and do the true/false exercise.

KEY

1 False. – The text suggests that the term *au pair* applies only to foreign girls.
2 True.
3 True.
4 False. – He had no idea the regulations existed.
5 False. – She thinks that boys are unsuited for this kind of work.

4 Get students to discuss this first in pairs and then in the class as a whole.

LANGUAGE STUDY: The third conditional and *wish*

1 Go through explanations and examples in the usual way. Then discuss questions 1 and 2, using the board to point out relevant features from the examples.

KEY

Both constructions use *had* + past participle (i.e. the past perfect form).

You may want to drill the sentences for pronunciation. Remember that we would probably contract *had had* → '*d had* and *would have* → *would've*.

2 Practice
• Students make sentences using the third conditional and *wish*.

KEY

1 He wished he hadn't been so lazy at school. If he had studied harder he would have passed his exams.
2 She wishes she hadn't drunk so much champagne. If she hadn't drunk so much champagne she wouldn't have/wouldn't have had a headache.
3 He wished he hadn't stopped Nigel Benn. If he hadn't stopped Nigel Benn he wouldn't have got into trouble.

SPEAKING: A woman's place

1 Students look at the list of jobs in the box and decide which are usually done by men, which by women and which by both. There is no right answer to this but here is a possible answer which would be common in many countries.

KEY

men: Soldier, Taxi-driver, Mechanic, Carpenter, Lorry driver, Coal miner, Bullfighter, Boxer
women: Secretary, Flight attendant, Au pair
both: Teacher, Doctor, Nurse, Shop assistant, Accountant, Cook, Hairdresser

2 Students discuss which jobs would only be done by men in their country.

3 Students discuss the view 'A woman's place is in the home'. Students may have differing view points on this depending on their nationalities!

HOMEWORK SUGGESTION

Imagine the interview between Arnie or Hoken and the journalist who wrote their story. Write the conversation. If you can, introduce sentences which use third conditional or *wish* + past perfect.

10 When in Rome

Aims and content

The overall aims are to deal with the future (a major notional area) and analyse ways of using *going to* and *will*; to provide practical writing pay-offs (menu, recipe, advice sheet for foreigners); to differentiate between *remind*, *remember*, *forget* in terms of forms and uses; to teach *in case*.

Set A

Aims: To launch the topic of customs and cultures through a discussion activity based on food; to practise listening through note-taking; to distinguish *will* (spontaneous decision) from *going to* (something already decided); to examine different uses of *will*; to write a local menu; to practise speaking through a role play.
Speaking: Could you eat it?
Listening: Toad-in-the-hole!
Language study: Going to or *will?*
Speaking: Role play
Writing: Making a menu

Set B

Aims: To teach vocabulary to do with cooking; to practise listening and note-taking; to write a recipe for a local dish.
Listening: Opinions on English food (FCE Paper 4, Part 3)
Vocabulary: Cooking
Listening: Bread-and-Butter Pudding
Writing: A dish from your country

Set C

Aims: To practise listening through a radio interview about international body language; to distinguish between *remember*, *remind*, *forget*; to practise reading based on an authentic advertisement.
Listening: Watch your body language (FCE Paper 4, Part 2)
Language study: Remember, forget and *remind*
Reading: Keep your hands in your pockets! (FCE Paper 1, Part 2)

Set D

Aims: To practise speaking based on a reading and information-gap activity; to teach *in case*; to practise writing through students producing an advice sheet for foreign visitors.
Speaking: Just good manners
Language study: In case
Writing: An advice sheet for foreigners

Set A

SPEAKING: Could you eat it?

• Students look at the types of food and associate them with countries. They will probably need help (from you or from a dictionary) with *toad-in-the-hole* (= sausages wrapped in a

kind of savoury 'cake' made of eggs, flour and water) and *tripe and onions* (*tripe* = the stomach of a pig, cow or ox).

KEY (other countries may be possible)

sheep's eyes – Saudi Arabia
snails – France
snake – China
veal cooked in milk – Italy
dog – China
birds' nests – China
toad-in-the-hole – Britain
tripe and onions – Northern England
brains – most of the world, but rare in Britain
raw fish – Japan
horse – France
turtle – Polynesia

• Have some whole-class discussion on the foods mentioned and foods in students' own countries. If you have mixed nationalities you could have students coming to the front of the class and giving a short talk about unusual (and to some tastes, off-putting) dishes from their own countries.

LISTENING: Toad-in-the-hole!

1 Discuss briefly students' opinions of English food (and manners). Then present the situation for the Listening task (Poppy at a restaurant with Martin and Moira).
• Draw students' attention to the menu of food available in the restaurant. Tell students to look through it and make a note of items which they do not understand. Most items can be found in a dictionary, but it will save time if you yourself have translations or explanations prepared.
• Tell students to listen and pick out who orders what. Play the tape in the usual way.

TAPESCRIPT

MOIRA: I wonder where Poppy is. I hope she hasn't got lost.
MARTIN: I'm sure she'll be here soon. Let's look at the menu.
MOIRA: I think I'll have the smoked salmon, then the duck. What about you, darling?
MARTIN: I think I'll have the cheese and onion tart and the roast beef.
POPPY: Hello. Sorry I'm late. I got lost.
MARTIN: Never mind. Do sit down.

MOIRA: Well, Yorkshire pudding – it's a sort of cake made from eggs and flour and water. You cook it in the oven and eat it when it's crisp and brown ...
POPPY: Oh, I think I see. And toad-in-the-hole? What a strange name!
MOIRA: Oh, that's Yorkshire pudding with sausages cooked inside.
POPPY: I see. I really can't make up my mind.
MOIRA: Why don't you have the duck? That's what I'm going to have.
POPPY: All right then. And I'd like to start with the soup.
WAITER: Are you ready to order, sir?
MARTIN: Yes, I think so. Will you bring us a bottle of dry white wine with the first course and we're going to have ...

POPPY: Thank you for a lovely meal. It was really delicious. I am afraid I am going to have to go.

MARTIN: What, so soon?

POPPY: I am sorry to leave in such a hurry but I am worried about getting home.

MARTIN: Come on, stay for coffee. It's going to rain soon and you'll get soaked. We'll give you a lift.

KEY

MOIRA: smoked salmon then duck

MARTIN: cheese and onion tart then roast beef

POPPY: soup then duck

2 Moira's exact words:

When she decides what to eat: 'I think I'll have the smoked salmon then the duck.'

When she tells Poppy what she has decided to order: 'Why don't you have the duck? That's what I'm going to have.'

NOTE: *I'll (I will) have.* The future with *will* is used at the moment when you decide something.

I'm going to have: The future with *going to* is used for something that has already been decided.

LANGUAGE STUDY: *Going to* or *will*?

1 Read through the examples of *going to* and check that the class understands. Elicit further sentences and contexts from the class. *Going to* is appropriate in a wide range of contexts, whereas *will* is limited to the situations which are discussed next.

2 Students do the matching exercise. Use the answers to reinforce the meanings of *will* and *going to*, eliciting parallel examples for each one.

KEY

1 – f; 2 – d; 3 – a; 4 – b; 5 – c; 6 – e

NOTE: When we use *will* to express determination, we always stress it and never contract it.

3 Explaining the uses of *will* and *going to* in the tapescript.

I'm sure she'll be here soon
I think I'll have ... } after certain verbs and adjectives.

I'll have/we'll give you a lift – spontaneous decision.

I'm/we're going to have ... – an intention; something that is already decided.

It's going to rain soon – prediction based on evidence now.

Will you bring us a bottle of wine? – request/order.

4 Ask the students to work individually then in pairs to compare their answers.

KEY

1 If you don't stop that noise I'll call the police. (Condition/threat)

2 Look! It's going to rain. (Prediction based on evidence now)

---

3 I'll help you. (Spontaneous decision)

4 I will lose weight. (Determination)

5 I know, I'll buy him a ... (Spontaneous decision)

6 I'm going to buy Dad a ... (Already decided)

SPEAKING: Role play

Present the situation, organise groups and allocate roles. If there is time, allow students to switch roles between customers and waiter.

WRITING: Making a menu

Present the task, eliciting examples of items which might go on a menu and a sample explanation or two. Students then proceed with the writing task. In an international class, put students of the same nationality together to allow them to confer over what to include in the menu.

HOMEWORK SUGGESTION

Choose three of the suggestions from Language study 4 and write short conversations.

Set B

LISTENING

1 Read out the question. Elicit some general views from different students in the class. Briefly discuss any stereotypes that emerge concerning English food.

2 Present the listening task. Students will hear five people talking about English food.
• Give students time to look at opinions A–E.
• Play the tape, several times if necessary. Students fill in their answers.
• Go through answers. You can play the tape again and pause at relevant sentences.

TAPESCRIPT

1 English food. Well, it's difficult to say what it is really. There's no such thing really. It's a mixture of all kinds of cooking. At home I think you could say that it is, erm, European. If English people go out they hardly ever go to an English restaurant. It's usually something like an Italian, Chinese or Indian one. French for special occasions

2 Well, before I came to England I'd always thought that, you know, the saying that the English don't eat, they just take nourishment, was true. But I must say I have changed my mind. The food here is not too bad at all.

3 Really, it's awful. It's a nightmare. The family where I am staying, well, really there is just one old lady... the food doesn't taste of anything. And the vegetables. All the time potatoes, potatoes, and other vegetables like carrots or cabbage... she cooks them for hours! All the stories people have about English food are true. I'm sorry, but it's true. One evening she said she wanted to give me pasta and she gave me spaghetti but from a tin – it was horrible.

4 Mmm, at Easter we usually go to France for a week, we go

to a cottage or something like that, but this year we decided to go to the countryside in, erm, England, on the east coast. Now, it was a nice holiday in many ways and there were lots of interesting places to visit, but the food! Finding somewhere to eat out was a problem and when we did, frankly the food was awful. All you could really get was fish and chips or steak and chips, stuff like that. A disappointing choice. Next year it's France again.

5 Definitely, it's things like roast beef and Yorkshire pudding on Sunday, or lamb with mint sauce. Then you've got delicious desserts like bread-and-butter pudding or apple pie or summer pudding, you know, made with all the soft fruits from summer. It's nonsense to say there's no such thing, cooked well they can be as delicious as anything from anywhere in the world.

KEY

A – 5; B – 4; C – 1; D – 2; E – 3

VOCABULARY: Cooking

1 Read out the words in the box and allow enough time for students to match words with the pictures.

KEY

CUTTING
A to chop
B to slice

PREPARING
C to mix
D to beat
E to spread
F to sprinkle

COOKING
G to fry
H to grill
I to boil
J to bake
K to stir
L to roast

EQUIPMENT
M a dish
N a bowl
O a saucepan
P a frying pan
Q a pot

2 Allow students to add any more words that they might know.

3 A *receipt* is a piece of paper that shows that you have paid for something; a *prescription* is a note written by a doctor which you take to the chemist's for medicine; a *recipe* is a set of instructions for how to make a dish.

LISTENING

1 Introduce 'Bread-and-Butter Pudding' as a well-known

dessert in England. Elicit ideas from students as to how it might be made – will it only be made of bread and butter? Make sure students understand *ingredients, utensils, method.* Then play the tape through one or more times. Students make notes under the headings.

TAPESCRIPT

Now, today's quick recipe is for Bread-and-Butter Pudding. It's a simple but delicious dessert. Now, you'll need the following ingredients: three quarters of a litre of milk, two hundred grams of butter, four large or six small eggs, two hundred and fifty grams of sugar, some dried sultanas, the big juicy ones, you'll need about one hundred and fifty grams – or, if you can't get sultanas, some little raisins. Oh, and I almost forgot, you'll need about half a dozen slices of white bread; it's actually better if it's a day old.

So what you do is this: break the eggs into a bowl and mix in the sugar, then add the milk and beat the mixture well until it's nice and smooth. Now take the slices of bread and spread them generously with butter, cut off the crust and cut each slice into three or four strips. Take a medium sized shallow dish, something that can go in the oven, and butter it so that it doesn't stick. Then put the strips of buttered bread along the bottom of the dish to form a layer. Take about half the sultanas or raisins and sprinkle them on ... you can be quite generous. Then put down another layer of bread and butter strips and sprinkle on the rest of the sultanas. Now pour the egg and milk mixture over the bread and butter and sultanas and leave it for a couple of hours. Then, when the bread is nice and wet, put it in a medium hot oven, around two hundred degrees, for about forty-five minutes or until it starts to rise and go nice and crisp. It's best not to eat it straight away, I think it tastes much better if it's warm rather than boiling hot.

KEY *(example notes)*

INGREDIENTS: 3/4 litre milk, 200g butter, 4 large or 6 small eggs, 250g sugar, 150g sultanas, 6 slices white bread
UTENSILS: mixing bowl, medium-sized shallow dish
METHOD: break eggs, mix in sugar, add milk, beat mixture, butter bread and cut into strips, put layer of bread in buttered dish then add sultanas, add another layer and rest of sultanas, pour in mixture, leave for 2 hours, cook for 45 min. in 200° oven, serve warm.

2 Students could check their notes against the tapescript on page 162. (It will be better if students check and correct each other's notes, not their own.)

WRITING

Students use the recipe they have just heard as a general model for writing recipes of their own. If there are students of the same nationality, allow them to work together for this.

HOMEWORK SUGGESTION

Finish the recipe you started in class or else write another one.

Set C

LISTENING: Watch your body language

• Introduce the topic of body language and gestures. See if students are aware of some everyday gestures and postures that have significance (Not simply well-known gestures expressing aggression or obscenity). Take one of the gestures shown in the pictures below as an example. Do students know what it might mean?

• Present the task. Give students a few moments to look at the notes for completion.

• Play the tape once through for general understanding.

• Play the tape again, several times if necessary. Students fill in the notes. They can check their answers in pairs.

• Go through answers, playing the tape again and pausing at relevant sentences.

TAPESCRIPT

CAROL JONES: When we're abroad, it's not just the spoken language that can cause problems. Most travellers can remember accidentally upsetting someone because a gesture which is harmless at home, causes great offence abroad. On 'Travel Wise' today we have Dr Ian Williams, an expert on international gestures.

DR WILLIAMS: Good evening.

CAROL JONES: Now, Ian, I believe that even experts like you are sometimes caught out.

DR WILLIAMS: Oh, indeed, Carol. Why, I remember being in India and misunderstanding a conversation. You see the person I was talking to kept shaking his head. I thought he was disagreeing with me. In fact it turned out to be the opposite.

CAROL JONES: So his head shake meant yes?

DR WILLIAMS: More than that, it meant 'carry on talking because I'm interested'.

CAROL JONES: So we can't even take simple head movements for granted. What about closer to home?

DR WILLIAMS: Well, in Europe some gestures are universal. Thumbing your nose means the same whether you are in Oslo or Madrid. But very often a gesture is either unknown or else means something entirely different. For example the thumbs up sign we use to mean OK is known throughout northern Europe. But if you go to Greece or Italy people won't understand what you're on about.

CAROL JONES: Mm ... talking of Italy, I'm reminded of that strange gesture, you know, the one where they hold the tips of their fingers together and move them up and down ...

DR WILLIAMS: Oh yes, the 'hand purse'. Um, we never see it over here but it's used all around the Mediterranean. Unfortunately it's probably the most confusing gesture around.

CAROL JONES: Why's that?

DR WILLIAMS: Well in Italy you'll remember it means 'What are you getting at?' or 'I don't understand' ... Yet in France it can mean that you are afraid, and if you go to Greece it means that something is good, while in Spain it simply means 'a lot'.

CAROL JONES: What a minefield! Sadly, the news is about to begin, so we don't have time to go into this any further. But Ian, what one piece of advice would you give to travellers going abroad?

DR WILLIAMS: Never copy local gestures as it can seem strange and cause offence. Steer clear of local taboo gestures too.

CAROL JONES: So probably the best thing on your next trip is to remember to keep your hands in your pockets. It's by far the safest way! Dr Ian Williams, thank you for coming in. And now we go over to the newsroom where ...

KEY

1 India; **2** shaking; **3** 'carry on talking because I'm interested'; **4** universal; **5** Oslo; **6** Madrid; **7** OK; **8** won't understand it; **9** confusing; **10** 'What are you getting at?'/'I don't understand'; **11** that something is good; **12** 'a lot'; **13** can seem strange and cause offence; **14** local taboo gestures; **15** keep your hands in your pockets

LANGUAGE STUDY: *Remember, forget* and *remind*

1 Discuss the examples and explanations for *remember* and *forget* in the usual way. Point out the structures and meanings using the board (*remember to do something, remember doing something*). Elicit further examples to make the distinction clear.

KEY

In sentence (a) Ian Williams remembers now what happened in the past: In the past he went to India; now he remembers it. In sentence (b) he is advising us about something we ought to keep in mind. (When we say *remember to do something* we are talking about using memory in the way it ought to be used; we can use the negative of *forget* in the same way: *I haven't forgotten to do something* means 'I have remembered to do what I ought to do'.)

2 Go through the explanation of *remind*, giving or eliciting examples.

3 Students do the exercise in the usual way.

KEY

1 remind; **2** remember; **3** forgotten; **4** remind; **5** forget; **6** Remember; **7** remember; **8** remember

READING: Keep your hands in your pockets!

• Introduce the text (on gestures). Generate interest in the text by asking the students to describe what is going on in the picture. Ask if there are any obvious nationalities that they can identify. Pre-teach the following items: *Yank:* slang for an American; *enrage:* make very angry; *choke:* when

food or drink goes down the wrong way; *maitre d':* head waiter; *skewer:* stab.
• Students read the text and answer the multiple choice questions. When you go through answers, get students to quote sentences from the text in support of their answers.

KEY

1 – A; 2 – C; 3 – B; 4 – C; 5 – A; 6 – C

• Finish by discussing any other interesting points from the text. See if students can work out the precise gestures described in the text.

HOMEWORK SUGGESTION

Write a short speech to a group of foreigners about the gestures they are likely to come across in your country.

Set D

SPEAKING: Just good manners

1 Do not discuss the pictures at this point, except to point out that they show rules that are being broken. Divide the class up so that some students read about Japan while others read about Arab countries.

2 Students explain the rules that are being broken in the pictures.

KEY

The social rules that are being broken are:
p.94 Top left – Kissing as a greeting; Top right – Bathing with soap; Bottom – Blowing your nose in public; sitting on a table.
p. 95 Top – Wearing shorts; Bottom – Picking up food with left hand/stretching out legs and showing soles of feet; not taking off your shoes.

3 Students read through the articles of their counterparts and check that they have been given all the essential information by their partners.

4 Students list items that express the idea of *must* and *mustn't.* They may need an example or two to get the idea across.

KEY

MUST	MUSTN'T
(the imperative is generally used for both)	
you should	you shouldn't; don't
always	never
make sure	whatever you do (never) ...
	on no account

LANGUAGE STUDY: *In case*

1 Take the example sentence and elicit its meaning.

2 Give or elicit the meaning of *in case* (roughly speaking it means 'in order to be safe if ...'). Go through the explanations and examples in the usual way. Students change sentences where possible.

KEY

1 I'll take my coat in case the weather changes.
2 I'll buy a thick paperback in case I have to wait a long time.
3 I won't take any cash in case it gets stolen. (We can't make a sentence using *traveller's cheques.*)
4 We might say 'I'd better take some tablets in case I get seasick.'
5 We cannot use an *in case* sentence here.

WRITING: An advice sheet for foreigners

1 Read through the situation. Elicit some examples of things foreigners *should/must/shouldn't/mustn't* do. Write these on the board. Point out the difference in strength between *must* (strong – something absolutely necessary) and *should* (weaker – something that is advised).
• Students work in groups to draw up items for the advice sheet.

2 Students continue the discussion. Pyramid discussion may be suitable at this point.

3 Students write the advice sheet, working individually, in pairs or in groups, using the texts in the Coursebook as a model.

HOMEWORK SUGGESTION

Finish/improve the advice sheet for foreigners.

Aims and content

The overall aims are to deal with the vocabulary of the environment and geography; to revise the formation/use of the passive, and the use of the article; to provide writing pay-offs (describing the geography of a country and describing a process).

Set A

Aims: To launch the topic (through speaking based on a questionnaire); to teach vocabulary connected with geography and climate; to practise reading based on authentic encyclopaedia entries, with an information-gap speaking activity to follow; to practise writing based on the geography of the student's own country.
Speaking: New Found Land: questionnaire
Vocabulary: Geography
Reading: Describing a country's geography
Speaking: The newest continent [P]
Writing: My own country

Set B

Aims: To practise reading based on a travel brochure (tour to Australia); to revise indefinite and definite articles; to practise listening based on a passage on Australian wildlife.
Reading: Discover Australia
Language study: Uses of *a/an, the* and *some*
Listening: The world's favourite Australians (FCE Paper 4, Part 2)

Set C

Aims: To practise reading based on a text about the Amazon rainforest; to revise the passive voice; to practise speaking based on the rainforest.
Reading: The Inuit
Reading: Xingu, the forbidden area (FCE Paper 1, Part 2)
Language study: The passive

Set D

Aims: To practise listening based on an argument about environmental problems; to teach verbs and dependent prepositions; to practise writing about a process.
Listening: Don't be so green!
Vocabulary: Verbs with prepositions
Writing: Describing a process

Set A

SPEAKING: New Found Land

1 Present this initial speaking activity, which launches the topic. Obtain some examples (humorous or serious) of possible laws before going on to the questions for discussion. Students discuss the questions in groups. In question 12 students decide on further questions for discussion.

2 Speakers' Corner
Help students to understand the activity, and organise the class for it. You may have to allow some discussion time first for students to choose speakers and topics, or for speakers to choose themselves! It is obviously best if students talk about subjects on which they have a strong opinion. You could also 'prime' the speakers in a previous lesson, so that they are ready to talk.

VOCABULARY: Geography

Students look up any meanings they are unsure of in the dictionary. Make sure that an adequate number of monolingual learner dictionaries is available for students. Elicit some additional examples, then encourage students to work together to come up with as many connections as possible. For example:
An oasis is a green place in the middle of a desert.
The tide completely covered the beach.

READING: Describing a country's geography

1 Students read and answer in the usual way.

KEY
A = China; B = Ecuador

2 Students make notes on the countries.

KEY
Name: China
Location: E Asia
Geographical features: low plains NE; high mountains (Tibetan plateau) W; 3 regions: Yellow River N, Yangtze centre, Xi Jiang S
Name: Ecuador
Location: NW South America, on Equator
Geographical features: coastal plain W; Andes (includes active volcanoes); Amazon Basin; also Galapagos Islands

SPEAKING: The newest continent

Use the usual procedure for information-gap work. The points of the compass (*north, south, east, west*) have already been revised in the reading task, but you can pre-teach *north-west, south-west, north-east, south-east.* Also pre-teach the construction: *X is south-east of Y.*

KEY

Complete map:

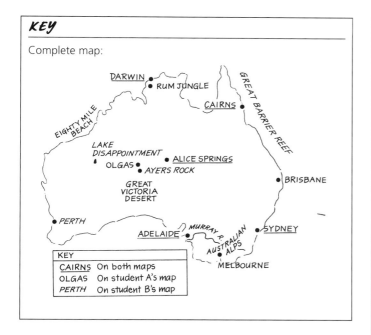

KEY	
CAIRNS	On both maps
OLGAS	On student A's map
PERTH	On student B's map

WRITING: My own country

By now students should have had enough input in terms of vocabulary, structure and text organisation to write a short text about their own country. Do not expect the same level of formality as in the 'models'.

HOMEWORK SUGGESTION

Write a conversation between yourself and a foreigner in which you give a description of your own country.

Set B

READING: Discover Australia

• Generate interest in the topic of Australia. Perhaps get students to identify the places in the photographs (Sydney Harbour and Opera House, Ayers Rock and the Great Barrier Reef). Find out if anyone has friends or relatives there.
• Students read the text and answer the true/false questions in the usual way.

KEY

1 False. You have to make your own way to the hotel.
2 True.
3 False. It is before Alice Springs.
4 False. You will have to travel by 4WD vehicle (= four wheel drive). (NOTE: *Vehicle* is an umbrella term which includes cars, buses, lorries, vans, Land Rovers, etc.)
5 True.
6 False. They are domes of rock.
7 False. You will see the sunset over Ayers Rock.
8 True.
9 True.

10 False. You will see them from a sub-sea vessel. (NOTE: *Vessel* is an umbrella term like *vehicle* and covers means of transport that go in the water, e.g. ship, boat, tanker, catamaran.)

LANGUAGE STUDY: Uses of *a/an*, *the* and *some*

Go through the explanations and examples and get students to do the exercise in the usual way. Students should be able to give reasons for their answers to the exercise.

KEY *(unnecessary articles in bold)*

1 Although I like **the** wildlife, I hate **the** dingoes.
2 **The** Ayers Rock is a most fascinating place.
3 **The** baby kangaroos are called joeys.
4 Have you ever eaten **the** kangaroo meat?
5 We travelled by **a** Landrover and I rode on a camel.
6 We took a boat to the Great Barrier Reef.
7 There's a postcard from **the** Sydney for you.
8 Kakadu is the most amazing place I've ever visited.
9 She is doing **the** research into the koala for her degree.
10 It loves **the** leaves, especially the leaves of the eucalyptus tree.
11 The water there is so beautifully clear that you can see the coral.
12 There were **a** millions of sheep at the farm.

LISTENING: The world's favourite Australians

1 Find out if students have heard of the duck-billed platypus, or if they recognise the animal from its picture. Then read through the sentences to be ticked or left alone on the basis of the listening passage. Students may know some of the answers from general knowledge – encourage them to apply this knowledge, but do not get them to shout out answers. It is probably best to begin by playing the first part of the tape, about the duck-billed platypus, rather than the whole thing.

TAPESCRIPT

When explorers came to Australia they couldn't believe their eyes. **The** continent was full of strange and wonderful creatures. There was **the** kangaroo which moved along in huge jumps, and all kinds of new snakes and insects. **The** strangest one of all was **the** duck-billed platypus, basically because nobody could work out what it was. Let me explain why. It's a bit like **a** duck because it has got **a** bill and webbed feet and lays eggs. It spends most of its time in **the** water digging around in **the** mud with its bill, but instead of feathers it is covered with fur so it can't be **a** bird. In the end scientists decided it was **a** mammal because it is warm-blooded and produces milk for its young.

Everybody's favourite, though, is the koala. Koalas are rather interesting. They are active at night and because of this, spend most of the daytime asleep in the fork of trees. They don't have tails, which is strange for animals which live in trees but they have a hard pad of skin which lets them sit for hours. They have pouches for their young like kangaroos but theirs open downwards! Baby koalas spend about six months in the pouches before riding on their mothers' backs.

Over the past two hundred years they have had a varied history.

In the old days dingoes ate them and they were hunted by the aborigines. When the Europeans colonised Australia they shot the dingoes and the aborigines started eating different food. This was great for the koalas and the population grew incredibly. Unfortunately they were hunted for their fur and in 1924 two million koala skins were exported.

Nowadays they are no longer hunted, but there are other dangers. Koalas eat enormous amounts of leaves from gum trees, but since many of the forests have been cut down food is getting scarce. Disease and cars are two other major threats. Luckily people are aware of the problems and are trying to protect them so their future doesn't look too bad.

Even though they look so cute and cuddly don't be taken in! One famous politician saw a koala and picked it up for a group of photographers. The koala wasn't interested and scratched him with its sharp claws. By the way, in case you were wondering, the name 'koala' comes from the aborigine language which means: 'I don't drink'. Even though they can drink water, they get most of the liquid they need from the leaves they eat.

KEY

1 a It has toes. No tick. (It has webbed feet, like a duck.)
  b It has fur. Tick
  c It has feathers. No tick
  d It gives birth to its young. No tick. (It lays eggs.)
  e It is cold-blooded, like a snake. No tick. (It is a mammal.)

2 Read out the sentence 'They are active at night' (= They move around at night, find food, etc.). Tell students to find out two other unusual things about the koala. Pre-teach the word *dingo*: an Australian wild dog. Play the second part of the tape about the koala.

KEY

2 1 at night; **2** asleep; **3** tails; **4** pouches (pockets they carry their young in); **5** downwards; **6** dingoes; **7** aborigines; **8** shot the dingoes; **9** hunted; **10** fur; **11** two million; **12** enormous amounts of leaves; **13** gum; **14** disease; **15** cars; **16** pick it up; **17** scratch you; **18** I don't drink

3 Students look at the tapescript on page 163. Discuss the use of the definite and indefinite article in the first paragraph.
The continent was full ... (Because Australia has already been referred to; we are speaking about a specific continent.) There was **the** kangaroo ... (The kangaroo is being referred to as a species.) ... and all kinds of **new snakes and insects.** (With plural nouns used in a non-specific way we don't use *the*.) **The** strangest one of all was ... (superlative construction) ... the duck-billed platypus (species – the same as for the kangaroo above). It's a bit like **a** duck ... (*a* = any duck, a single non-specific duck) ... because it has got **a** bill ... (*a* = one) ... and **webbed feet** ... (non-specific plural, so no article) ... and lays **eggs** (non-specific plural, so no article) ... in **the** water ... (the water specific to a particular place) ... so it can't be **a** bird (*a* = one non-specific member of a family) ... decided it was **a**

mammal (*a* = one non-specific member of a family)

HOMEWORK SUGGESTION

Write six questions based on the text about Australia. Give two choices for each of the questions.

Set C
READING

1 Give students time to look at the text. They can discuss it briefly among themselves, helping each other to understand the general idea.
• Elicit some opinions about why the text is different from the ones we usually hear about the environment.

KEY

In this case, it is a native people, not outsiders, who wish to exploit the natural resources to be found on their land.

2 Present the task. Write on the board the four words which are given (*experiment, given, further, each*).
• Tell students to do a first reading of the text and work out where the four given words go. (2 = each; 6 = given; 10 = further; 12 = experiment).
• Students look at the text again in detail, and try to work out the missing words. They can work in pairs or groups for this, as some of the missing words are quite difficult.
• Discuss answers.

KEY *(other answers may be possible)*

1 way; **2** each; **3** without; **4** attacked/killed/injured; **5** most/much; **6** given; **7** take; **8** own; **9** fiercely/strongly; **10** further; **11** past; **12** experiment; **13** well; **14** all; **15** involved/concerned

READING: Xingu, the forbidden area

1 Discuss the lead-in picture and questions in the usual way.

KEY

Sting is a pop star, with long fair hair, dressed in western clothes. Raoni, the Indian chief, has long hair, a headdress and tribal jewellery. Between his chin and his bottom lip is a large wooden plate, worn as a custom of the tribe. He is holding a pipe in his hand.
Students discuss what they think the rainforest is like and how dangerous they think it is. They may suggest dangers such as poisonous snakes and spiders, and hostile Indians.

2 Get students to read the text and answer the multiple choice questions. Go through answers in the usual way. Discuss briefly any points of difficulty or interest that arise.

KEY

1 – C; 2 – A; 3 – C; 4 – B; 5 – C; 6 – C; 7 – B; 8 – B

LANGUAGE STUDY: The passive

1 Go through the examples and elicit answers to the questions below. At each question, elicit further, parallel examples. Write them on the board and get students to identify the elements (subject, object, verb, past participle, verb *to be*) within them.

KEY

1 We change the verb in the active sentence to the past participle and add it to an appropriate form of the verb *to be*.
2 It becomes the subject.
3 It becomes the agent. (Sentence (**b**) has no object.)
NOTE: Some students may feel uncomfortable with a formal grammatical explanation. In this case, you should write the sentences up on the board and show by means of arrows and different colours what happens to the active sentence when it is transformed to the passive, and keep grammatical explanation to a minimum.

2 Students do the transformation exercise. When you go through answers, write them up in the form of a 'chart' as in the key below. Students complete the chart.

KEY

ACTIVE	PASSIVE
1 The Indians protect the forest. (Present simple)	1 The forest is protected by the Indians.
2 Guns and disease are wiping out the Indians. (Present continuous)	2 The Indians are being wiped out by guns and disease.
3 Human greed will rob children of the earth's beauty. (*Will* -future)	3 Children will be robbed of the earth's beauty by human greed.
4 Very few people have seen this place. (Present perfect)	4 This place has been seen by very few people.
5 Alcohol destroyed thousands of Indians. (Past simple)	5 Thousands of Indians were destroyed by alcohol.

3 In other words

Point out that this exercise once again involves changing from active to passive, and from passive to active. Students write the sentences. When you go through answers, you can get students to write the sentences on the board if you wish.

KEY

1 Rivers and lakes are polluted by factories.
2 The forest was destroyed by fire.
3 The nuclear explosion affected many countries.
4 Oil from tankers kills thousands of sea birds.
5 The ozone layer has been damaged by gases.
6 ... (so) skin cancer will probably kill more people.

7 Changes in the weather have affected some countries.

HOMEWORK SUGGESTION

Write a short composition about the environmental problems of your country. If appropriate, include details about over-development from tourism or industry.

Set D

LISTENING: Don't be so green!

1 Discuss the meaning of the title of the listening before students listen. The title is a 'pun' (play on words). Green is of course a colour, but has two other meanings: (a) concerned about the environment and the damage being done to it, (b) naive, lacking in knowledge.
• Play the tape through for general understanding. As the passage contains fairly complex arguments, you may want to play it through twice.
• Give students time to look at the notes for completion.
• Play the tape again, several times if necessary. Students complete the notes. They can check their answers in pairs or groups.
• Go through answers, playing the tape again and pausing as necessary.

TAPESCRIPT

FRANK:	Just look at these pictures! Why doesn't your government do something?
MARIA:	Are you accusing me of burning down the forest again?
FRANK:	It's somebody's fault. You can't blame us.
MARIA:	But I do. Indirectly you're responsible. Your banks lent us too much. And we can't pay it back ...
FRANK:	What are you getting at?
MARIA:	Well, interest rates are high and we're desperate for dollars. We have to clear the forest to provide land for cattle.
FRANK:	That's still no excuse. You shouldn't have borrowed so much. Anyway, what about coffee? Couldn't you export that?
MARIA:	We do. But there's more money in beef than coffee.
FRANK:	Come off it! I paid two pounds sixty p for this jar.
MARIA:	But we get hardly anything ... about fifty p, I think.
FRANK:	How come?
MARIA:	It's the processing – the roasting and the grinding – which adds value. That's done over here.
FRANK:	So why not process it yourselves? Or put up the price?
MARIA:	Because importing countries are too powerful.
FRANK:	Even so ... there must be another way.
MARIA:	Yes and no. You can't prevent people from clearing the forest if that's the only way they've got of making a living. We have to show there's an alternative by encouraging people to buy more products which grow in the forest; you know – like nuts and rubber.
FRANK:	No morality, just economics. You're a hard woman, Maria.
MARIA:	And you, Frank, darling ... sometimes you're just a bit too green!

KEY

1 indirectly; **2** loans; **3** the forest (to provide land for cattle); **4** fifty p (= fifty pence); **5** roasting; **6** grinding; **7** powerful; **8** nuts; **9** rubber; **10** economics

2 Students read the questions and discuss. Play the tape again if necessary.

KEY

Students discuss whether they agree or disagree with Maria and how far they think Frank accepts the responsibility which developed countries have. Students may feel that Maria wins the discussion by being able to give more arguments in support of her point of view.

VOCABULARY: Verbs with prepositions

1 Students match the halves to form complete sentences.

KEY

1 – c; 2 – d; 3 – e; 4 – b; 5 – a

2 Students expand the sentences. It will be easiest if students use the past tense of the verb in each sentence.

KEY

1 He blamed the government for cutting down the trees.
2 He thanked the Indians for welcoming them to their village.
3 He congratulated the local people on working to protect their forests.
4 He accused the politicians of not understanding the problem.
5 The politicians prevented the Indians from living in a traditional way.

WRITING: Describing a process

1 Point out that passive forms are often used in describing a process (e.g. an industrial process, or a procedure for doing something in an organisation, government department, etc.). Find out from students if they have encountered any such processes or procedures in their studies or work.
• Point out that when a passive is repeated in the same sentence, the verb *to be* is not normally repeated. (This occurs in sentences **e**, **g**, **c**, **f**.) Start students off by taking sentences as examples if necessary. Then students work on the sentences, writing the correct verb form and putting the sentences in order to form a complete paragraph.

KEY

Coffee is grown in a warm climate but the beans are exported to make instant coffee. **(g)** When (the coffee) trees are several years old, they flower, and green berries are produced which ripen into 'cherries'. **(d)** The 'cherries', each containing two coffee beans, are picked and dried in the sun. **(f)** When dry, the beans are separated from their shells, put into sacks and exported. **(b)** When they arrive at their destination, the beans are bought by a coffee dealer and sold to a coffee processor. **(e)** These imported coffee beans are roasted and ground. **(h)** In order to produce instant coffee powder, huge pots of fresh coffee are made. **(a)** This coffee is sprayed into hot air. **(c)** The hot air evaporates the water and coffee powder is left and freeze-dried.
NOTE: This is a very simplified version of coffee-making processes.

2 For this task, students will probably need vocabulary from the teacher. If the composition of the class allows, students can discuss in single-nationality groups and draw up a list of suitable products as you go round the groups. They could then work on the written paragraph as a group task. If the students are of mixed nationalities, you will have to allow some minutes of 'thinking time' and if possible, discuss with each student individually before any writing is done.

HOMEWORK SUGGESTION

Write about a process with which you are familiar.

12 Dog Eat Dog

Aims and content

The overall aims are to explore the topic of 'the media', providing sufficient vocabulary; to introduce verbs for reporting; to develop the skill of writing and planning discursive compositions; to give practice in a variety of reading styles.

Set A
Aims: To teach vocabulary around newspapers; to practise listening and extending awareness of sentence stress; to practise speaking and sentence stress through an information-gap activity.
Vocabulary: Newspapers
Listening: The British Press (FCE Paper 4, Part 2)
Listening: How to get an interview
Speaking: Getting the facts straight (FCE Paper 5, Part 3) [P]

Set B
Aims: To practise the vocabulary of headlines and examine the grammar of headlines; to practise the reading skill; to teach and practise reporting verbs.
Vocabulary: Understanding the headlines
Reading: The scoop!
Language study: Reporting verbs

Set C
Aims: To practise reading and speaking based on newspaper articles; to practise letter writing and giving advice.
Reading: Tricked!
Speaking: Discussing newspaper articles
Writing: I thought you should know ...

Set D
Aims: To practise the listening skill; to provide guided practice of several FCE exercise types (Paper 3, Paper 4); to practise planning and writing compositions.
Listening: The news
Writing: Newspaper articles
Writing preparation: Composition writing

Set A

VOCABULARY: Newspapers

• Explain what the title of the unit means. A 'dog eat dog' world is a world which is very competitive and in which people often behave cruelly or immorally to achieve their aims. In Britain, the competition between popular papers means that journalists often behave in this way – *Dog Eat Dog* is the title of a book about journalism.
• As a lead-in to the topic, students complete the words in the sentences. Most of the words should already be known to them.

LISTENING

1 After reading through the task, it will be helpful to ask questions orally which draw on any existing knowledge which students may have. They may already know about some newspapers in Britain, e.g. that the *Times* belongs to the 'quality' press, and that the *Sun* is one of the tabloids. They may also have some idea about the political leanings of the newspapers; they might also guess that the *Independent* aspires to be in the centre.
• Play the tape through for general understanding. Then play it again, perhaps twice. Students complete the notes, checking their answers in pairs. Go through answers briefly, but do not discuss the tape in detail at this point as there are further tasks to come.

TAPESCRIPT

HANS: Can you tell me something about newspapers in Britain, Jackie?

JACKIE: Right, well, there are two types of newspaper. There are the popular papers, you know the tabloids like the *Sun* and the *Daily Mirror* and the quality papers like the *Times, Guardian* and *Independent*. Oh, and I almost forgot the *Daily Telegraph*.

HANS: Are there big differences politically?

JACKIE: Um, the *Mirror* and *Guardian* are the only two which are fairly left wing. All the rest are on the right, you know, the *Sun, Times* are right wing in my opinion. So is the *Telegraph*. The *Independent,* a fairly recent paper, tries to be independent of all the major parties and is in the centre.

HANS: And who reads which papers?

JACKIE: Well, I think this is largely to do with social class, education and, of course, which political party you tend to support. Tabloids are mostly read by ordinary working class people but there is a middle class tabloid called the *Daily Mail*. The tabloids are dreadful, they're full of pictures of pretty girls and competitions, stories about the private lives of famous people, TV stars and so on. They've got no real news in them.

HANS: And do political parties own newspapers?

JACKIE: No except for some papers with tiny circulations. Most papers are owned by rich businessmen. All the same, national papers support a party particularly at general elections. In fact the *Sun* claims that it won a general election for the Conservative party.

HANS: Really! And do many people buy the *Sun?*

JACKIE: Goodness, yes. It has a circulation of about 4 million; its left wing equivalent the *Mirror* sells about 3 million, I think. All the quality papers added up together don't equal the circulation of the *Sun*.

HANS: And do you have any kind of censorship?

JACKIE: Not really. I suppose it's because we have a long tradition of freedom of the press. And in a way this can be a problem. Recently there was an awful photo on the front of several of the tabloids of a woman news presenter. She was sitting on a beach somewhere hot and sunny, looking very fat and unattractive, a million miles from her normal TV image. I think it's unfair to print pictures like that. After all, she was just a private person trying to relax on holiday. But in Britain we have far too much of this; there aren't really any privacy laws which can protect people from the press. Telephoto lenses mean that nobody is safe.

KEY

1 Guardian; **2** Independent; **3/4** Times/Telegraph; **5** Mirror; **6/7** Daily Mail/Sun

2 Play the tape again, twice if necessary. Students complete the sentences. They can check their answers in pairs.

KEY

8 ordinary working class people; **9** middle class; **10** social class; **11** education; **12** political party; **13** rich businessmen; **14** about 4 million; **15** about 3 million; **16** Sun; **17** Conservative; **18** censorship

3 Students consider their answers to the question.

KEY

19 Jackie thinks it's awful/unfair.

4 Form students into introduction groups of three or four, preferably of mixed nationalities. Students briefly tell the rest of the group something about the newspapers they have in their country.
• If students all belong to the same nationality, get groups to work together on a set of notes, suitable for giving an oral presentation about newspapers in their country.
• Be aware of possibilities for developing this task into a project in which students volunteer to give an oral presentation to the class as a whole. Students may even be able to obtain and show examples of the newspapers they talk about.

LISTENING: How to get an interview

1 Find out if any students already know who the people in the photographs are (but do not let them shout out answers). Then play the conversation.

TAPESCRIPT

JULIAN: What's so funny?
ANNABEL: It's this book. It's about this journalist who would do anything for a story.
JULIAN: Who did he work for?
ANNABEL: The tabloids, the popular papers.
JULIAN: One of those ...
ANNABEL: Anyway, he got up to some real tricks.

JULIAN: Like what?
ANNABEL: Well, you know Oliver Reed?
JULIAN: The film director?
ANNABEL: That's Oliver Stone. Oliver Reed, the actor.
JULIAN: Oh, him? ... a bit of a playboy wasn't he?
ANNABEL: Mm that's right. There was a lot of gossip a few years ago; he married a schoolgirl ...
JULIAN: Who, this reporter?
ANNABEL: No, Oliver Reed.
JULIAN: What! He must have been twice her age.
ANNABEL: Three times, actually. Anyway, Wensley, you know, the journalist, he realised that this would be a great story so he followed them to the West Indies.
JULIAN: Oliver Reed can't have been happy.
ANNABEL: You're right. He refused to talk to anyone. Of course Wensley couldn't go back to England without a story – his editor would have killed him.
JULIAN: I can imagine ...
ANNABEL: Anyway, Wensley was desperate. What he did was invite Reed's minder, you know a kind of bodyguard, to his hotel.
JULIAN: Crafty.
ANNABEL: And guess what. His minder actually turned up with the girl and Wensley got them to tell him the whole story!
JULIAN: And where was Reed while this was going on?
ANNABEL: At home in bed with a cold. Anyway, the best bit is that Wensley told the other two ...
JULIAN: The girl and the minder?
ANNABEL: Yeah ... so he told them that he was going out to get some food because everyone was feeling hungry. Anyway, instead, he went off to find Reed. He just walked into the villa.
JULIAN: What a cheek!
ANNABEL: Reed was furious and chased him out of the house. All the while though, Wensley was asking him questions.
JULIAN: And did he get him?
ANNABEL: No, he got away, although Reed spent the next day checking every hotel on the island. It was worth it though, Wensley had his interview and his editor was happy. The story made the headlines.

KEY

1 Wensley (Wensley Clarkson); **2** Oliver Reed (a well-known actor); **3** Oliver Reed's wife

2 Students look at questions 1 – 4 and think whether they know the answers. (note: In Question 3, *get round* means to solve a problem). Play the tape again and discuss.

KEY

1 He went to the West Indies to try to get an interview with Oliver Reed.
2 Reed refused to speak to anybody.
3 He invited Reed's 'minder' (a colloquial word for bodyguard) to his hotel for a drink. The minder came with Reed's girlfriend and they had a drink. Wensley Clarkson said he was going out for some food but instead went into the villa and had an 'interview' with Reed (which in fact consisted of Reed

telling him to go away).

4 It probably wasn't a fair way of getting an interview, but it was successful.

3 *Get* is used in the following ways: He *got up to* some real tricks; to do something (usually bad or illegal). Wensley *got them* to tell him the whole story: to encourage/persuade.
He was going out *to get* some food: to find/obtain.
And did he *get him*: catch. No, he *got away*: to escape.

4 Play the tape of the first extract. Elicit the fact that in the third sentence, there is a strong stress on Stone. This is an example of 'contrastive' stress, used here to correct someone.
• Play the second extract. Students mark in the stress.

• Play the two extracts again. Students repeat, then practise in pairs.

SPEAKING: Getting the facts straight

Follow normal procedures for pairwork information-gap activities. Point out that the activity involves correction of information, so contrastive stress will be appropriate. Illustrate with an example from the situation if necessary. The Editor should read his information to Kit who should correct and contradict him.

HOMEWORK SUGGESTION

Write a speech in which you tell a foreigner something about the newspapers in your country.

Set B

VOCABULARY: Understanding the headlines

1 If you have any popular British or American newspapers ('tabloids') available you can illustrate the point about headlines being short and dramatic with genuine examples. (Point out that the short word may also save space, but that is not the only reason for using it.) Then students see if they can match the headline words with their synonyms.

KEY

a – 8; b – 3; c – 4; d – 6; e – 2; f – 9; g – 5; h – 7; i – 1

2 Go through the examples, making sure students see what the grammatical terms relate to (i.e. where the infinitive occurs, etc.).

3 First of all students try to expand the headlines so that they make sense in normal English.

KEY

1 A government minister is going to close down some hospitals.
2 A prince and princess (royal couple) deny that there is any problem between them.
3 The head of the fire brigade is going to resign because of the way he handled a big fire.
4 A teacher is being questioned by the police over a scandal (probably cheating) to do with examinations.
5 Members of the government are angry as differences grow between them.
6 A princess has got married in unusual and exciting circumstances.

• Now students give their ideas about the actual events that took place. Encourage students to be as inventive as they can over the origin of the stories.

4 This activity can be carried out in groups. You could help students by giving them a few ideas to begin with, but it is better if they invent stories of their own, starting off with a bare situation and a dramatic headline. The headline and stories can be read out to the rest of the class. The class can decide on the headline/story which is most dramatic/amusing, etc.

READING: The scoop!

1 Present the background to the text. Elicit the fact that Paul McCartney is a well-known singer (a former member of *The Beatles*). Read out the titles to choose from. Then students read the text. The aim here is to encourage swift reading for gist. The way students support their arguments for different titles should give insight into how well they have understood the text. Pre-teach *nutter*: crazy and dangerous person; *muckspreader*: someone who tells unpleasant stories and gossip. Students have met the verb *to spread* in Unit 10, Set B (to spread butter); *yep* in this text means 'Yes'.

KEY

a and **b** would both make good titles (NOTE: **b** means roughly 'A journalist will do anything to get a good story').

2 Students match what actually happened with what the journalist wrote. This is quite a difficult exercise, as it requires the students both to understand the sentences and to deal with choices which are similar, but not the same.

KEY

1 – e; 2 – a; 3 – d; 4 – c; 5 – b

LANGUAGE STUDY: Reporting verbs

1 and **2** Go through the patterns and examples in the usual way, using the board and eliciting further examples from the class.

3 Students do the transformation exercise in the usual way.

KEY

1 He advised me not to print the story.
2 She denied taking/having taken/that she had taken the photographs.
3 She asked me not to print her name.
4 He warned me not to give him an interview.
5 Julian admitted inventing the story/to having invented the story/that he had invented the story.
6 He suggested phoning/that I/he/she should phone the editor.
7 The editor told her secretary to get her a photograph of the accident.
8 He persuaded me to tell him what had happened.

HOMEWORK SUGGESTION

Write ten true/false statements based on the text about Paul McCartney.

Set C

READING: Tricked!

1 Organise students to work in pairs so that one student reads article **A** (on p. 108) and the other reads article **B** (on p. 109). Point out that they will only be able to answer some of the questions 1 – 8 from the article they read – they must find out the other answers by asking their partner the questions.

KEY

	ARTICLE A	ARTICLE B
1	Oxford	no information
2	Rare – only 50 female birds are known to exist	near extinct parrot
3	no information	12 ounces
4	hysterical	feels she has been tricked
5	no information	in a box of luxury chocolates
6	no information	London
7	no information	Norman
8	*Kathy:* long prison sentence *Jennifer:* deportation	no information

2 Students read the article they have not yet looked at. Discuss.

KEY

Article **A** comes from a 'popular paper', Article **B** from a 'quality paper'.
Article **B** carries more information.
Article **A** has more human interest.
Article **A** is more emotional.
Article **A** is likely to be found more difficult (because of the high level of descriptive language).

SPEAKING

Students discuss Kathy's story and give their opinions.

WRITING: I thought you should know ...

This task leads out of the speaking task above. In the writing, students can take any suitable role – a friend, or perhaps a worried relative, e.g. cousin, grandfather/grandmother, uncle/aunt.

HOMEWORK SUGGESTION

Complete/improve the letter which begins: 'I thought you should know ...'

Set D

LISTENING: The news

1 These news items are obviously a joke. Note the date – 1st April (= April Fools Day).
• Students listen to the opening sentences from the news and write down the headlines. Encourage them to suggest what the stories might be about.

TAPESCRIPT

This is the eight o'clock news on Wednesday 1st April. First the main news headlines read by Arthur Robinson.
• New regulations for Britain's motorists are to come into force from midnight tonight.
• A blaze has destroyed examination buildings in Cambridge.
• Bad weather has caused the destruction of Italy's spaghetti crop.
And now for the news in depth from your newscaster Annie Mcleod.
The Minister of Transport, Mr Alfred Murphy, has announced that as of midnight tonight new regulations for road users will come into force. From midnight cars and buses will have to drive on the right-hand side of the road. To avoid unnecessary confusion bicycles and lorries will not have to comply with the changeover until February 29th of next year. All traffic will be banned from roads between 11.30 this evening and midnight to ensure that the changeover goes smoothly.

A (1) *blaze* at the Local Examinations Board (2) *has destroyed* a wing of the building. The (3) *mystery* fire (4) *broke out* at around three o'clock this morning and it took until nine o'clock for fire-fighters to bring it (5) *under* control. Fortunately damage (6) *appears to be* limited to the Science examinations section. A (7) *spokesperson* has said that a (8) *thousand*, I'm sorry I'll read that again, a hundred (9) *thousand candidates* who took the November (10) *examinations* will have to re-sit. A group of students is (11) *helping* police with their (12) *enquiries*.

Bad weather has caused the destruction of this year's spaghetti crop in Northern Italy. The crop was destroyed by exceptionally cold weather for this time of year. Farmers woke up this morning to find that the spaghetti had frozen on the branches of their trees. This means ruin for thousands of Italian farmers who were depending on this year's harvest to rescue them from economic difficulties. This is the third year that the spaghetti harvest has been a disaster and farmers must be wondering if they will be rescued by the European Community again.

KEY

See tapescript above.

• Students discuss what they think they will hear about each item from the news in depth. Students can work in pairs or small groups to work out their predictions.

2 Students listen to the news in depth and check their predictions.

3 Now students listen in detail to the first news item and answer the questions.

KEY

The regulations come into force at midnight.
They apply to cars and buses.
To avoid confusion, other road users will not have to change until next February.

4 Students listen to the item about the fire and fill in the gaps.

KEY

See tapescript – the missing words are in italics.

5 Play the tape again, or get students to look at the tapescript. Students work out the tenses used, looking particularly at the first two sentences in each news item.

KEY

A variety of tenses is used, but elicit the fact that the present perfect is often used to introduce news items. Then when detail is covered, the newsreader will move into another tense – often the past simple, as in the item about the fire.

NOTE: The reason is that the present perfect gives to events in the past a sense of having some general importance now – which is also the broad aim of a news broadcast. By contrast, the past simple is concerned with specific details and specific times.

WRITING: Newspaper articles

1 Take the first sentence as an example if necessary. Then students continue, expanding the notes. Students should not look at the tapescript at the back of the book until they have done the exercise. They can then check their answers.

KEY

1 Bad weather has caused the destruction of this year's spaghetti crop in Northern Italy.
2 The crop was destroyed by exceptionally cold weather for this time of year.

3 Farmers woke up this morning to find that the spaghetti had frozen on the branches of the trees.
4 This means ruin for thousands of Italian farmers who were depending on this year's harvest to rescue them from economic difficulties.
5 This is the third year the spaghetti harvest has been a disaster.
6 Farmers must be wondering if they will be rescued by the European Community again.

2 Students continue with this further set of notes to expand into an article.

KEY

1 Finally, the World Animal Fund has announced plans to save penguins from extinction.
2 They want to build an electric fence around penguin breeding grounds in the Antarctic.
3 They believe this is the only way of preventing hungry polar bears from eating all the penguins.
4 The polar bears will be given bananas to eat instead.
5 Next Monday, a group of international pop stars will make a record to raise money for the project.

• Students discuss the kinds of words omitted from the notes (they are 'grammar' words like *a, the, have, (announced,* etc.), *to (build,* etc.).

3 Students work on the news item as instructed. You can organise the task as though it is a TV news programme with students pretending to be newscasters.

WRITING PREPARATION: Composition writing

1 Give students time to read through the text. You could ask them as they read to underline the key words in each paragraph (this will make it easier for them to understand how the plan on the right relates to the text).
• Briefly go through the text with students, paragraph by paragraph, helping them to see how the plan 'produces' the final text, sometimes using different words, but the same ideas.

2 The procedure is similar to (1), but this time, students read the text and work out for themselves the kind of plan which will produce the text. Once again, it may help if students underline key words and phrases in each paragraph.

KEY (example plan)

Paragraph 1: TV important invention – many people feel slaves to TV
Paragraph 2: TV has killed conversation – people turn to TV for entertainment
Paragraph 3: TV informs/educates, e.g. about life in other countries
Paragraph 4: Both advantages and disadvantages – depends on us

3 Discuss the composition topic. Depending on the level of the class, you can spend time eliciting points for and against: in this way, through discussion, you and your students together will arrive at points which might go in the plan. However, a good class may manage without much guidance, perhaps with students only having some brief discussion among themselves.
• After you have checked students' plans they could write the composition, perhaps for homework.

HOMEWORK SUGGESTION

Improve the first draft of the composition you started in class.

13 Evolution

Aims and content

The overall aims are to revise the future continuous and perfect; to revise ways of making logical deductions and sympathising; to review various ways of linking, contrasting and explaining covered in earlier units.

Set A

Aims: To practise speaking, based on cartoons; to practise understanding dictionary entries for key vocabulary, with a speaking activity to follow.
Reading: What's the joke? – cartoons
Vocabulary: Understanding dictionary definitions/ Science and scientists
Speaking: Time travellers

Set B

Aims: To practise listening, and ways of expressing sympathy; to practise the language of logical deductions; freer speaking practice to incorporate the above.
Listening: Living dinosaurs – expressing sympathy (FCE Paper 4, Part 2)
Language study: Making intelligent guesses

Set C

Aims: To practise reading based on an article about the future evolution of mankind; to practise future continuous and perfect forms.
Speaking: Mystery cultures (FCE Paper 5, Part 3) [P]
Reading: 'Man After Man' (FCE Paper 1, Part 1 & 2)
Speaking: Predictions
Language study: Future predictions

Set D

Aims: To revise ways of linking, explaining and contrasting from previous units; to practise listening based on a talk (the evolution of armour); to write a text combining the above elements.
Language study: Linking, explaining and contrasting
Listening: The evolution of armour (FCE Paper 4, Part 2)
Writing: Composition from notes

Set A

READING

As a lead-in to the unit, students try to explain the jokes to someone who hadn't seen them.

Explanations
Top left: Cartoon shows some dinosaurs all smoking cigarettes. The caption says: *The real reason the dinosaurs died out,* so the joke is that the dinosaurs died from smoking cigarettes.

Top right: Cartoon shows a dinosaur wearing a baseball cap and glove and carrying a baseball bat. He is standing outside the caves where he thinks his friends live, but

unfortunately, they are all extinct! That's why it says: *Suddenly Bobby* (the dinosaur) *felt alone in the world.*

Bottom: Cartoon shows a funny-looking woman from the 20th century surrounded by a lot of dinosaurs. She is standing by a machine. The caption says: *Disaster befalls Professor Schnabel's cleaning lady when she mistakes his time machine for a new dryer.* This means that she made a mistake – she thought the time machine was a washing machine/tumble dryer. She is probably going to be eaten by the dinosaur behind her!

VOCABULARY

1 Dictionary definitions

• Read out the words so that students hear their pronunciation. (Do not obtain meanings at this stage.) Then students read the definitions below and match the words to them.
• With a good class you may want to spend some time on the definitions – perhaps also comparing the definitions found in other dictionaries.

KEY
1 reptile; **2** dwell; **3** meteor; **4** fossil; **5** drought; **6** genetics; **7** mammal; **8** ancestor

2 Science and scientists

• Elicit some words for different branches of science in English. Do students know what we call the scientists associated with these branches? Then students try to complete the sentences.

KEY
1 astronomer, astronomy; **2** anthropologists, anthropology; **3** Geology, Geologists; **4** Archaeology, archaeologist

• Students discuss the sciences they consider most or least interesting from their own point of view, and most or least useful.
• As a further activity, you could ask your students to look the words up and find where their stress lies.

SPEAKING: Time travellers

1 This activity can be carried out in groups, perhaps as a pyramid-discussion procedure.

2 Students could choose roles and write speeches individually; however, speeches could also be composed as a group activity (groups appoint a speaker).

HOMEWORK SUGGESTION
Write about what you saw and what happened when you travelled through time.

Set B

LISTENING: Living dinosaurs

1 Part A

• Find out if any students have read about dinosaurs, or been to any dinosaur exhibitions. Read out the situation and the questions. Play the tape in the usual way.

TAPESCRIPT

PART A

POP OSBORNE:	Hello Pat. What have you been (1) *up to*?
PATRICIA:	I've just taken Katie to an exhibition.
POP OSBORNE:	(2) *Poor you*, you (3) *must be tired*.
PATRICIA:	Tired! (4) *I'm exhausted*.
POP OSBORNE:	(5) *Never mind*. I'll make a nice cup of tea. So, what did you see?
PATRICIA:	Well, it was called 'Living Dinosaurs'.
POP OSBORNE:	Living dinosaurs! You (6) *can't be serious!*
PATRICIA:	Of course they were models which look like dinosaurs ... They're operated (7) *by computer*. They do all the right things though. Move and (8) *breathe* and make horrible (9) *noises*.
POP OSBORNE:	Katie (10) *must have been scared*.
PATRICIA:	Actually she (11) *loved* it. One little chap was (12) *terrified*. He (13) *can't have been* more than four.
POP OSBORNE:	Oh (14) *dear*, (15) *what a shame*. He'll probably have (16) *nightmares*.

KEY

It is an exhibition on 'Living Dinosaurs' (i.e. it has true-to-life models which move and make noises like living dinosaurs). The exhibition is suitable for children, but is perhaps frightening to very young children.

• Play the tape again. Students fill in the blanks in the conversation.

KEY

See tapescript above – the missing words are in italics.

2 Sincerely sympathetic!

1 Play the tape. Students listen to the pronunciation of the phrases on the tape. Point out that the phrases show sympathy. Play again. Students mark the intonation, as in the first example, and practise repeating the phrases.

KEY

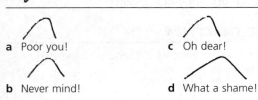

a Poor you! **c** Oh dear!

b Never mind! **d** What a shame!

2 Students decide on the phrases which complete the sentences. After this they can briefly practise the sentences and responses in pairs.

KEY

a Poor you!/Oh dear!/What a shame!
b Never mind!
c What a shame! (or *Poor you!* if we are thinking about the owner rather than the dog)
d Never mind!/Oh dear!
e Oh dear!

3 Part B

Give students time to look at the questions. Pre-teach *die out* (= to become extinct). Check that students remember *fossil* and *ancestor* from Set A. Play the tape.

TAPESCRIPT

PART B

POP OSBORNE:	So did you have a nice time, Katie?
KATIE:	Yeah. It was great. Can I tell you all about dinosaurs?
POP OSBORNE:	If you like, dear.
KATIE:	Well, they died a long time ago. Sixty million years.
POP OSBORNE:	Well, fancy that.
KATIE:	I bet you don't know why they died.
POP OSBORNE:	You are going to tell me anyway, I expect.
KATIE:	Well, people used to think it might have been a change in the weather. You know, an ice-age.
POP OSBORNE:	Oh, really.
KATIE:	Nowadays they think it could have been a meteor.
POP OSBORNE:	A meteor, from outer space? Why's that?
KATIE:	'Cos lots of other things died at the same time. They know that 'cos geologists dug up lots of fossils of things that died. So it must have happened suddenly.
POP OSBORNE:	Fancy that. People have some funny ideas, don't they?
KATIE:	So what happened is that it fell in the sea – splash – and made it boil.
POP OSBORNE:	Well, I never.
KATIE:	There was lots of steam and stuff. It killed most of the plants. The 'vegetarian' dinosaurs died out, so did the meat eaters – like tyrannosaurus rex – he was a meat eater – he's my favourite – well, they all died. It got too humid too.
POP OSBORNE:	I don't like the heat either!
KATIE:	But you're not a reptile! Dinosaurs were reptiles; you know, cold-blooded like snakes. We're mammals.
POP OSBORNE:	That's nice.
KATIE:	So the dinosaurs couldn't cope. The heat made them slow.
POP OSBORNE:	Oh dear!
KATIE:	But the mammals, they were warm-blooded, they could control their temperature better. My dad says they were our ancestors. But the dinosaurs, they died!
POP OSBORNE:	What a shame. Who would have imagined it? The

KATIE: Well, mum says we shouldn't feel sorry for them. They did last over a hundred and sixty million years!

POP OSBORNE: Even so, it can't have been nice for them. Anyway, talking of vegetarians and meat eaters, what do you want for lunch? Spaghetti or a hamburger?

KEY

1 60 million years ago.
2 Perhaps because of a meteor. Previously people thought that they died because of a change in the weather, i.e. with the occurrence of an ice age.
3 The theory is that a meteor fell into the sea and boiled off large amounts of water. The water vapour blocked out the sun and most plants died. Those dinosaurs which fed off plants died; those which fed on the plant eaters then starved to death as well.
4 Scientists changed their minds because geological evidence suggests that the extinction happened very quickly, rather than as part of a slow change.
5 Mammals are warm-blooded (i.e. their bodies stay at a constant temperature) and were able to survive. Dinosaurs are cold-blooded (i.e. their temperature changes with the temperature of their environment) and could not deal with a dramatic change in temperature.
6 160 million years.

NOTES:
1 Not all scientists accept the idea of 'sudden' extinction. The process may have taken thousands of years.
2 The change in temperature could have been a fall, not a rise as the tape suggests.

LANGUAGE STUDY: Making intelligent guesses

1 Point out that this section deals with structures used when you make a guess about something – e.g. what caused the dinosaurs to become extinct, what a person is feeling, etc.
• Read out sentences 1 – 6. Take the first sentence as an example. Ask (a) if it is certain or uncertain, (b) if it is positive or negative, (c) if it is talking about the past or the present.
• Take other sentences as examples if necessary. Then students work applying the certainty/uncertainty, positive/negative, past/present distinctions to the sentences for themselves.

KEY

1 certain, positive, present
2 uncertain, positive, past
3 certain, positive, past
4 certain, negative, past
5 uncertain, positive, past
6 certain, negative, present

• Write up the structures on the board. Elicit what happens when we move from present to past. Students should be

able to see that we move from *be* to *have been* (= *have* + past participle of *be*). For example:

BE
She must be scared.
HAVE BEEN
She must have been scared.

• Help students to see that *must* is associated with certainty (positive), *might* with uncertainty (positive), and *can't* with certainty (negative). (NOTE: The examples omit *might not*, which is uncertain in a negative sense; there is no need to deal with this, as it will only confuse.)
• Elicit further examples of guesses about the present or past, and the situations in which we might make these guesses.

2 Stress patterns
• Play the tape. Elicit the fact that the stress is on *must* and *tired* in (1) and *might, change, weather* in (2). Also elicit the fact that *be* in (1) is weakened to /bɪ/, while *have been* in (2) is weakened to /əv bɪn/.
• Students copy the pronunciation and practise the sentences. Elicit ideas about how the remaining sentences are pronounced. Students practise saying the sentences in pairs.

3 Present the task. You will probably have to go through one or two examples for students to understand what is to be done. Point out that in this passage they can use *could* as an alternative to *might* for 'possibly' forms (but not for the 'definitely not' form in number 9, where *could* must be used in reported speech). Students complete the text.

KEY

1 must have been
2 must have been trapped
3 might have/could have fallen
4 can't have died
5 must have gone
6 must have been caught
7 must have been
8 could have/might have had
9 could not have
10 must have told/must have been telling

HOMEWORK SUGGESTION

Imagine you are the journalist who reported the story about the prehistoric bird which had been trapped in the rock. Write a dialogue between you and the engineers who saw it. Remember to ask them to explain what they think had happened to the bird.

Set C

SPEAKING: Mystery cultures

Divide students into pairs, A and B. They make their minds up about the objects they see, then show their partners the objects and announce their conclusions. In so doing they should try to use the various structures for deduction ('intelligent guessing') covered previously.

READING: 'Man after Man'

1 Read through the introductory paragraph: 'We know ... makes some suggestions'. Before thinking about the future of mankind, see if students themselves have any knowledge of the evolution of mankind up to the present. Have they heard or read about man-like fossils? Do they know where any of these fossils have been found? (Many have been found in Africa.) Have they any idea when 'modern man' evolved? (According to some scientists, less than 200,000 years ago.)

• Read out the questions (How much longer ...?; What do you understand ...?). Elicit students' ideas. (NOTE: According to the *Longman Dictionary of Contemporary English, genetic engineering* means 'the changing of the nature of a creature or of its organs, cells, etc. by the artificial changing of its genes'.)

• Pre-teach *tundra* and *woodland*. Check that students remember the word *dwell*, which was introduced in Set A, and understand the derived word *dweller*. Also pre-teach *descendant*: remind students of the word *ancestor*, then move on to *descendant*, for example:
Apes are the ancestors of humans.
Humans are the descendants of apes.

2 Introduce the reading task, making it clear that one of the headings A – E is not used. Students read the text and match headings to paragraphs. When you elicit answers, you can ask for sentences which provided clues, but do not discuss the text in detail, as there is a further task to come.

KEY

1 B (Evidence: *Civilisation will have broken down and billions of people will starve and die.*)
2 D (Evidence: *they genetically engineer five new species.*)
3 E (Evidence: *These two eventually depend on each other ...*)
4 A (Evidence: *the men who left Earth return in a giant spacecraft.*)

3 Students do the multiple choice reading task in the usual way. When you go through answers, students should be able to provide evidence from the text.

KEY

1 – B; 2 – C; 3 – B; 4 – A; 5 – A; 6 – A

• This may be a good time to point out the use of tenses in the text. In the first paragraph, two main tenses are used: (1) simple future ('will do'), because we are dealing with predictions; (2) future perfect ('will have reached', 'will have broken down'), used to predict a situation in the future when something has already happened. These tenses will be looked at further in the Language study section. Notice that in later paragraphs, the present simple is used, because the 'time frame' has been clearly established.

4 Word search
• Students find ways of expressing the ideas 'dying' and 'ending', and write them down, with line references.

KEY

break down (line 7), die (lines 7, 41), become extinct (line 12), no longer exist (line 15), die out (lines 31, 38)

SPEAKING

Get students to give their opinions on Dixon's ideas.

LANGUAGE STUDY: Future predictions

1 Go through the example sentences and explanations in the usual way, copying sentences and the 'time line' onto the board to make points clear. Then students do the exercise.

KEY

She'll have: eaten 75,000 food pills.
written in her diary 25,000 times.
played chess 2,500 times.
watched 500 videos.
drunk 50 bottles of Happy Juice.

2 Students make predictions about their own lives. They can think about finishing school/university, marriage, children, job, etc.

HOMEWORK SUGGESTION

Write a short composition about life in the distant future. If you like, you can discuss how you feel about Dougal Dixon's predictions.

Set D

LANGUAGE STUDY: Linking, explaining and contrasting

Remind students about ways of joining sentences. Elicit from them linking expressions for cause and effect, etc. and examples of sentences using them. Then students choose the linking words and expressions in the text below. When you go over answers, discuss – sometimes different answers are possible, and sometimes students may not immediately see why an answer is wrong.

KEY

1 B *Once upon a time* is best; **D** *In the beginning* is possible.
(**A** *First of all* comes at the beginning of a series of actions or before the first point in an argument; **C** *Firstly* comes before the first point in an argument.)
2 B *Of course* and **C** *Naturally* are both possible.
(**A** *Sincerely* comes at the end of a letter.)

3 **C** *that's why* introducing a result.
(**A** *so that* introduces a purpose; **B** *because* introduces a reason.)

4 **C** *Eventually* meaning 'finally, after a long time'.
(**A** *Lately* means 'in recent times'; **B** *Once* means 'at one time'.)

5 **C** *to* = to-infinitive after comparative form of adjective, as in 'It is easier to speak English than Chinese.'.
(**A** *for* comes before a clause or a gerund; **B** *in order to* expresses purpose.)

6 **B** *otherwise* meaning 'in any other situation'.
(**A** *unless* means 'if ... not'; **C** *instead* means 'as an alternative to the situation already mentioned'.)

7 **C** *not ... until* to show the start of something after a time when nothing happened.
(**A** *before* shows that something happened at an earlier time; **B** *by* refers to achieving something before a point in time.)

8 **A** *During* and **B** *Over* are both possible, showing that things happen in course of a period.
(For **B** *By* see 7 above.)

9 **B** *so* is best; **D** *that's why* is acceptable; both express result, but *so* fits 'traditional' punctuation better.
(**A** *because* introduces reason; **C** *so that* introduces purpose.)

10 **A** *As* and **C** *Because* are both possible, expressing a reason; however, **A** *As* is more likely to begin a sentence. **B** *While* is possible if you think the meaning is 'during the time that ...'.

11 **A** *so* for degree construction *so* + adjective + *that* + clause.
(The others do not occur in this construction.)

12 **D** *who* is best, **C** *that* is possible.
(**A** *which* refers to things or animals, not people. **B** *whom* cannot be the subject of a relative clause.)

13 **B** *Afterwards* meaning 'later', and followed by what happened next.
(**A** *After* introduces a subordinate time clause expressing what happened before.)

14 **B** *as* meaning 'in such a way that they actually became money'.
(Choices **A** and **C** suggest mere substitutes for money; **D** *instead* does not fit structurally – we must say *instead of*.)

15 **A** *Eventually,* meaning 'finally, after a long time'.
(**B** *Lastly* means 'coming last in a list of reasons'.)

16 **B** *Although,* meaning 'in spite of the fact that ...'
(**A** *Because* comes before a reason; **B** *Despite* comes before a noun phrase or gerund, not a clause.)

17 **B** *although*
(**A** *despite,* see 16 above; **C** *while* is used to contrast two otherwise similar people or things, for example: 'Gold always stays shiny, while silver tends to lose its shine.')

18 **D** *as* is the best answer;**B** *because* is possible, though not very suitable with a reason given to back up a statement.
(**A** *so* and **C** *that's why* are completely wrong, as they introduce a result.)

19 **D** *Nowadays* and **B** *These days* are both possible.
(**C** *Actually* does not refer to the present time; it introduces the truth.)

20 **A** *In fact,* to strengthen the previous statement, meaning 'I would go even further and say that ...'.
(**B** *Really* does not strengthen a previous statement – it indicates the truth of the statement it is in; **C** *Nevertheless* comes before a surprising or contradicting fact.)

LISTENING

1 Present the task. Elicit the meaning of *armour*. Try to put across the idea that, just as animals have evolved over time, other things have evolved too – for example, weapons and armour.
• Give students a few moments to look at the pictures and see how many items they can find. Students may be able to give some idea of the purpose of the various pieces of equipment. In a single-language class you might also elicit mother-tongue translations of some items.

2 Introduce the task. As there are several of technical terms in the listening text, it may be helpful for students to look at the notes for completion, and to take a note of words which belong to the area of warfare and weaponry. You can allow students to check the meaning of these words if you wish.
• Play the tape once through for general understanding.
• Play the tape again. Students complete the notes, then compare their notes with a partner.
• Play the tape again. Students check their notes.
• Go through answers, playing the tape and pausing as necessary.

TAPESCRIPT

Unfortunately, human beings have always been very good at finding new ways of killing each other. When weapons improve and become more effective armour has to improve too.

(slide one)
In classical times most fighting was done on foot by soldiers fighting hand to hand with spears and swords, so armour had to give protection but be fairly light so the soldier could move. That's why armour from this period only protects the head and upper body.

(slide two)
This shows a beautiful helmet from Greece. Even though it covers most of the face there is still plenty of room for the soldier to see through.

(slide three)
In Roman times, better-equipped soldiers wore body armour made up of strips of metal, which was far more flexible – each piece moves – they could move their bodies much more easily than in the armour made just from one piece.

(slide four)
During the Middle Ages, cavalry became more important and a lot of the fighting was done on horseback. This meant that armour could be heavier and give greater protection. A knight would wear a suit of chain mail which covered the whole body. Chain mail was popular for about four hundred years up to thirteen hundred.
A knight would also have worn a heavy helmet like this one. It gave protection against heavy swords. Of course it was quite difficult to see because there was only a little hole to look through.
However, as bows became more powerful they were able to penetrate chain mail, so they had to find an alternative. The result was a return to plate armour.

(slide five)
For the next two hundred years, plate armour became more and more sophisticated. The best armour of all was made in Italy and Germany and shows remarkable craftsmanship.

(slide six)
The invention of gunpowder and guns changed the face of warfare. For a time it was possible to provide more protection by making thicker armour. But as guns improved, armour became less and less effective. Look at this breastplate from the English Civil War of the sixteen forties. The bullet has gone straight through and must have killed the poor soldier wearing it.

(slide seven)
People quickly realized that the best protection against a bullet is to be a fast moving and difficult target. Because of this, over the next few centuries we see a return to fast and lightly armed soldiers with very little protection.

(slide eight)
However, the last fifteen years or so have seen new developments. Some new materials are so strong that they can offer protection against bullets and flying metal. Look at this picture of an American foot soldier wearing a flak jacket and a helmet.

KEY

1 on foot; **2** spears and swords; **3** light; **4** head and upper; **5** Greece; **6** see through; **7** more flexible; **8** horseback; **9** heavier; **10** suits; **11** bows; **12** Italy and Germany; **13** thicker; **14** fast moving target/difficult target; **15** (very) little protection; **16** fifteen years; **17** flying metal

WRITING

It is not possible to give a model composition, as this is a freer writing activity. However, it is important that students use the ways of linking, explaining and contrasting covered previously.

HOMEWORK SUGGESTION

Complete the assignment on the evolution of armour as homework.

14 *Pedigree*

Aims and content

The overall aims are to teach the forms/uses of *make, let* and *allow*; to revise time propositions; to help with essay preparation and planning; to practise writing a discursive composition.

Set A

Aims: To launch the topic (family and royalty) through a speaking activity; to revise kinship vocabulary; to practise reading and develop skills for FCE Paper 3, Part 1
Speaking: Talking about family relationships
Reading: Heirs to the throne

Set B

Aims: To practise the skills of scanning and more intensive reading; to introduce seven new phrasal verbs through their context; to deal with obligation, focusing on *make, let, allow*; to provide freer speaking practice from the above.
Reading: Forbidden love (FCE Paper 1, Part 3)
Vocabulary: Phrasal verbs in context
Speaking: Evaluating the text
Writing: Writing about the abdication
Language study: Make and *let*
Speaking: Marriage customs

Set C

Aims: To contrast pairs of time expressions; to practise writing a story from notes, selecting material.
Language study: Time expressions
Writing: Writing a story from notes
Language study: Subject-object questions

Set D

Aims: To practise reading and evaluating the content of a text, moving on to writing an article; to practise speaking about photographs; to practise listening; to write a composition examining two sides of an argument.
Reading: The best job in the world? (FCE Paper 1, Part 1)
Speaking: Spitting Images
Listening: The British Royal Family
Writing: Balancing arguments

Set E

Aims: To practise listening for specific information and answering multiple choice questions; to practise reading and matching information.
Listening: Henry VIII and his six wives. (FCE Paper 4, Part 1 & 2)
Reading: Royal Biographies. (FCE Paper 1, Part 4)

Set A

SPEAKING: Talking about family relationships

1 Introduce the subject of family trees. Make sure students understand how they work, taking some examples of family relationships (e.g. from students themselves) and copying a simple tree onto the board. Also elicit a little background about Queen Victoria (Queen of the United Kingdom for most of the 19th century). Then students study her family tree and answer the questions.

> *KEY*
> _____
> **1** Alice of Battenberg.
> **2** He is her nephew; she is his aunt. She was Edward VIII's niece; he was her uncle.
> **3** Peter.
> **4** Great-great-grandson.
> **5** Father and son.
> **6** Peter, Zara, Beatrice and Eugenie.

2 Vocabulary
• Students should be able to brainstorm words for family relationships, including:
mother, father, son, daughter, brother, sister, grandmother, grandfather, grandson, granddaughter, uncle, aunt, nephew, niece, cousin.
• You will probably have to teach the *in-law* addition to *son, daughter, mother, father, brother, sister*. Point out that we cannot say e.g. 'grandmother-in-law'. Also show how the prefix *great-* is used.
NOTES:
1 In English the children of your parents' cousins are your second cousins.
2 Students may want to know the distinction between *Mummy, Daddy, Mum and Dad, Ma and Pa*, etc. *Mummy* and *Daddy* are usually used by small children, and *Mum* and *Dad* by older children within the home. *Mom* and *Pop* are American, and *Ma* and *Pa* mainly American.

3 If there is a royal family in the students' own country, this may make for an interesting discussion, but handle with care!

4 An interesting variation on the 'draw your family tree' task would be for students to tell their partner about their family, and for the partner to draw the family tree.

READING: Heirs to the throne

1 You may have to spend some time on the questions, checking that students understand 'in line to the throne', etc. Then students read and try to answer in the usual way.

> *KEY*
> _____
> **1** Prince William is second and Prince Harry third in line after Prince Charles.
> **2** In around 2030.
> **3** He'll be the most English monarch for about 400 years.

4 32.5% (6.5% of each).
5 Quite often. Three instances are given in the text.

2 Students fill in the blanks.

KEY

1 after; **2** to; **3** the; **4** for; **5** of; **6** this; **7** who; **8** nearly; **9** in;
10 that; **11** of; **12** has; **13** but; **14** because/when; **15** the;
16 had/decided/wanted; **17** could; **18** of; **19** able/allowed;
20 same

HOMEWORK SUGGESTION

Draw your family tree and write sentences describing the relationship between its members.

Set B

READING: Forbidden love

1 Find out if students have heard of the Duke/Duchess of Windsor, King Edward VIII, or the Simpsons. (The events in the passage have been made into a TV series which students may have seen.) Then students read and make notes on the main dates and events.
NOTE: You pronounce *heir* exactly the same as *air*.

KEY *(important dates and events)*

1929: The Simpsons go to London.
December 1935: Edward inherits the throne.
December 11th, 1936: Edward VIII abdicates. They go into exile.
1972: Edward dies.
1986: Duchess of Windsor dies.

2 Students match the sentences with the gaps. They can check their answers, working in pairs. When you go through answers, get students to say which sentences provided clues to the answers.

KEY

1 – B; **2** – E; **3** – A; **4** – D; **5** – C

3 Students find answers to the questions from the text.

KEY

1 Wallis probably had a difficult childhood because her mother had to cope with the sudden loss in fortune.
2 Because of her charm and skill as a hostess. Obviously, without her husband's wealth she wouldn't have been able to do anything.
3 The newspapers kept the story secret out of loyalty to the Royal Family.
4 He joined Wallis in the South of France and they led a life in exile.

VOCABULARY: Phrasal verbs in context

1 Students pick out the meanings of the phrasal verbs.

KEY

1 take after; **2** come into; **3** look down on; **4** bring up; **5** call off;
6 turn out

NOTE:
It is worth pointing out that the three-part phrasal verb, i.e. *look down on*, is transitive inseparable, taking this form:

VERB	ADVERB	PREPOSITION	OBJECT
look	down	on	someone

2 Students make sentences containing the phrasal verbs.

3 Word search
Students look back at the reading text for words connected with royalty.

KEY

Paragraph 1: Duchess, abdication
Paragraph 2: Prince, heir to the throne
Paragraph 3: King, Royal Family, Queen
Paragraph 4: throne, King, abdicated
Paragraph 5: Duke, Your Royal Highness, throne, coronation, Queen

SPEAKING: Evaluating the text

Students discuss among themselves briefly, then have some whole class discussion. You might want to find out from students what they think would have happened nowadays. Would a similar relationship have similar consequences?

WRITING

This will need careful setting up. The first thing to do is to find out which characters the students want to be. Next, get them to work in sub-groups according to their chosen character and brainstorm things they want to say.

LANGUAGE STUDY: *Make* and *let*

1 Go through examples and explanations in the usual way.

2 Students rephrase sentences as in the example.

KEY

1 Brothers and sisters in ancient Egyptian and Inca royal families were allowed to marry each other.
2 Some societies let men have more than one wife.
3 Her parents made her marry him (even though she didn't love him).
4 Gypsy communities let (their) children marry.
5 Tallensi tribes make their young men look outside the tribe for a wife.
6 The prince wasn't allowed to marry the actress.

SPEAKING: Marriage customs

Make sure students understand the meaning of the actual words describing the custom. Then give them time to think of and write down the possible significance of the custom for themselves (not in groups at first, but they should confer in groups later). Complete the activity with general discussion. Students should be able to give their ideas reasonably fluently and accurately.

KEY *(possible significance of the custom)*

the loaf of bread: perhaps a symbol of fertility, perhaps a signal to the wife as to her duties in the kitchen!
the beer: again fertility; or perhaps to show that the husband should be able to brew – or perhaps that he is expected to enjoy drinking beer!
sawing the log in two: perhaps a symbol of sharing, perhaps to symbolise warmth in the house

---

HOMEWORK SUGGESTION

Using the information in the Language study and Speaking exercise, write a composition about marriage customs in different cultures. Include your own opinions.

Set C

LANGUAGE STUDY: Time expressions

This exercise revises expressions which students should have covered at previous stages of learning.

KEY

1 for; **2** during; **3** While; **4** Meanwhile; **5** eventually; **6** lately; **7** after; **8** Afterwards; **9** before; **10** previously

---

WRITING: Writing a story from notes

This is a fairly free writing activity and it is pretty much up to the students which points they decide to include in their stories. Ideally, they should include some of the time expressions which were covered in the previous exercise; however, this should not be forced upon them.

LANGUAGE STUDY: Subject-object questions

1 Find out if students know the story of Romeo and Juliet (if they have read/seen the play, or seen the film). Then give them time to read through the text and find the number of characters – and deaths!

KEY

There are nine characters.
There are five deaths.

---

2 Use the board to go through the explanations and examples. Point out subjects, objects, verbs and auxiliaries. Elicit parallel examples. For example, using *what*:
What happens in Romeo and Juliet? (*What* is the subject of the sentences.)
What does Romeo do? (*What* is the object of the sentence.)

3 Students make questions to fit the answers.

KEY

1 Where did the lovers meet? – At a feast.
2 Who married them? – Friar Laurence.
3 Who killed Mercutio? – Tybalt.
4 What does Romeo do? – He kills Tybalt to avenge Mercutio.
5 What happens to Romeo? – He is banished from Verona.
6 What makes Juliet appear dead? – A drug Friar Laurence gives her.
7 Who does Romeo kill? – Prince Paris.
8 Why does Romeo kill him? – Because he blames him for Juliet's death.
9 What kills Romeo? – The poison he drinks.
10 What happens when Juliet wakes up? – She sees Romeo's body and kills herself.

HOMEWORK SUGGESTION

Complete the 'Writing a story from notes' activity.

Set D

READING: The best job in the world?

Introduce the text. Get students to say quickly what it is about (the Queen). Ask if students have read articles about the Queen in their own newspapers. Do they think her job is 'The best job in the world?'

1 Make sure the task is understood – the sentences A–G are the missing opening sentences of the paragraphs 1–7. Give students time to match sentences with paragraphs.

KEY

1 C (Evidence: This sentence introduces the topic by making students think about it.)
2 E (Evidence: *She gets a 'salary' of four million pounds a year ...*)
3 B (Evidence: This paragraph gives examples of power.)
4 F (Evidence: *The Queen travels all round the world ...*)
5 G (Evidence: This is the paragraph that introduces the negative aspects of the job – the 'minuses'.)
6 A (Evidence: *... there are always photographers ...*)
7 D (Evidence: *would rather live in peace and quiet, enjoying her wealth.*)

---

2 Students look at the text again, and form a general impression about whether it is basically humorous, basically serious, or half-and-half.

KEY

Opinions may differ, but perhaps the text is basically serious, although some of the points are lighthearted, and others are expressed from a humorous angle.

3 Students look at the text in greater depth. Of course, what is important, of secondary importance, or light/humorous is largely a matter of personal opinion, but see suggestions in key below.

KEY *(suggested answer)*

Paragraph 2
To begin with ... have to pay a penny. (I)
What's more ... secrets off it! (LH)

Paragraph 3
Then of course ... power and foreign travel ... in prison (I)
It is the perfect job ... all for nothing. (SI)
Incidentally ... two hippos. (LH)

Paragraph 4
There are lots of boring formal dinners to attend (I)
bad news if you've a weight problem (LH)
and speeches to give (I)
She always has to be ... speak her mind. (I)
It must also be hard ... 'yes men'. (SI)

Paragraph 5
Possible the worst thing ... family life. (SI)

Paragraph 6
Complete paragraph. (I)
Note: Since April 1993, the Queen has paid tax on her income.

4 **Understanding the organisation of the text**
Students go through the text and note down words and phrases under each heading, as in the key opposite.

KEY

Ways of ordering points
To begin with (*para 2*)
What's more (*para 2*)
Then (*para 3*)
Now (let's look ...) (*para 5*)

Ways of giving opinions
Possibly, the worst thing ... (*para 6*)
While I wouldn't mind the money, it must be ... (*para 7*)
I'm sure there is part of her ... (*para 7*)
Fortunately ... (*para 7*)
I wouldn't want the job (*para 7*)

Balancing arguments and drawing conclusions
Let's weigh up its good and bad points (*para 1*)
Now let's look at the minuses (*para 5*)
... on the one hand ... but on the other (*para 6*)
While I wouldn't mind ..., it must be ... (*para 6*)

5 **Writing**
This task will benefit from some preliminary discussion of points to cut. Encourage disagreement – do not insist on a single way of doing the task.

HOMEWORK SUGGESTION

Using the plan you started in class, write an article about the Queen.

SPEAKING: Spitting images?

In some countries there are satirical television programmes similar to the one mentioned here. Discuss briefly. Then students match photographs.

KEY *(matching pictures)*

The Spitting Image photo shows from left to right: Prince Andrew; Prince Charles; Prince Philip; The Queen
The Royal Family photo shows, from left to right: Prince Charles (the Prince of Wales), the Queen, the Duke of Edinburgh, Prince Andrew (the Duke of York).

• Students give their opinions of the satirical photographs and cartoons. Do public figures deserve to be made fun of in this way?

LISTENING: The British Royal Family

1 Give students a few moments to look at the photographs and think about the kind of people they might be. Then play the tape.

TAPESCRIPT

1 Excuse me madam, have you got a moment? What do you think of the Royal Family?

I think they're absolutely marvellous. I mean, they are wonderful ambassadors for this country and represent everything that is good and great in Britain ... not to mention all of the wonderful things they do for charity. And just think of all the tourists who come here because of the Royal Family. I really don't know what we would do without them. And the royal babies, I think it's just marvellous when a new one comes along, bless them.

2 Could you tell me what you think of the Royal Family?

The Royal Family. What, that lot? I mean, they cost the country millions, don't they? There are so many of them too. Me, I'm unemployed and I have to live off fifty pounds a week but they've got millions and we still have to pay them. If I had my way I'd ...

3 And you sir? Do you think the Royal Family does a good job?

To tell you the truth I don't think much about them at all. They're all right I suppose. They do a pretty good job .... I wouldn't like to be one, I mean, they're always in the public eye aren't they?

4 Would you mind telling me what you think of the Royal Family?

They're harmless, I suppose. The only thing is, they're a bit out of date. They don't really mean much in the modern world, do they? It's not like in the old days when the king led his armies into battle. They're not much use but at least we know what we've got though. We don't have the circus the

Americans have every four years when they elect a new president. That really makes me sick. The only real thing I don't agree with is that we have to pay for them. Taxpayers, I mean. After all, they're rich enough already.

KEY *(who said what)*

A – 1; B – 4; C – 2; D –3

• Present the next, more substantial task – students listen, list points and decide whether they are positive, negative or neutral. Play the tape several times if necessary.

KEY

POSITIVE POINTS
good ambassadors, work for charity, good for tourism, good example of family life, Britain doesn't have the United States presidential circus

NEGATIVE POINTS
expensive, too many of them, out of date

• Encourage students to add further negative and positive points. Then get them to say which they think are most important.

2 Leading questions

Play the tape. Students mark in stress and intonation.

KEY

1 Could you **tell** me what you **think** of the **Royal Family**?
2 Do you **think** the **Royal Family** does a **good job**?
3 Would you mind **telling** me what you **think** of the **Royal Family**?

3

Students carry out a survey on each other – you can get them to extend the survey to people outside the class if you wish. Later, have a discussion in which students summarise the opinions they encounter.

4 Linking words in connected speech

• Play the tape and point out how, in speech, the sounds of words join up. Students can also say the phrases themselves, with words joined.
• Play the next extract. You can get students to try to repeat the words as said on the tape. Students mark in stresses and places where the sounds of words join together.

KEY

Me, **I'm** unem**ployed** and **I** have to live off **50** pounds a **week**, but **they've** got **mil**lions.

NOTE: Bold type indicates stressed syllables.

WRITING: Balancing arguments

Present the task. Read out the introductory paragraph which will begin the article. Then students form into pairs or groups and go through the procedures as instructed.

HOMEWORK SUGGESTION

Finish the Writing activity 'Balancing arguments'.

Set E

LISTENING: Henry VIII and his six wives

1 Present the background briefly. Give students a few moments to look at the table. Play the tape. Students fill in the table.

TAPESCRIPT

INT: Henry VIII was the founder of the Royal Navy and established the Church of England. However, he is best remembered for his six wives. He was a difficult man, but was he as cruel as some people think?
B: Certainly. He was capable of tremendous cruelty. His reign is full of dead bodies. Wife number two – Anne Boleyn – and Catherine Howard, wife number five, both had their heads chopped off. Most of Catherine's family was executed too. Many ministers met the same fate. It seems to be the way he solved problems. However, we should remember this was a cruel age and it was common for princes to use their powers in this way.
INT: I see. And what made him marry so often?
B: Basically he was desperate for a son. His first wife Catherine of Aragon could only give him a daughter and so he had to re-marry. The Pope wouldn't let Henry divorce Catherine so Henry formed his own church so that he could *go ahead* with it anyway. It also gave him the excuse to close down all the monasteries and steal all their enormous wealth. His chief minister, Thomas Cromwell, helped him with this.
INT: And what sort of reward did he get?
B: Well, for a long while Cromwell was the second most powerful man in the kingdom. Even though the great lords *looked down on him* as the son of a butcher they feared him. He made them obey the king and attend his special courts. But, as usual, in the end Henry *turned on him* and he lost his head.
INT: How come?
B: Well, Henry finally got a son from wife number three, Jane Seymour. Sadly, she died shortly after the birth so he was on the lookout for a wife again. English families either couldn't *keep up with* his demands or were suspicious of Henry. Diplomats had to look abroad. She couldn't be a Catholic of course so there was a limited choice. Cromwell eventually *talked the king into* marrying Anne of Cleves. She looked OK from her portrait so a diplomat married her on Henry's behalf.
INT: So what went wrong?
B: Well, when she arrived Henry was horrified. He said that she looked like a horse and refused to have anything to do with her.
INT: So that was the end of Cromwell. And wife number six?
B: Catherine Parr? Well she had the good luck to outlive him.

KEY

Wife's name	What happened to her
Catherine of Aragon	*divorced*
Anne Boleyn	*executed*
Jane Seymour	*died*
Anne of Cleves	divorced

| Catherine Howard | executed |
| Catherine Parr | *survived* |

2 Students listen again and answer the multiple choice questions.

KEY

1 – A; 2 – A; 3 – B; 4 – B; 5 – B; 6 – C

3 Students turn to the tapescript on page 166.
• Students can work in pairs or groups to find the ways used to express obligation.

KEY

(a) he *had to* remarry; The Pope *wouldn't let* Henry divorce Catherine; he (Cromwell) *made* them obey; Diplomats *had to* look abroad; she *couldn't* be a Catholic

• Students work in pairs to find the relevant phrasal verbs.

KEY

(b) (i) go ahead; (ii) look down on; (iii) turn on; (iv) keep up with
NOTE: *talk someone into something* (= to persuade) is another phrasal verb in the passage

4 Working in groups, or addressing the whole class, students talk about a 'larger than life' figure from their country's history. Someone who is 'larger than life' is a real person whose actions and character make him/her into a legend.
• Notice that this task also has possibilities for written work (essay or project). The 'biography' of the larger than life person could be prepared as a homework task.

READING

NOTE: as the reading section is fairly long, you may want to pre-teach some of the vocabulary at the end of the previous lesson, e.g.

Boudicca lead a revolt, dye
Alfred   hearth, tell someone off (= scold)
William   establish, feudalism, loyalty, survey, ruthless
Elizabeth intrigue, power (= powerful country), plot, flowering of artistic talent, manipulative
Charles   absolute power, raise (= impose) taxes, Roundheads, Cavaliers, execute, stubborn
Victoria virtually (= almost), constitutional monarch (= king or queen who is subject to the will of an elected parliament), symbolise, hardship, devoted

1 Introduce the task by getting students to scan the biographies quickly and think which, if any, of the monarchs they have heard of. (Queen Elizabeth I and Queen Victoria may be the most likely.)
• If students in the class have a good knowledge of history, read through 1–7 and find out if any of the questions can be answered without reading the texts. If not, get students to read the texts and find out answers in the usual way. Students can check their answers in pairs.

2 Students discuss the question in groups and then report back to the class. Encourage groups to give reasons for their answers.

3 Students could begin this exercise in class working in pairs. They should finish it for homework.

KEY

1 – E, V; 2 – B, C; 3 – C; 4 – A; 5 – W; 6 – A, E (also B); 7 – V

HOMEWORK SUGGESTION

Student's could make notes about a past or present ruler of their country and then write a brief biography.

15 | *After Dark*

Aims and content

The overall aim is to practise reading, and develop awareness of logic/cohesion factors; to prepare students for a fluency writing activity: to teach causative *have* and *needs doing/to do* forms; to preview question tags (to be taken up in *Think First Certificate*); to provide more exam-oriented revision of some key elements from previous units.

Set A
Aims: To practise reading for overall understanding and text completion (FCE Paper 3, Part 1); to teach vocabulary related to common sounds; to practise writing through a fluency writing activity.
Reading: The ghostly piper
Vocabulary: Common sounds
Writing: A night to remember

Set B
Aims: To practise reading and to develop awareness of cohesion/coherence by separating out and ordering two different texts; to teach causative *have something done* and *needs doing/to do* forms.
Reading: Haunted houses (FCE Paper 1, Part 2)
Language study: Have something done and *need*

Set C
Aims: To teach vocabulary for rooms and furnishings; to practise describing a room and letter writing; to practise expanding a text from notes; to practise the listening skill and introduce question tags.
Vocabulary: All around the house
Writing: A room of my own (FCE Paper 2, Part 2)
Writing: The story of Princess Elizabeth Balthory
Listening: What a bargain!

Set D
Aims: To practise reading and listening (dialogue); to provide a final revision of key structures.
Reading: The late arrival
Language study: Revision of key language
Listening: Vampire rumours

Set A

READING

1 Elicit some comments on the picture. What country do students associate with pipers and castles? (*Answer:* Scotland) Would they expect ghosts to be found there? Let students speculate briefly about the connection between the piper and the castle.

2 Students read the text and choose the correct answers.

> ### KEY
> 1 – **C** the; 2 – **B** whose; 3 – **C** who; 4 – **C** so; 5 – **C** was; 6 – **B** whom; 7 – **A** outside; 8 – **C** as; 9 – **B** what; 10 – **C** back; 11 – **C** that; 12 – **A** When; 13 – **C** had; 14 – **B** still; 15 – **B** where

3 Discussion
The discussion of the first three questions can be brief. But if students know of haunted houses, castles, etc. in their own country, spend some time on this question. Give students time to prepare their story. They may be able to work in groups for this.

VOCABULARY: Common sounds

• Point out that the verbs for sounds often themselves give some idea of the sound (elicit one or two examples from the students' mother tongue(s)). Give students a few moments to look at the sound verbs **a – i**, or briefly go through the verbs. Then students listen to the tape and write down the order of the sounds.

> ### KEY *(the order of the sounds)*
> 1 – **c** gasp; 2 – **g** squeak; 3 – **b** slam; 4 – **f** snore; 5 – **h** tap; 6 – **a** bark; 7 – **d** rattle; 8 – **i** yawn; 9 – **e** scream

• As a diversion, the way different languages imitate the sounds of different animals and birds may be of interest (e.g. dog: 'bow wow', cock: 'cock-a-doodle-doo', sheep: 'baa-aah', etc.).

WRITING: A night to remember

1 The aim of this is imaginative writing and fluency composition work. It is important to set the scene to exploit the picture as much as you can. The questions are designed to help you do this.

2 Play a little bit of the tape to help students to get the idea, and discuss. (NOTE: The task would also work well as a group writing activity, so you can organise students to work in groups at this point if you wish.)
• Play the tape. Students make notes. They will need to listen to the 'sound story' at least twice. The sounds are as follows:

Sound of car driving along (couple in it chatting about how far it is home) and engine gradually stuttering to a halt. Owl hooting in the background. Car stutters to a halt and engine goes dead. The two passengers in the car (one male, one female) groan more or less in unison – Oh no! Man says: Not again! This car is hopeless! Then woman says: look over there! Man says: Wow! Let's go and ... Car doors open and shut. Two passengers walk across the gravel. Couple gasp. Exchange ... 'Yes?' Muffled ums and ers from the original couple (male/female). Androgynous person says: You'd better come this way. Door squeaks on hinges as it shuts. Door slams echoingly behind them. Three pairs footsteps go across the hall and up creaking staircase, as a grandfather clock somewhere strikes midnight. Couple asleep in bed (man snoring lightly) as grandfather clock strikes three. Sounds of twigs or branch of a tree tapping on the window of the couple's room and the barking of a dog and the rattle of chains somewhere in the house. Snoring stops and man yawns as he half wakes up. Woman wakes up also and gasps. Man says sleepily: What's that? as woman screams.

• After students have listened to the sounds and made notes, they can work the notes up into a complete written story, using past tense forms for narrative.

HOMEWORK SUGGESTION

Write the history of a place with a mysterious history in your country.

Set B

READING: Haunted houses

Generate interest in the text by exploiting the title 'Haunted Houses' – ask if anyone believes in haunted houses or that there is always a logical answer to everything. See how many of the class have seen the film *Ghostbusters*. Pre-teach the words *sewer* and *tide*.

1 Go through the instructions, and quickly see if students can identify an example paragraph from each story. Then students read the paragraphs, separate them out, and order them.

KEY

Story 1: **A – I – F – E – C**
Story 2: **D – G – B – J – H**

2 Have a short period of whole-class discussion. Students indicate the clues in the texts which seemed to connect one paragraph with another. (e.g. 'strange noises' in paragraph A connects with 'loud explosions and the sound of banging' in paragraph I.)

3 Students read the paragraphs again and decide on the correct answers. They can check their answers in pairs. When you go through answers, get students to quote evidence from the paragraphs.

KEY

1 – B; 2 – B; 3 – B; 4 – C; 5 – C; 6 – A
The picture illustrates story 1, the one set in England.

LANGUAGE STUDY: *Have something done* and *need*

1 Copy the examples onto the board. Elicit answers to the questions. Point out the *have something done* structure on the blackboard. Elicit further examples as necessary to make clear how the structure works.

KEY

a means 'someone did it for them'.
b means 'they did it themselves'.

2 Use the board to go through the two structures: *need doing* and *need to be done*. Elicit further examples of sentences using the two structures, getting students to transform one structure into the other.

3 Students re-phrase the sentences.

KEY

1 We had the roof repaired (by some workmen).
2 The wall needs to be fixed.
3 A painter re-decorated the hall.
4 We had the pipes and central heating fixed by a plumber.
5 We had the old sewer filled in.
6 The garden needs to be dug/needs digging.

4 Students discuss the house and give their opinions.

HOMEWORK SUGGESTION

You are a member of the Lutz family (Reading passage). Write a letter to a friend in which you tell them about your experiences.

Set C

VOCABULARY: All around the house

Students look at the picture and label it. This could be done individually or in pairs.

KEY

1	cooker
2	fireplace
3	wallpaper
4	desk
5	bookcase
6	sofa
7	basin
8	bed
9	rug
10	radiator
11	wardrobe
12	chest of drawers

WRITING: A room of my own

1 You may have to give or elicit an example or two so that students get the idea. Then students proceed with detailed comparison of the information in the letter, and the picture above.

KEY

Martina has forgotten to mention the bed, the rug, the wardrobe and the chest of drawers.
Students decide what changes they would make.

2 Students write the letter as instructed.

WRITING: The story of Princess Elizabeth Bathory

Go through the background. Find out if students know about the people mentioned – Elizabeth Bathory, and (more likely to be known) the Dracula family. Then they try to expand the notes.

KEY

1 When she was fifteen she married a famous count who was Hungary's greatest general and who was often away.
2 At the age of twenty-five her beauty started to disappear.
3 She believed she could stay beautiful by having baths in the blood of young girls!
4 She sent servants to find young women who were promised good jobs.
5 Once they reached the castle they were thrown into deep dungeons.
6 The poor girls' blood was drained for the countess' bath.
7 After five hundred girls had disappeared, the King heard rumours.

8 When he had the castle searched, many terrible things were found.
9 Because of her noble position she was not executed but she was sealed in a small room until she died.
10 Nowadays on dark nights, you can hear the screams of the countess and her victims near the ruins of the castle!

LISTENING: What a bargain!

1 Present the situation briefly. Explain *estate agent* (= a person whose business is to buy or sell houses for people). Tell students to listen and make notes on the good and bad things about the house. You may have to play the conversation several times.

TAPESCRIPT

LIZ BALFOUR:	Well, here we are. Let me open the door for you. Mind the step. Here's the sitting room.
MIRANDA SHORT:	Wow, it's really big isn't it?
LIZ BALFOUR:	Yes, but it could be really cosy. It needs to be re-decorated.
MIRANDA SHORT:	Are all the rooms this large?
LIZ BALFOUR:	Yes, but you could always divide them.
MIRANDA SHORT:	It's been empty quite a while, hasn't it?
LIZ BALFOUR:	Only a few weeks.
MIRANDA SHORT:	It's freezing. What's that funny smell?
LIZ BALFOUR:	Oh, just a little damp.
MIRANDA SHORT:	Do you think you could turn the central heating on?
LIZ BALFOUR:	Actually, it doesn't have central heating.
MIRANDA SHORT:	Oh, doesn't it? I thought it did.
LIZ BALFOUR:	No, I'm afraid not. But the previous owners had the roof and the attic restored. That's why it's such a bargain.
MIRANDA SHORT:	Oh, really. I thought it was because of the stories.
LIZ BALFOUR:	Those silly stories. You don't believe those, do you?
MIRANDA SHORT:	But there had been a murder, hadn't there?
LIZ BALFOUR:	Oh, yes. But ...
MIRANDA SHORT:	And the other people. They only stayed six weeks, didn't they?
LIZ BALFOUR:	I'm not terribly sure. Anyway, let's look at the rest of the house ... Let's begin with the cellar.
MIRANDA SHORT:	OK then ... as I'm here.

LIZ BALFOUR: Watch out, the door's a bit low. After you!
MIRANDA SHORT: Oh, thank you very much.

KEY (example notes)

GOOD THINGS
big sitting room, sitting room could be cosy, rooms could be divided, roof and attic restored, cheap

BAD THINGS
needs redecoration, cold, damp, no central heating, murder took place in house, possibly haunted, door to cellar rather low

• Students discuss the questions which follow.

KEY (possible answers – students give their own opinions)

Miranda is cautious, and perhaps rather nervous. Liz is rather 'pushy', and perhaps not very honest or trustworthy (because she is keen to sell).

• Students give their own opinions about what happens next and whether or not they would be willing to live in the house.

2 Checking and confirming

Play the sentences. Students try to copy the intonation. They decide which one is a 'real' question and which is just checking on facts already known. Discuss the intonation features associated with each category, playing the tape again as necessary. A fall is used for just checking/confirming; a rise for a real question.

KEY

a is just checking.
b is a real question.

3 Students listen to further sentences and decide if they are 'real questions' or 'just checking'.

KEY

1 It's been empty for quite a while, hasn't it? *Just checking.*
2 You don't believe that, do you? *Real question*
3 But there had been a murder, hadn't there? *Just checking*

4 Students work in pairs and read through the dialogue. You could also get one or more pairs to 'act out' the dialogue in front of the class.

HOMEWORK SUGGESTION

You are one of the 'Ghostbusters' who went to visit the doctors' surgery in Yorkshire. Write a conversation between you and the doctors about the house and its problems. Try to include checking and confirming endings, e.g. *isn't it, don't you,* etc.

Set D

READING: The late arrival

Students read the text and answer the questions.

KEY

1 The vampire.
2 He/She was bitten by the vampire.
3 The one on the right.

LANGUAGE STUDY: Revision of key language

1 Students complete the second sentence so that it means the same as the first.

KEY

1 I had a headache so I went to my room.
2 While I was sleeping, I heard a sound.
3 I cried out because it was such a surprise.
4 She managed to come through the window.
5 If it hadn't been a fancy dress party, I would have been terrified.
6 She had the strangest eyes I'd ever seen.
7 Although I was shocked, I was attracted to her.
8 Unless you come closer, you won't see my teeth.
9 I can't remember what happened next.

2 Students check their answers by looking through the text about 'the late arrival'.

LISTENING: Vampire rumours

• Check if students have any 'knowledge' about vampires – myths relating to them, how to protect oneself against them, etc. Give them time to look through sentences 1–6 and think of how they would answer the questions from their own knowledge.
• Play the tape. When you go through the answers, students should give reasons for their answers, correcting false answers from information on the tape, and quote from the tape as necessary.

TAPESCRIPT

INTERVIEWER: Would you mind if I asked you some questions?
VAMPIRE: Not at all, dear boy; after all that's why we're here.
INTERVIEWER: How long have you been, um, a creature of the night?
VAMPIRE: Since 1327, that's six hundred and seventy years.
INTERVIEWER: Wow! And how were you 'born' if I can say that?
VAMPIRE: Well, I happened to knock at the door of Count Dracula's castle in the middle of the night.
INTERVIEWER: Why, were you lost?
VAMPIRE: Not at all, I was a tax collector for the King at that time – so you can see I've always been a blood sucker, ha-ha. Anyway, I wanted to catch the count at home.
INTERVIEWER: I see. So he bit you and that was that.

VAMPIRE:	Quite.
INTERVIEWER:	Now, I'd like to turn to your powers. Is it true that you can fly through the air?
VAMPIRE:	Absolute nonsense.
INTERVIEWER:	And what about being scared of crosses?
VAMPIRE:	Rubbish too – they have absolutely no effect on us.
INTERVIEWER:	But what are you scared of then? I mean, what about the sun.
VAMPIRE:	Ah, yes, that's true. We have to be tucked up in our coffins before the first rays of sun, otherwise we burn.
INTERVIEWER:	We have heard, do excuse me for bringing this up, that the only way to kill a vampire is with a wooden stake through the heart.
VAMPIRE:	Oh dear, you have been watching too many horror films – but actually you are right.
INTERVIEWER:	And what about garlic, you know, protecting people against the attention of vampires?
VAMPIRE:	It depends on the tastes of the vampire – my English cousins can't stand foreign food, but I love a bit of garlic or paprika myself!
INTERVIEWER:	And finally, is being a vampire lonely?
VAMPIRE:	Not really, I have my family. There's my wife Lucretia and my boy Vlad Junior ...
INTERVIEWER:	Your wife ... Where did you meet her?
VAMPIRE:	In Rome, back in 1430, I think. Anyway, there she was across the room. I had to have her. It was love at first bite ...

KEY

1 False.
2 False. (Crosses have no effect.)
3 True.
4 True. ('... but actually you are right.')
5 False. (The vampire likes garlic.)
6 False. (He has a family.)

HOMEWORK SUGGESTION

Write a short entry about vampires for an encyclopaedia. Include how they are 'born' and what they can and can't do, and what they are afraid of.

Key to Activity Reference Section

Irregular Verbs

Missing words are in *italics*.

INFINITIVE	PAST SIMPLE	PAST PARTICIPLE	INFINITIVE	PAST SIMPLE	PAST PARTICIPLE
be	was/were	been	lead	*led*	led
become	*became*	become	leave	*left*	left
begin	began	*begun*	let	let	*let*
break	broke	broken	lose	*lost*	lost
bring	*brought*	brought	make	made	*made*
build	built	*built*	*meet*	met	met
buy	*bought*	bought	pay	*paid*	paid
catch	caught	caught	put	put	*put*
choose	chose	*chosen*	read	*read*	read
come	came	*came*	*ring*	rang	rung
cost	*cost*	cost	run	*ran*	run
do	*did*	done	say	*said*	said
drink	drank	*drunk*	see	saw	*seen*
drive	*drove*	driven	sell	sold	*sold*
eat	ate	eaten	sing	*sang*	sung
fall	*fell*	fallen	sit	sat	*sat*
feel	*felt*	felt	sleep	*slept*	slept
fight	fought	*fought*	speak	spoke	*spoken*
find	*found*	found	spend	*spent*	spent
fly	flew	*flown*	stand	stood	*stood*
forget	forgot	*forgotten*	steal	stole	*stolen*
get	got	*got*	swim	*swam*	swum
give	*gave*	given	take	took	*taken*
go	went	*gone*	teach	*taught*	taught
have	had	had	*think*	thought	thought
hear	*heard*	heard	wear	*wore*	worn
hide	hid	*hidden*	*win*	won	won
hold	*held*	held	write	wrote	*written*
hurt	hurt	hurt			
keep	*kept*	kept			
know	knew	*known*			

Prepositions

1 in; **2** underneath; **3** into; **4** out of; **5** over; **6** onto; **7** through; **8** across; **9** between; **10** towards; **11** among; **12** around; **13** onto

Narrative tenses

See page 20 for answers.

Phrasal verbs

1 **1** – e; **2** – m; **3** – q; **4** – t; **5** – i; **6** – g; **7** – r; **8** –o; **9** – l; **10** – p; **11** – c; **12** – c; **13** – a; **14** – v; **15** – f; **16** – k; **17** – w; **18** – h; **19** – x; **20** – b; **21** – n; **22** – d; **23** – s; **24** – u; **25** – j

2 **1** find out T3; **2** get on with T4; **3** take on T3; **4** look for T2; **5** give away T3; **6** turn up T1; **7** set of T1; **8** run out (usually followed by *of*) T1; **9** hold on T1; **10** put through T3 (usually, we would not put the object after the particle); **11** come across T2; **12** make out T3; **13** look after T2; **14** give up T3; **15** cut down T2 (usually followed by *on*); **16** take up T3; **17** get over T2; **18** make up T3; (remind students that the same phrasal verb may have a very different grammar according to its meaning. *Make up* = make the peace/reconcile is Type 1.) **19** come up with T4; **20** tell off T3; **21** be up to T4; **22** look down on T4; **23** bring up T3; **24** take after T2; **25** come into T2

3 **1** made up; **2** came across; **3** came into; **4** looked for; **5** found out; **6** given up; **7** takes after; **8** tell off; **9** up to; **10** set off; **11** brought up; **12** get on with; **13** look after; **14** make out; **15** hold on; **16** took up; **17** take on; **18** turned up; **19** look down on; **20** put you through; **21** get over; **22** come up with; **23** ran out; **24** cut down; **25** giving away

'Language Study' Index

Adjective + preposition: UNIT 7, SET C.
Ratan Patel is *good at* languages.

After and afterwards: UNIT 1, SET E.
I put the blindfold on her. *Afterwards* I went into the audience.
After I had put the blindfold on her, I went into the audience.

Comparatives and superlatives: UNIT 7, SET C.

Countable and uncountable: UNIT 4, SET A.
I'm looking for treasure.
How much luck have you had so far?
Well, *a little*.

Describing physical appearance: UNIT 7, SET A.
Angela *had* beautiful blue eyes, long red hair, pale skin and freckles.
Mr Gilbert, a big man *with* a bald head and glasses.

Despite and although: UNIT 4, SET C.
Despite the poor man's warning, Shovell kept on his course.
Although he escaped drowning, he was murdered.

Different types of description: UNIT 9, SET B.
What's she like?
How is she?
What does she look like?
What does she like?

Expressing ability: UNIT 6, SET D.
She *was able* to hum the melody.

First and second conditional: UNIT 8, SET C.
If you move to Rome, *you'll become* a Roman too.
If you moved to Rome, *you'd become* a Roman too.

Future predictions: UNIT 13, SET C.
A few specially chosen human beings *will leave* Earth.
Civilisation *will have broken down*.

Going to or will?: UNIT 10, SET A.
I'm going to be a policeman when I grow up.

Have something done and need: UNIT 15, SET B.
She *had* her picture *taken* by a professional photographer.
The roof *needed* repairing.

If, unless and otherwise: UNIT 5, SET A.
If you don't eat more fruit, your teeth will fall out!
Unless you eat more fruit, your teeth will fall out!
You'd *better* eat more fruit, *otherwise* your teeth will fall out!

In case: UNIT 10, SET D.
I'll take a map *in case* I get lost.

Indefinite pronouns: UNIT 7, SET B.
Say you're sorry when you hurt *somebody*.
Share *everything*.

Indirect questions: UNIT 4, SET D.
Could you tell me where he was from?

Do you know what it's worth?

The infinitive and the gerund: UNIT 3, SET B.
Casanova *managed to keep* him quiet.
They *succeeded in lifting* one of the roof-tiles.

Linking, explaining and contrasting: UNIT 13, SET D.

Make and let: UNIT 14, SET B.
She and the Prime Minister tried to *make* Edward end the relationship.
Public opinion would not *let* a twice-divorced American woman become Queen.

Making intelligent guesses: UNIT 13, SET B.
You *must be* tired.
It *might have been* a change in the weather.

Narrative tenses: UNIT 3, SET E.
Paul *was buying* drinks at the bar, when disaster struck.
Within seconds, a fire *broke out* and *spread* to lots of gas-filled balloons, which *started* to explode.
Paul *had proposed* to me at midnight.

Passive: UNIT 11, SET C.
They *are protected by* the hostile tribes of the Lower Xingu.

Prepositions of position and direction: UNIT 3, SET A.
Then he climbed *over* the edge and *down* onto the floor.

Present perfect and past simple: UNIT 5, SET C.
I *used to be* a pharmacist.
I *trained* as one and *practised* for a few years.

Remember, forget and remind: UNIT 10, SET C.
I *remember* going to India.
Don't *forget* to keep your hands in your pockets.
Can you *remind* me to post this letter?

Reported speech: UNIT 6, SET B.
Jane said (that) it was awful and (that) she didn't like it at all.

Reporting verbs: UNIT 12, SET B.
He *insisted* on paying the bill.
She *persuaded* him to tell the truth.
He *denied* stealing the handbag.
His teacher *suggested* (that) he should become a journalist.

Revision of adverbs: UNIT 7, SET D.
He plays *badly*.
She writes *well*.

Revision of key language: UNIT 15, SET D.

Revision of past forms: UNIT 2, SET C.

Separable phrasal verbs: UNIT 6, SET D.
Ellen Boudreaux knows when to *turn* the radio *on*.

Sequencing/Reason and purpose: UNIT 2, SET B.
Wanda was always sick *because* she was so nervous.
She slept in car parks *in order to* save money.

Past simple passive: UNIT 6, SET A.
Hamlet *was written by* Shakespeare.

So and such: UNIT 2, SET C.
It was *such* a challenge that it took four months to film.
It was *so* challenging that it took four months to film.

Subject–object questions: UNIT 14, SET C.
Who loves Romeo?
Who does Romeo love?

Subjects, verbs and objects: UNIT 3, SET C.
We drove the car.
Night had fallen.

Tense review: UNIT 1, SET D.

Third conditional and *wish*: UNIT 9, SET E.
If he *had had* an EC passport, probably nothing *would have* happened.
He *wished* he *had known* about these regulations.

Time expressions: UNIT 6, SET C AND UNIT 14, SET C.
We always eat *at* 7 o'clock.
I'll wait *until* 7 o'clock.
Queen Victoria reigned *for* 64 years.
The Prime Minister changed twenty-seven times *during* her reign.

Uses of *a/an, the* and *some*: UNIT 11, SET B.
She's *a* travel agent.
The kangaroo was running fast.
There's *some* water in this bottle.

Uses of *used* to: UNIT 2, SET C.
I *used to* watch *The Flintstones* when I was a kid.

Key to Workbook

Unit 1

Set A

1
A checked blouse
B plain vest
C striped shirt
D patterned skirt
E checked suit
F striped cardigan

2 She was dressed really strangely; she was wearing an old skirt and a pair of trainers. But instead of wearing tights she had a pair of plain socks on her feet. She was also wearing a funny old checked pullover with a man's striped shirt underneath. She was quite pretty really but her hair was untidy.

Set B

1 1 take (people) in 2 made out 3 found out 4 got on with 5 took (him) on 6 look into

2 1 found out 2 look into 3 give up 4 made out 5 took on/has taken on 6 gave (him) away 7 looked for/have looked for 8 get on with

3
1 He once made out that he was an international banker.
2 He was born in the poorest part of New York.
3 A wealthy German aristocrat fell in love with *him*.
4 Interpol hired a private detective.

Set C

1 A: SA B: C C: C D: C E: C F: SA G: SA H: SA I: SA J: C
1 D 2 A 3 J 4 G 5 B 6 F 7 C 8 I 9 E 10 H

2 *Requesting*
1 Could you change them for me, please?
Complaining
1 But they've shrunk and I can't wear them.
2 I bought these jeans here last week and they've shrunk.
Apologising
1 No, I'm sorry. I threw it away.
2 I'm sorry to hear that, madam.
3 I'm afraid we can't change anything without a receipt, madam.

3
1 CAN I HELP YOU
2 TORN
3 MANAGERESS
4 RECEIPT
5 SALE
6 IMITATION
7 BARGAIN
8 SHRANK
9 SCRATCHED
10 REFUNDS

Set D

1
1 Of course, I took it back to the shop to change it and the manageress told me it was a fake.
2 I'm just writing to thank you for the cheque you sent me for my birthday.
3 Well, mum, that's all my news.
4 You won't believe what happened today!
5 Simone and I are going up on the train to do some shopping.

2 *Possible letter*

28 Nelson Road
Hornsea
Suffolk
24th February 199–

Dear Fran,

How are you? I'm fine. I'm just writing to thank you for the money you sent me for my birthday. I'm looking forward to spending it in London this weekend. Tom is driving me there to do some shopping.

That reminds me. You won't believe what happened today! Tom bought me a really expensive 'Reiko' watch for my birthday and after two days it stopped! Of course, I took it back to the shop to change it and the manager told me it was a fake. I thought the name on the watch face meant it was genuine, but he said it was an imitation and that I should ask Tom where he bought it. I'm seeing him this evening so I'll ask him then. I can't wait to find out where he bought it so I can take it back and complain.

Well, Fran, that's all my news. Thanks again for the money – it was very kind of you.
Love,
    Clare XXX

3 1 was watching 2 heard 3 retired 4 live 5 don't open 6 went 7 opened 8 were standing 9 explained 10 had smelt/had smelled 11 had come 12 let 13 offered 14 accepted 15 left 16 went 17 came 18 had gone 19 realised 20 had disappeared

Set E

1 1 E 2 D 3 A 4 C

2 1 made out 2 find out 3 took in 4 take 5 fake 6 took in 7 genuine 8 made out

3 1 F 2 T 3 F 4 F 5 T 6 F 7 T

4 1 after 2 afterwards 3 after 4 after 5 afterwards

Unit 2

Set A

1 Line 3 – it Line 5 – to Line 6 – on Line 8 – any Line 9 – of

3 1 B 2 A 3 B 4 B 5 A

2 Fiona: love stories
Kate: westerns
Tom: horror films
Pete: musicals
Jane: science fiction films
Paul: comedies
Susan: documentaries
Frank: adventures
Joe: cartoons
Lucy: thrillers

Set B

1 1 It's very dangerous because you can be killed or injured as a result of one mistake.
2 They use airbeds and mattresses to break their fall and make sure that fire extinguishers and doctors are available in case anything goes wrong.

2 1 because 2 That's why 3 First of all 4 After that/ then 5 Then/After that 6 in order to 7 so that 8 Finally

3 1 that's why 2 in order to 3 because 4 so that

Set C

1 1 It was an experiment in 'seeing music and hearing pictures'.
2 A nature documentary.
3 On television.
4 Julie Andrews.
5 1966.

2 1 comic 2 inventive/imaginative 3 viewers
4 remarkable 5 genius 6 monument

3 1 used to behave
2 's used to getting
3 are used to living
4 used to be
5 is used to getting up
6 used to make

4 1 such 2 such 3 so 4 such 5 so 6 so 7 so 8 such

Set D

1 1 who created Mickey Mouse.
2 whose films made him well known all over the world.
3 which made Judy Garland famous.
4 where I saw my first film.
5 whose creations gave pleasure to millions.
6 who was the star of the film?
7 which I saw on the flight to New York.
8 who played Dracula.

2 Marty McFly, Doc Brown and Jennifer travel in the time machine to 2015 because the Doc has discovered something alarming about their future. Marty stops his son from getting involved in a robbery and then discovers that he is a middle-aged failure. Biff steals the time machine and becomes a dominant character in the Hill Valley of 1985. It's a complex story, giving Michael J. Fox three parts to play, and with plenty of fast, noisy, exciting action.

3 1 director 2 villain 3 script 4 plot 5 actor 6 heroine
7 cinema 8 character

Unit 3

Set A

1 1 A 2 B 3 A 4 B 5 B

2 1 into 2 to 3 in 4 on 5 to 6 at 7 from 8 in 9 to 10 on

3 1 up 2 preparing/making/cooking 3 brushed/cleaned
4 on 5 left 6 to 7 caught/took 8 got 9 before/after
10 would 11 as/while 12 drinking 13 no 14 same
15 booked 16 without

Set B

1 1 to escape 2 to hijack 3 participating 4 in moving
5 to capture 6 to deal 7 to review 8 having

2 1 D 2 A 3 F 4 B 5 C 6 E

3 1 to be; going 2 damaging 3 sitting 4 to meet; being
5 to seeing

Set C

1 1 E 2 A 3 D 4 B 5 F

2 *Date of accident:* Tuesday 21st January 1992
Type of aircraft: A320 Airbus
Reason for crash: Unknown
Previous altitude: 5,000 feet
Rate of descent: 2,300 feet per minute

3 1 F The pilots had chosen a standard landing.
2 T
3 F Any one of four computers can fly the plane on its own.
4 F In 1988 an A320 Airbus crashed in France.
5 T

Set D

1 1 I'm phoning about
2 Hold the line
3 if you'd like to give me your name
4 Let me see
5 I'll pass the message on
6 Let me see

2 *Missing animal:* Abyssinian Boa
Reported by: Albert Smith
Occupation: Zoo keeper
Description of animal: Two metres long. Bright green.

Time of disappearance: Around 1 p.m.
Other information: Very poisonous. Do not touch.

Set E

1 1 was sitting 2 was talking 3 were listening 4 were thinking 5 began 6 realised 7 didn't want 8 told 9 was feeling/felt 10 left 11 escaped 12 had to 13 couldn't 14 was 15 knew 16 made 17 had come 18 was 19 climbed 20 had just closed 21 heard 22 had heard 23 was 24 wanted 25 was going

2 1 Earlier that day her father had told her she couldn't go to the disco because she had to study for her exams.
2 She made a rope from the sheets on her bed and climbed out of the window.
3 She was crossing the garden when she realised she had left her purse in her bedroom.
4 As she was climbing back up the rope, her father saw her from the kitchen window.
5 When she climbed through the window, her father was waiting for her. He laughed so much that he decided she could go out after all.

Unit 4

Set A

1 1 Some 2 Few 3 any 4 many 5 few 6 some 7 a few 8 many 9 a little 10 much

2 (1) There are a few small bars of gold and a bag full of old Spanish coins. (2) There aren't any diamonds on their own but there are some earrings and bracelets. (3) There is a lovely necklace which I would like to keep. (4) The best thing of all is Lady Gertrude's tiara with the famous Poohba of Ashrami's Ruby. (5) I don't think many people would buy it. (6) There is a suitcase full of US dollars but unfortunately there aren't any Swiss Francs. (7) There are a few old Persian and Chinese carpets. How many do you think we carry in the van? (8) There are several modern paintings and one of a clown I liked by Picasso; ask Wilma how much it is worth.

Set B

1 1 D 2 B 3 F 4 E 5 C

2 1 B 2 A 3 B 4 B 5 B

3 1 looking for 2 came across 3 take (them) in 4 make (anything) out 5 give away

Set C

1
1 STEER
2 PIRATE
3 SHORE
4 CARGO
5 SILVER
6 HARBOUR
7 WRECK
8 JEWELLERY

2 1 had seen 2 arrested 3 had spent 4 escaped 5 had hidden 6 had stolen

3 1 Despite being wealthy, he spent very little money.
2 Although they had had a long journey, they stayed up until midnight.
3 Although they had the map, they couldn't find the box.
4 Despite searching all morning, they found nothing.
5 Although she was very hungry, she ate nothing all day.

4 Line 2 – for Line 3 – been Line 6 – a Line 7 – of Line 9 – the

Set D

1 1 Where did you find the money?
2 What time is it?
3 Where did you hide the necklace?
4 What was she wearing?
5 Where did he find her?
6 What's going to happen?
7 Where have they gone?
8 What have you found?
9 Where did my golf ball go?
10 Is this Jeremy's teddy bear?

2 *Possible answers*
1 Can you tell me what people leave on trains?
2 Would you mind telling me what happened to that?
3 I wonder if yours is an interesting job.
4 Could you tell me what happens when someone loses something?
5 Can you tell me what you do then?
6 I wonder if people are happy to get their lost property back.

3 1 B 2 A 3 C 4 B 5 A 6 A 7 B 8 C 9 C 10 B

Set E

1 1 It's a tall, patterned, porcelain vase. C
2 It's an expensive, new, Japanese camera. E
3 It's a small, brown, compact umbrella. D
4 It's a black, leather, Italian handbag. B
5 It's an old, wooden, rectangular box. A

2 1 It's a white, leather, French handbag. G
2 It's a new, square, metal box. H
3 It's a small, white, oval case. I
4 It's an old, black, English camera. J

Unit 5

Set A

1 1 unhealthy 2 If 3 lung 4 unless 5 wards 6 diseases
7 lives 8 otherwise 9 used 10 treat

2 1 otherwise you won't lose weight.
2 doesn't take regular exercise, she won't get better.
3 give up smoking, otherwise your liver will suffer.
4 doesn't come to the gym, I won't see her.
5 get fit unless he takes up jogging.
6 take tablets, he'll get very tired.
7 use the sports centre unless you're a member.
8 don't eat less chocolate, you'll put on weight.

3 1 himself 2 yourselves 3 themselves 4 myself
5 ourselves 6 herself 7 yourself 8 himself

Set B

1 *Possible answers*
1 *The answer here will depend on the country concerned.*
2 I'm sorry but you can't/you shouldn't/mustn't
smoke in here.
You aren't allowed to smoke in here.
3 You should give up smoking/cut down on the
cigarettes you smoke.
You should see a doctor about your cough.
4 Why don't you go to bed/have a sleep/have an early
night?

2 1 B 2 A 3 B 4 C

3 *Possible answer*

The Surgery,
Grange Road,
Epping
5th July 199–

Dear Mr Tyler,
   If I were you I'd contact my G.P. and arrange to have a
check-up. I don't think you can be as fit as you suppose you
are. Why don't you cut down on the cigarettes you smoke
or, better still, give up smoking altogether? Smoking can
cause heart disease and lung cancer. Have you thought
about drinking mineral water with your dinner instead of
wine? It's really not a good idea to drink so much alcohol. I
think you should also consider taking up some form of
regular exercise – swimming, for example, or cycling.
   You seem to have got over this first attack, but if you don't
want your wife to spend the rest of her life looking after a
sick husband you really must make some serious changes to
your present life-style.
   Yours sincerely,
   Dr Dann

Set C

1 1 He's been living in London for six months.
2 They've been dieting since Christmas.
3 She's been here since last week.
4 He's had a moustache since last year.
5 She's been jogging for two hours.
6 He hasn't smoked for six months.
7 She's been swimming since she retired.
8 They've been waiting for half an hour.

2 1 qualified 2 went 3 trained 4 worked 5 has lived
6 has worked 7 specialised 8 has been working 9 have lost
10 are/have been 11 have asked 12 gave 13 invited/has
invited 14 has not (yet) accepted

3 1 He has studied in London and New York and worked
in California and a clinic near London.
2 He has specialised in treating children and
adolescents and helping adults who have lost a family
member.
3 He has become famous because his methods are
successful.
4 He might not be able to go to Vienna because he has
a lot of patients to treat.

Set D

1 1 F 2 F 3 T 4 F 5 T 6 T 7 T 8 T

2 *Common cause of skin cancer:* spending too long lying in
the sun
Statistics (the world): increasing by 5 per cent a year; cases
have doubled in last ten years
Reason for increase in cases of skin cancer in Britain: more
and more people spending holidays in hot countries
Statistics (Britain): more than 1,000 deaths every year
Facts about skin cancer: can attack people ten years or more
after exposure to sun's rays; one of the hardest cancers to
treat; surgery can only deal with problem if caught at early
stage.
Measures taken against skin cancer: attempts to create
vaccines which could enable human body to destroy
cancerous cells; make people more aware of dangers of
sunbathing.
People at risk from skin cancer: people with a lot of moles,
red or fair hair, blue eyes, fair skin and freckles; people who
find it difficult to go brown and burn easily; people with a
history of the disease in the family.

3 *Possible answer*
Skin cancer can be caused by spending too long in the sun.
It is becoming more and more common as more people
spend their holidays in hot countries. In Britain alone more
than a thousand people die from it every year.
Unfortunately, surgery can only deal with problems if the
disease is caught early. As a result, the authorities are trying
to make the public more aware of the dangers of
sunbathing. Red or fair haired people are among those most
at risk if they spend too long lying in the sun.

Test One

1 1 taken in 2 ran 3 notorious 4 in order to 5 used to
6 setting 7 such 8 has travelled 9 whose 10 telling
11 shrank 12 looked after 13 few 14 none 15 took on

2 1 playing well 2 stealing 3 whose mother 4 to wash
5 in leaving 6 used to 7 had paid the bill 8 order to spend
9 work hard 10 a brilliant student

3 1 C 2 B 3 C 4 B 5 A

4 1 fashionable 2 wooden 3 designer 4 comfortable
5 shiny

5 1 across 2 through 3 see 4 used 5 make 6 in 7 look
8 order 9 off 10 for

6 1 When she moved to the coast she took up sailing.
2 He never got over (the shock of) losing his job.
3 She made out that she had no money.
4 He came to an hour after the accident.
5 They feared their food supplies would soon run out.

7 Line 2 – did Line 3 – it Line 5 – the Line 8 – more
Line 10 – it

Unit 6

Set A

1

```
A R T(M U S I C I A N)A
R(P H I L O S O P H E)R
C O M N O R C M O R X T
H I O V A L I P L O P I
I N T E R S E O I T L S
S C I N T A N S T R O T
(W R I T E R)T E I C R E
M U S O R T I R C A E S
A R(T R A N S P I R R)E
E X P L O R(T R A I N E
(D I R E C T O R)N B O R
A M U S I C A L T R R M
```

2 1 Dante wrote *The Divine Comedy*.
2 The part of Ilse Lund in *Casablanca* was played by Ingrid Bergman.
3 Dali produced many great surrealist works of art.
4 Marie Curie discovered radium.
5 Wimbledon was won by Steffi Graf in 1991.
6 Mozart composed *Eine Kleine Nachtmusik*.
7 *Psycho* and *The Birds* were directed by Alfred Hitchcock.
8 *Sunflowers* was painted by Van Gogh.

3 1 scientist 2 scientific 3 musical 4 musician 5 artist
6 arts 7 director 8 production 9 surprising 10 musical

Set B

1
JP: What did you think of the exhibition?
AB: I enjoyed it very much. I found the sculptures particularly fascinating.
JP: Did you find the exhibition interesting, Mr Barrett?
GB: I saw nothing that I liked at all. All the paintings are terrible. Amanda produced better work at the age of five.
JP: What do you think about your father's opinions, Amanda?
AB: He's always been very traditional. He doesn't approve of anything less than a hundred years old.
GB: That isn't true. But much of the art of the twentieth century leaves me cold. On the other hand, I think the art of the Renaissance is marvellous.

2 1 Amanda was enthusiastic about everything she saw while her father hated it.
2 Gerald seems to have conservative tastes. According to Amanda he doesn't like anything from this century.
3 He admires the work of Renaissance artists the most.

Set C

1 1 in 2 to 3 in 4 until 5 during 6 in 7 by 8 before
9 for 10 after/during 11 as 12 Since

2 1 When did he live in Peru?
2 What did he do in 1883?
3 Where did he live in Brittany?
4 Who did he spend two months with in Arles?
5 Why did he go back to Paris?
6 How did he suffer serious injuries?
7 When did he die?
8 How did he try to express the simplicity of the lives of the natives of Tahiti?

Set D

1 1 T 2 F 3 F 4 T 5 F 6 F

2 1 apply 2 post 3 advertised 4 CV 5 graduating
6 knowledge 7 secretarial 8 skills 9 personal assistant
10 unable

Unit 7

Set A

1
1 correct
2 He's got a grey moustache.
3 Her hair is dark and curly.
4 correct
5 correct
6 She's got long, fair hair.
7 The twins have (got) curly, fair hair.
8 correct
9 He's got a black and white tie.
10 correct

2 1 told 2 to 3 got 4 with 5 gave

3 1 backed him up 2 told her off 3 got away with 4 was up to 5 look after 6 gave it up 7 passed out 8 got over it 9 took up 10 cut down

Set B

1 1 E 2 B 3 A 4 D

2 1 T 2 F 3 T 4 T 5 T

3 1 everybody/everyone 2 Someone 3 nobody/hardly anybody (studies) 4 Anyone/Anybody/Everyone/ Everybody 5 everything

Set C

1

H M P J V L E O F R E N C H H
P K I N D E R G A R T E N I
H L K E L E C T U R E D M S
Y W W C E R V E F G R Y O T
S D R A W I N G T E O E M O
I B G A E S C I E N C E M R
C T O A C H E M I S T R Y
S S E C O N D A R Y G T J B
P W B Q L C M Y Y D E Y Z I
R H O T L M G S C H O O L O
E A O B E M N I K J G G L L
N K K I G M A T H S R M L O
S P E L L I N G R N A A C G
B S K T E A C H E R P I C Y
S C I P P L Y X E C H M I C
G B A T I N A B L E Y B Z K

2
1 English is the most interesting subject.
2 Her mathematics result wasn't as good as her handicrafts result.
3 Is this your best mark?
4 There isn't a bigger primary school in the area.
5 Lucy was less disappointed with her exams than Cathy.

3 1 in 2 at 3 to 4 at 5 to 6 in 7 of 8 at

Set D

1 1 hard 2 beautifully 3 fast 4 badly 5 slow 6 lately

2 1 C 2 B 3 I 4 J 5 G 6 E 7 D 8 A 9 F 10 H

3
Sachiko
Japanese
Fulchester Language Academy
three months
very good
ten
four
English
not cheap; you have to pay more for a good school
trip to Oxford and Brighton and school discotheques
an hour's homework most days

4 *Possible answer*
I spoke to Sachiko, a Japanese student. She's been studying at the Fulchester Language Academy for three months. She's from Osaka and likes her school. She says her teacher is very good and she's learning a lot. There are ten students in her class and four of them are Japanese. Most of the time she speaks English in class. She doesn't think her school is cheap but understands that you have to pay more for a good school. She's been to Oxford and Brighton with the school and there are discotheques every weekend. Most days her teacher gives her an hour's homework.

Unit 8

Set A

1

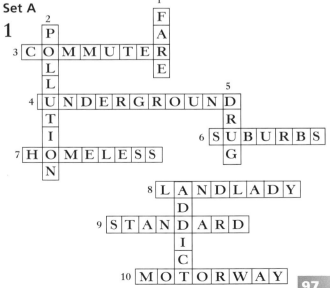

2
1 In a very small village.
2 It's very peaceful
3 London

3 *Possible answer*
Dear Chris,
It was great to receive your card. I'm glad you're enjoying life in the country. London is as busy as ever. There's more and more traffic and the streets are more and more crowded. It would be good to spend some time in the country. Can I come and stay the weekend after next?
David

Set B

1 *Suggested answers*
1 Do you live in the country?
2 And do you enjoy it?
3 What do you like best?
4 Why is that important to you?
5 How do you spend your evenings?
6 You live in London, don't you?
7 And are you happy there?
8 Where do you work?
9 What do you do?
10 What time do you start work?
11 How do you spend your evenings?
12 How do you get to work?

2 *Possible answers*
1 Jim Judd likes living in the country because he doesn't like cities. He likes the peace and quiet of the countryside. He likes to relax by reading and listening to the radio. In summer he often goes to the pub for a drink.
2 Tony Smith lives in London because he likes living in a city. Also, he has a business there. In his free time he likes to go to the opera and visit Greek restaurants.

Set C

1
1 If I eat more, I'll get fat.
2 If I get fat, I'll need bigger clothes.
3 If I need bigger clothes, I'll look awful.
4 If I look awful, I'll feel depressed.
5 If I feel depressed, I'll start smoking.

2
1 If I bought a farm, I'd keep cows.
2 If I kept cows, I'd have lots of milk.
3 If I had lots of milk, I'd make wonderful cheese.
4 If I made cheese, I'd win prizes.
5 If I won prizes, I'd be on TV.

3 1 crowded 2 homeless 3 Commuters 4 banned
5 buildings 6 Arrangements

4
1 If the air wasn't so polluted, I'd go jogging.
2 If I move to the country, I'll work from home.
3 If the trains weren't so crowded, I'd get a seat.
4 If alcohol was banned, the underground would be safer.
5 If they raise train fares, I'll have to cycle to work.

Set D

1 1 C 2 D 3 A 4 E 5 B
2 1 T 2 F 3 F 4 T 5 F 6 F 7 T 8 T 9 F 10 T
3 *Sample answer*
London was built on water and now has a rising water table. As a result the foundations of many of the capital's tall buildings could move. Their design was based on the design of Lever House in New York but conditions there are quite different. The water table under Central London has risen dramatically in recent years. Consequently, many tall buildings and deep tunnels in the capital are in danger of flooding. (72 words)

Unit 9

Set A

1 *Down* 1 yellow 2 black 3 green
Across 2 blue 4 red 5 white

2 1 out 2 sounded 3 myself 4 rather 5 let 6 although
7 again 8 had 9 ask 10 only 11 would 12 at 13 make
14 turned 15 hard 16 least 17 call 18 however

3 1 although he was 2 saw red 3 dressed more smartly, he would/might 4 was in/went into the red 5 has been banned

Set B

1 1 dull 2 arrogant 3 fair 4 sensitive 5 sympathetic
6 shy 7 cruel 8 suspicious 9 greedy 10 mean

2
1 How tall is she?
2 How old is she?
3 What's she like?
4 What does she like doing?
5 What food does she like?
6 What does she like to wear?

Set C

1 *Letter to Jane:* 1B 2J 3D 4G 5K 6E 7M
Letter to hotel manager: 1I 2H 3A 4F 5L 6C

2 *Possible letter*

24 King Street,
Cambridge,
CA24 3PA
4th April 199–

Working Holidays for Foreign Students,
5 Tottenham Court Road,
London W1

Dear Sir or Madam,
I am writing to enquire if you have any vacancies for summer work in the UK. I am nineteen years old and I have previously worked as a shop assistant. I would be happy to supply references.
I hope you have a suitable vacancy and I look forward to hearing from you.
Yours faithfully,
Jenny Brown

Set D

1 1 A 2 B 3 A 4 A 5 B

2 1 demonstrate 2 fatal 3 on the rocks 4 measures up
5 work shy 6 stick together 7 superficial
8 (job) absenteeism

Set E

1 1 If he hadn't been late, he wouldn't have driven really fast.
2 If he hadn't driven so fast, he wouldn't have been stopped by the police.
3 If he hadn't been stopped by the police, he wouldn't have been late for his meeting.
4 If he hadn't been late for the meeting, he wouldn't have made a bad impression on his clients.
5 If he hadn't made a bad impression on his clients, he wouldn't have lost the contract.
6 If he hadn't lost the contract, he wouldn't have lost his job.

2 1 hairdresser 2 au pair 3 carpenter 4 mechanic
5 cook/chef 6 soldier 7 flight attendant 8 boxer

3 1 has; will give
2 told; would believe
3 hadn't been; wouldn't have stopped
4 had known; wouldn't have given
5 had to; would drive
6 gets; will start

Unit 10

Set A

1 1 A 'll go
   B 's going to be
2 B 'm going to live
3 B 'll have
4 B 's going to rain
5 B 's going to talk
6 A 'll enjoy
   B 'll miss
7 A 'm going to miss
   B 'll drive
8 A 'll go
   B 'm going to spend

2 Dear Marina,
Great news. (1) Michael and I are going to get married next Thursday. (2) The next day we are going to fly out to Gadavia. (3) I am going to work at the embassy and Michael has already found a teaching job. (4) The political situation doesn't look very good. (5) Everyone says that there is going to be war but I hope we'll be safe.
(6) The wedding is going to be in the register office at Hammelring Town Hall at 3.30 so I'm going to wear an ordinary dress. (7) We are going to have a reception at the Goldhawk Hotel. (8) I'd like to invite Sasha but I don't know where he is living now. (9) I think I'll phone his mother. (10) If you see Maggie and Charlie will you tell them too?
I'd better post this letter and invitation to you otherwise I'll miss the post.
Lots of love,
Gemma

Set B

1 1 First of all 2 bowl 3 beat 4 Crush 5 slice 6 Peel
7 Chop 8 frying pan 9 until 10 Meanwhile 11 When
12 pour 13 stir 14 Sprinkle 15 serve

2 1 First 2 Then 3 Next 4 Meanwhile 5 Finally

Set C

1 1 an old blue jacket
2 tiny people in the picture wearing strange hats and riding horses
3 a massive vehicle on eight wheels
4 a moving picture
5 strange blue trousers
6 moving her thumb backwards and forwards
7 a wide path
8 shiny, black circles over his eyes

2 *Sample answers*
1 You put a small, rectangular thing into a little box and put some things over your ears. Then marvellous music fills your head!
2 This is a kind of box which sometimes makes a screaming noise. When it starts to scream someone picks up its lid, puts it near their mouth and talks to it.
3 This is a funny square box with numbers on it. At night, when it is dark, you can see them. It makes a strange ticking sound. When you are sleeping it suddenly makes a loud ringing noise like a bell and wakes you up!

4 This is an enormous bird made of metal. People go into its stomach and are eaten alive. When it flies, its wings don't move but it makes a loud and terrible noise.

Set D

1 1 C 2 B 3 A 4 B 5 B 6 C 7 A 8 B

2 *Sample answer*
If you visit Batavia, try to remember these rules. When you greet people, men should only kiss men and women should only kiss women. Members of the opposite sex should never kiss in public.
If you are invited to a house in Batavia you must enter with your left foot first and leave with your right foot first.
You don't need to wear a tie, even on formal occasions. However, always wear socks as it is bad manners to show your feet. Take a jacket in case you go to a smart restaurant for dinner.
Batavians never eat eggs and fish at the same meal. You should remember to chew your food with your mouth open and make lots of noise too. This means that you think the food is delicious and it is good manners.
Whatever you do, never touch your ear when you are speaking to a man. This is a terrible insult. Never touch your lips when speaking to a woman either (unless you want to marry her!). It is a terrible thing to touch a child's head as this brings bad luck. Whatever you do, never talk about the dead as this will bring the devil into the house.
If you go to Batavia you should take tea and electrical goods as gifts.

Test Two

1 1 B 2 A 3 A 4 C 5 B 6 A 7 B 8 C 9 A 10 B
11 B 12 C

2 1 lecturer 2 fascinating 3 actor 4 sympathetic
5 courageous 6 instructor 7 polluted 8 fried

3
1 he would/could have seen
2 here for
3 was found by a
4 hard/harder you'd/you would get better
5 plays the violin very
6 claimed to have come/(that) he'd/he had come.
7 before our arrival at
8 the fastest runner in
9 not to believe a word
10 up a story to explain

4 1 sensitive 2 ever 3 who 4 shining 5 in front of 6 for
7 bored 8 until 9 on 10 make 11 with 12 remind

5 1 A 2 F 3 B 4 H 5 E 6 C 7 G 8 D 9 I

6 1 gave (her) away 2 told (him) off 3 pay (it) back 4 try
(the dress) on 5 turn (it) down 6 backed (him) up

7 Line 1 – the Line 4 – of Line 6 – when
Line 9 – some Line 12 – was

Unit 11

Set A

1 1 jungle 2 forest 3 coast 4 range 5 desert 6 island
7 plain 8 harbour 9 bay

2 *Suggested answer*
New Zealand is a country in Australasia, which occupies part of the South Pacific Ocean. Lying east of South-East Australia, it consists of two main islands, North Island and South Island, together with Steward Island, Chatham Island and others. The islands are mountainous and their scenery is varied and beautiful. The climate is healthy. There are active volcanoes in North Island.

Set B

1 1 The 2 the 3 an 4 the 5 the 6 the 7 a 8 the 9 –
10 – 11 the 12 – 13 an 14 the 15 the 16 the 17 the 18 –
19 – 20 a 21 a 22 the 23 the 24 – 25 the 26 the 27 the
28 The 29 the 30 a 31 – 32 the

2 1 A 2 C 3 B 4 C 5 B

Set C

1
1 A complex of greenhouses created to simulate the different environments of the earth.
2 In the Arizona desert.
3 Eight.
4 To investigate how our earth sustains itself by recycling air, water and nutrients; to find out which forms of life can best be sustained in a closed system; to try out new crop varieties.
5 About 60 million dollars.

2
1 They are dominated by an Amazonian rainforest.
2 The Amazonian rainforest contains several hundred different varieties of plant. The savanna contains termites.
3 The marsh was created by transporting parts of the Everglades in Florida.
4 They have been sealed into Biosphere II to investigate how our earth manages to sustain itself.
5 Up to a third of the life forms inside Biosphere II will become extinct outside Biosphere II during the experiment.

3
1 Mineral deposits were discovered there in 1986.
2 The children are now (being) educated by volunteer teachers.
3 Since 1990 some new plantations have been established.
4 Food supplies are/were brought in by helicopter every week.
5 No trees have been cut down in recent years.

Set D

1
1. They have discovered a new species of fish off Tasmania.
2. The child was brought up in the outback by aborigines.
3. The lost city was discovered in the middle of the jungle.
4. They are going to build a new plant in the forest.
5. The creature is often seen in the distance by villagers.
6. Trees were being felled in the woods.
7. Eskimos have always hunted the animals.
8. The rainforest had been cut down.

2 1 are grown 2 are picked 3 are transported 4 are dried 5 are passed 6 have been rolled 7 are laid out 8 (are) left 9 are dried 10 is graded 11 being exported 12 (being) sold

Unit 12

Set A

1

```
A N Q U A L I T Y A R E B
O P R I N T N H E A D D A
F H O P O L I T A G H I S
D E J O U R N A L I S T V
C A H P T A B R E D C O Y
R D T U R R C E N S O R M
N L A L O O M P R O O T P
S I T A R T I C P A P G E
I N A R T I C L E T A N S
G E A W I N T E R V I E W
E P O T A B L O I D I P E
```

2 1 T 2 T 3 F 4 T 5 F 6 T

Set B

1
1. An attempt to climb Everest has been unsuccessful.
2. A minister has resigned following exciting events in the House of Commons.
3. The Prince is going to marry a model.
4. There have been arguments in the government after the fire at a London disco.
5. The manager is very angry after being sacked.

2
1. Will you write the report by midnight, please?
2. Why don't we work on the report together?
3. If I were you, I'd sell the story.
4. Don't forget to check your facts.
5. Don't publish the story.
6. I didn't steal the car.
7. I'm sorry for being late/I'm sorry I'm late.
8. Don't give the dog chocolate.

3 1 suggested 2 reminded 3 told 4 warned 5 encouraged 6 denied 7 insisted 8 persuaded 9 asked 10 admitted

4
1. He denied talking to the press.
2. He insisted (that) they were not going to get divorced.
3. He suggested selling the story.
4. He admitted agreeing to do the interview.
5. He advised me not to say anything.
6. He warned me not to trust journalists.
7. He encouraged me to tell him who did it.
8. He reminded me to look in the paper.

Set C

1 1 C 2 B 3 A

2
A 1 has decided 2 ended 3 is claiming 4 was not told 5 has worn 6 will work
B 1 married 2 has been described 3 chose 4 appeared 5 wore 6 was designed/had been designed
C 1 have smashed 2 has cost 3 were arrested 4 (were) seized 5 will appear 6 have been charged/are charged 7 was still being questioned 8 said 9 hadn't made 10 would have lost

Set D

1 *Possible answers*
1. 'Don't eat the food,' she said.
2. 'Why don't you talk to a reporter?' they said.
3. 'I made up the story,' he said.
4. 'I've never met the man,' she said.
5. 'If I were you, I'd talk to the editor,' she said.
6. 'Go on. Give me the details,' he said.

2 1 A 2 F 3 F 4 A 5 F 6 F 7 A 8 F 9 A 10 A

3 1 I 2 C 3 C 4 I 5 I

4 *Sample answer*
People in the UK have very different opinions concerning the freedom of the press. Some believe a free press is essential to a healthy democracy. Others feel that journalists may abuse their freedom.
It has been argued that politicians should have no secrets from the people they represent and that it is the duty of journalists to expose corrupt politicians who do not deserve the confidence of the public.
On the other hand, many people feel that even public figures deserve some privacy and that journalists may be selective about what they report. In addition, some things must remain secret for reasons of national security.
In conclusion, this is a complex subject and one about which politicians and journalists will probably always hold opposing views. (125 words)

Unit 13

Set A

1 1 A 2 B 3 B 4 A 5 B 6 A

2 1 force 2 compound 3 indications 4 evolution
5 various 6 rapid

Set B

1 1 Gliding lizards.
2 Over 100.
3 They used air currents to glide and possibly controlled their flight by moving their back legs.
4 Close to water.
5 About 65 million years ago – perhaps!

2 1 There must have been over a hundred species of pterosaur.
2 They might have controlled their flight by moving their back legs.
3 These legs can't have been very strong because the creatures spent very little time on the ground.
4 They might have been able to both dive and swim.
5 They could have hatched from eggs like birds.
6 They might have fallen out of their nests and drowned.
7 Pterosaurs must have died out about 65 million years ago.
8 Pterosaurs can't be extinct because scientists have seen them.

Set C

1 1 will have reached 2 will die out 3 will have proved
4 will have landed 5 will be

2 1 In 2003 he will graduate from university and start his first business.
2 By 2010 he will have sold his business and become a Member of Parliament.
3 By 2015 he will be/will have become a member of the government.
4 By 2025 he will have become the youngest prime minister ever.
5 By 2035 he will have won at least three elections.
6 In 2035 he will retire from politics.
7 In 2040 he will win the Nobel Prize for Literature.
8 By 2050 he will have retired to Florida.

Set D

1 A 6 B 3 C 1 D 5 E 2 F 8 G 7 H 4

2 *Sample answer*
It was in the sixteenth century that an inventor called Johann Hautach constructed the first 'clockwork' car. In the late eighteenth century Cugnot built a three-wheel 'steam carriage' and about sixty years later Summers and Ogle built a car which could travel at 60 kph.

Following the development of the internal-combustion engine in 1876 a petrol-engined three-wheeler and a two-cylinder V engine were built and by 1900 motorists could choose steam, petrol-driven or electric cars.
Between 1905 and 1910 the first Rolls Royces were produced in Britain and the first Fords in the United States. By 1925 steam and electric cars had almost disappeared. The 1930s saw the production of small Riley and MG sports cars, powerful BMWs and the Fiat 'Topolino', and after 1945 cars with more powerful engines were manufactured. Nowadays hatchbacks like the Renault 5 are popular all over Europe.
(149 words)

Unit 14

Set A

1 1 Frederick 2 Augusta 3 Charlotte 4 George IV
5 Caroline 6 Edward 7 Victoria of Saxe-Coburg-Gotha
8 Adolfus 9 Marie 10 Francis

2 1 Victoria was George III's granddaughter.
2 Victoria of Saxe-Coburg-Gotha was William IV's sister-in-law.
3 Caroline was George III's daughter-in-law.
4 Adolfus was Frederick's grandson.
5 Marie was Augusta's great granddaughter.
6 Marie was William IV's niece.

Set B

1 1F Her mother and brother-in-law were killed in accidents.
2F When her brother-in-law was killed Stephanie was in the USA.
3T
4F Stephanie used to live in California.
5T
6T
7F Stephanie is very proud of *Words Upon The Wind*.
8T

2 1 Her parents made her go to parties and balls.
2 They didn't let him socialise/allow him to socialise with other students.
3 He was made to go into exile.
4 Their son is allowed to do what he wants.

Set C

1 1 Who does Jane love?
2 Who loves Sally?
3 Who does Sally love?
4 Who did Penny love?
5 Who does Mark love?

2 1 during 2 until 3 By 4 After 5 until 6 While
7 when 8 meanwhile

Set D

1
1 In bed.
2 For a short walk around the garden.
3 Hot soup.
4 Shooting or fishing.
5 Relaxes with a glass or two of Scotch and discusses the day's sport.

2 *Suggested answer*
My day usually begins at about 6.30. I get up, wash, shave and get dressed and I'm ready for breakfast with my wife at seven. We have bacon and eggs with strong tea. After this I'm ready for work!
I'm a gardener and I cycle to the park where I work. This takes about fifteen minutes so I often arrive a bit early. I don't mind starting before eight if the weather's good. I usually have lunch outside, in the park. I love watching things grow and always feel sad when it's time to cycle home. I finish work at five and when I get home I have a bath before eating dinner with my wife, usually around six. In summer I work in my garden till late. In winter we go to bed after the 9 o'clock news on TV. (147 words)

3 1 turned on 2 came into 3 carry on 4 took after
5 brought up

Set E

1 1 C 2 A 3 E 4 B 5 D

2 *Suggested answers*
1 In what way? *or* How?
2 Do you think they deserve the money they receive?
3 Do you think they all spend their money responsibly?
4 What do you think?/Could you tell me what you think?
5 Do you like the Queen?
6 Why is a president (would a president be) better than a queen?
7 What do you think?
8 Do you think history and tradition are important?

3 1 F 2 A 3 A 4 F 5 A

4 Line 1 – it   Line 4 – of   Line 6 – they   Line 7 – such
Line 9 – the

Unit 15

Set A

1 1 B 2 A 3 B 4 A 5 A

2 1 skeleton 2 slammed 3 tapping 4 barking 5 snoring
6 screamed

3 1 ever 2 when 3 staying/living 4 had 5 alone 6 felt
7 round 8 nobody/no-one 9 door 10 have

Set B

1 1 B 2 A 3 A

2
1 The window frames need replacing.
2 The phone needs fixing/mending.
3 The garage needs cleaning out.
4 The shower needs mending/fixing.
5 The garden needs weeding.

3
1 She had the window frames replaced last Thursday.
2 She's going to have the phone fixed next week.
3 She had the garage cleaned last week.
4 She had the shower mended yesterday.
5 She's going to have/having the garden weeded tomorrow.

Set C

1
1 He said it was very warm in winter.
2 He said the old rug by the sofa could easily catch fire.
3 He said there would be no problem about changing the wallpaper.
4 He said the bed was very comfortable.
5 He said he could get a desk and a bookcase.
6 He said Mick might hear some strange noises at night.

2 1 fireplace 2 wallpaper 3 wardrobe 4 chest of drawers
5 radiator 6 sofa 7 rug 8 desk 9 basin 10 electric

Set D

1 1 look into 2 made out 3 passed out 4 got over
5 came across 6 brought in 7 taken on 8 told (the children) off 9 make (anything) out 10 find out 11 came into 12 taken in

2 1 As 2 so 3 scared 4 otherwise 5 when 6 Suddenly
7 towards 8 terrified 9 faint 10 turned.

3 Line 1 – that Line 4 – to Line 6 – on Line 8 – the
Line 9 – it

Test Three

1 1 B 2 C 3 A 4 C 5 B 6 B 7 C 8 A 9 C 10 A

2
1 can't be
2 really need cleaning
3 tell me who you saw
4 might be snow
5 said (that) he had stolen
6 prevented him from posting
7 tell me where you met
8 allowed her son to do

3 1 accused 2 headlines 3 for 4 been 5 looking
6 behaving 7 prevent 8 from 9 on 10 was 11 to
12 exclusive

4 1 D 2 E 3 A 4 C 5 B

5 1 popularity 2 censorship 3 cooker 4 relationship
5 densely

6 1 took after 2 brought (him) up 3 came into 4 looked
down on 5 look into

7 Line 1 – was Line 3 – a Line 6 – in Line 7 – to Line
9 – at Line 10 – used Line 11 – out

8 1 popularity 2 relationships 3 receptionist
4 censorship 5 correspondent 6 freedom 7 democracy
8 politicians